Vakhtang Kipiani (ed.)

World War II, Uncontrived and Unredacted
Testimonies from Ukraine
Translated by Zenia Tompkins and Daisy Gibbons

UKRAINIAN VOICES

Collected by Andreas Umland

18   Mykola Davydiuk
      Wie funktioniert Putins Propaganda?
      Anmerkungen zum Informationskrieg des Kremls
      Aus dem Ukrainischen übersetzt von Christian Weise
      ISBN 978-3-8382-1628-7

19   Olesya Yaremchuk
      Unsere Anderen
      Geschichten ukrainischer Vielfalt
      Aus dem Ukrainischen übersetzt von Christian Weise
      ISBN 978-3-8382-1635-5

20   Oleksandr Mykhed
      „Dein Blut wird die Kohle tränken!"
      Über die Ost-Ukraine
      Aus dem Ukrainischen übersetzt von Simon Muschick
      und Dario Planert
      ISBN 978-3-8382-1648-5

21   Vakhtang Kipiani (Hg.)
      Der Zweite Weltkrieg in der Ukraine
      Geschichte und Lebensgeschichten
      Aus dem Ukrainischen übersetzt von Margarita Grinko
      ISBN 978-3-8382-1622-5

The book series "Ukrainian Voices" publishes English- and German-language monographs, edited volumes, document collections, and anthologies of articles authored and composed by Ukrainian politicians, intellectuals, activists, officials, researchers, and diplomats. The series' aim is to introduce Western and other audiences to Ukrainian explorations, deliberations and interpretations of historic and current, domestic, and international affairs. The purpose of these books is to make non-Ukrainian readers familiar with how some prominent Ukrainians approach, view and assess their country's development and position in the world. The series was founded and the volumes are collected by Andreas Umland, Dr. phil. (FU Berlin), Ph. D. (Cambridge), Associate Professor of Politics at the Kyiv-Mohyla Academy and Senior Expert at the Ukrainian Institute for the Future in Kyiv.

Vakhtang Kipiani (ed.)

WORLD WAR II, UNCONTRIVED AND UNREDACTED
Testimonies from Ukraine

Translated by Zenia Tompkins and Daisy Gibbons

Bibliografische Information der Deutschen Nationalbibliothek
Die Deutsche Nationalbibliothek verzeichnet diese Publikation in der Deutschen Nationalbibliografie; detaillierte bibliografische Daten sind im Internet über http://dnb.d-nb.de abrufbar.

Bibliographic information published by the Deutsche Nationalbibliothek
Die Deutsche Nationalbibliothek lists this publication in the Deutsche Nationalbibliografie; detailed bibliographic data are available in the Internet at http://dnb.d-nb.de.

УКРАЇНСЬКИЙ ІНСТИТУТ КНИГИ

Dieses Buch wurde mit Unterstützung des Translate Ukraine Translation Program veröffentlicht.
This book has been published with the support of the Translate Ukraine Translation Program.

© Vivat Publishing Ltd, 2018
ISBN-13: 978-3-8382-1621-8
© *ibidem*-Verlag, Stuttgart 2021
Alle Rechte vorbehalten

Das Werk einschließlich aller seiner Teile ist urheberrechtlich geschützt. Jede Verwertung außerhalb der engen Grenzen des Urheberrechtsgesetzes ist ohne Zustimmung des Verlages unzulässig und strafbar. Dies gilt insbesondere für Vervielfältigungen, Übersetzungen, Mikroverfilmungen und elektronische Speicherformen sowie die Einspeicherung und Verarbeitung in elektronischen Systemen.

All rights reserved. No part of this publication may be reproduced, stored in or introduced into a retrieval system, or transmitted, in any form, or by any means (electronic, mechanical, photocopying, recording or otherwise) without the prior written permission of the publisher. Any person who does any unauthorized act in relation to this publication may be liable to criminal prosecution and civil claims for damages.

Printed in the EU

Contents

Vakhtang Kipiani
The Truth About War — 9

Romko Malko
My Family's War Began in 1939 — 12

Oleh Kotsarev
How My Great-Grandfather Helped Establish the Third Reich in Kharkiv — 19

Pavlo Solodko
Over the Course of Their Wartime Separation, My Grandma and Grandpa Wrote Two Hundred and Fifty Letters to One Another — 24

Dmytro Krapyvenko
"The Infantry Had Deserted Us, but We Had Already Taken Our Positions, So We Weren't about to Retreat." — 37

Taras Shamaida
A German Tried Persuading My Grandfather to Marry His Daughter—So That the Red Army Wouldn't Touch Her. — 41

Serhii Taran
"One Grandfather Went to Fight in Bessarabia in 1940, While the Other Joined Stepan Bandera's Insurgent Army." — 47

Taras Antypovych
A Life Bought with Milk and Cheese — 54

Oleh Pokalchuk
"The Officer Showed My Mother How Germany Planned to Expand Its *Lebensraum*." — 58

Iryna Slavinska
They Used Girls to Help "Get the German Tongues" or Obtain Information. — 65

Elina Slobodianiuk
A Wartime Fairytale: "Cinderella? That's My Grandma." — 73

Sevhil Musaieva
My Crimea: "They Can't Really Want to Take Our Homeland Again, Can They?" — 76

Ihor Shchupak
Why a Nazi Officer's Daughter Would Visit Ukraine to
Investigate Her Father's past Crimes   81

Oleksandr Zinchenko
Petro Movchan, a Man Who Won Us the War   86

Sviatoslav Lypovetskyi
"The Most Terrifying Moment Was When They Bombed
Their Own Artillery"   91

Valentyn Stetsiuk
War, Occupation, and Evacuation   95

Eleonora Koval
A Potato on a Tree: Happy New Year 1942!   111

Yurii Kolomyiets
War Has Broken Out! Alas, War Has Broken Out!   114

Anastasia Lebid
When Bolshevik Rule Was First Installed,
It Was Initially Quite Benign   124

Nataliia Popovych (Natalka Talanchuk-Hrebinska)
"Oh Mama, Life Is So Hard without You ..."   134

Oles Kulchynskyi
As She Watched the News Years Later, My Grandma Used
to Say, "I'm Stupid for Not Having Grabbed a Revolver after
the War!"   143

Stepan Semeniuk
Seventy-Nine Days in a Death Cell   147

Yevhen Klimakin
"My Grandfather Was in the SS." "And Mine Was
Killed in Auschwitz."   157

Volodymyr Parkhomenko
Surviving Fire and Water: My Father, Who Escaped
Bombing and Drowning in the Dnipro   170

Boris Artemov
The Two Lives and One Victory of Yukhym Eisenberg   178

Danuta Kostura
"My Father Carried His Rifle in the Red Army the Way
He Had Learned to in the Galician Division of the German
Armed Forces."   186

Maria Matios
Peace, War, and People   195

Dmytro Stembkovskyi
"My Grandpa Was in the Underground Resistance in Kyiv
and Blew up a Dnipro River Bridge."   203

Ihor Lubkivskyi
My Grandfather Fought in Both the First and
Second World Wars   210

Iryna Yatsyshyn
"Many Families Were Deported to Siberia. Some People
Were Punished by Their Own Families for Their Alleged
Cooperation with the NKVD."   219

Volodymyr Ushenko
Three Stories about My Family: An Officer, a Partisan,
and a Murdered Teacher   229

Liudmyla Taran
Vasyl Taran: "How I Made It through the War"   232

Eduard Zub
The German Attack Wasn't Unexpected: "We All Knew That
There Would Be a War. How Did Stalin Not Know?"   244

Vladyslav Faraponov
My Family's War: Their Unheard Memories and Their
Heroic Deeds Have Now Been Uncovered.   249

Bohdan Ivchenko
The History of Victory Day in the Soviet Union (1947 – 1965)   253

Contributing Authors   261

The Truth About War

When I was a child of about seven, I would find myself feeling rather awkward on May 9 and June 22. Over thirty years had passed since the end of "the most terrible war in human history," as we were taught at the time. All of my classmates had grandmothers and grandfathers that had fought on the front. Some of these veterans were still coming to school for the ceremonial assemblies in honor of the war, while others were already long dead and buried. But they had once existed, these heroes of the Great Patriotic War; yet my grandmothers and grandfathers had not fought. Three of them were too young to be sent to the front, and one of my grandfathers was exempted from service as an energy specialist and head of a strategic state facility. I was very jealous that everyone had someone in their family who had fought, whereas I did not.

Only many years later did I come to appreciate what a blessing it is when an all-encompassing catastrophe bypasses your family; when your loved ones are all still alive and your grandparents can share with you their own version of what transpired and what they witnessed and lived through. This very human truth about the war that was void of lofty epithets often didn't match up with what they said on TV, what was being shown in movies, and the stories we were spun at school as the only possible version of events.

Naturally, there were films and books that contradicted the fabrications of the Soviet General Staff's propagandists and their "parrots" among the Soviet General Staff—but these ideas were merely a drop in the ocean. It felt as if most people born in the USSR only knew what the party allowed them to know and remember. Fortunately, this was indeed not the case. At home, parents and elders would share stories with their children that didn't make it into the official canon—often accompanied by the proviso, "But don't tell anyone outside of this house or at school!" Later, these uncontrived and unredacted stories would act as the yeast that gave rise to freedom of thought, speech, and action.

Obviously, in order to fully comprehend World War II, one must read a multitude of academic monographs, as well as the memoirs of Winston Churchill, Erich von Manstein, Gregory Zhukov, and so on. But not everyone has time for that. Sometimes a brief paragraph will suffice to entice someone into reflection and research. A photo story by the renowned journalist and photographer Yuri Rost, which appeared in the pages of the then very popular Russian *Literaturnaya Gazeta* ("Literary Newspaper"), once made an incredible impression on me. In the Cherkasy region of

Ukraine, he had met a certain Lysenko family: the mother Yevdokiia and her ten sons Andrii, Pavlo, Mykhailo, Todos, Mykola, Petro, Oleksandr, Ivan, Stepan, and Vasyl. When the war began, all ten—Andrii, Pavlo, Mykhailo, Todos, Mykola, Petro, Oleksandr, Ivan, Stepan, and Vasyl—went off to fight. And when the war ended, all ten—Andrii, Pavlo, Mykhailo, Todos, Mykola, Petro, Oleksandr, Ivan, Stepan, and Vasyl—returned home, to the house they had grown up in, where their mother was waiting for them. Some time after the war, a memorial to the mother was constructed in the village of Brovakhy in the Korsun-Shevchenkivskyi District. Ten poplars were also planted there in honor of her ten sons, and five willows in honor of the daughters she raised (this woman gave birth to seventeen children in total). Unfortunately, I haven't had the opportunity to travel to those places and bow my head before this symbolic memorial to all the mothers who bore children for love and happiness and, as it turned out, for war as well. We are not the ones to choose the times we live in.

The Ukrainian edition of this book went to print in April 2018. Yet back in the spring of 2010, an announcement appeared on the pages of several popular websites and newspapers about the start of the project "1939 – 1949: Unwritten Stories: Share Your Family's Story of World War II." It was a short and very simple text:

> World War II left its mark on every Ukrainian family. As a general rule, those who participated in these events, regardless of which side they fought on, do not want to share the details till this day. Only on occasion would they entrust their truth of the war to their closest relatives.
> On the eve of the national celebration of Victory Day, we encourage Ukrainian journalists to publish their family stories and lore about what their parents, grandparents, and great-grandparents lived through during the war.
> We also encourage our readers to participate in this project.

The idea resulted in over one hundred publications. The voices of both the living and of those who are now long gone were heard. Eyewitnesses to the war's events—soldiers of the various armies (the Red Army, the Ukrainian Insurgent Army, the German Army's "Galician Division"); residents of the territories occupied by the Nazis, their allies, and the Bolsheviks; *Ostarbeiters*; children; women—all spoke up. And, very importantly, people's children and grandchildren finally found the time to sit down and listen to their loved ones, and to write down the testimonies of a time that seemed so far away, yet one that is somehow still close at hand. Because Ukrainians argue till this day about whether it should be called World War II or the Great Patriotic War; Ukrainians are still divided, as a quarter of Ukraine's citizens still consider Stalin to have been an effective leader and inspirer of "the victory of the people." At the same time, many people recall the other dimensions of this tragedy—from the heroism of some to the baseness of others. Yet others continue to remain silent about what they saw—about the death and the fear and the tears. Such things are not forgotten, even if they are not spoken of out loud.

The stories published in this collection are just a portion of the texts published on the popular-history websites *Ukrainska Pravda* ("Ukrainian Truth"), *Teksty* ("Texts"), and *Istorychna Pravda* ("Historical Truth"). In reality, there are many more such texts that can, if the opportunity presents itself, be published in a second and third volume. If you haven't yet shared your loved ones' stories of World War II in Ukraine, you can always do so by emailing istpravda@gmail.com.

Vakhtang Kipiani
Editor-in-Chief, *Istorychna Pravda*
www.istpravda.com.ua

Romko Malko

My Family's War Began in 1939

The war encountered my Grandma Vira's family in Ternopil, in their new house. And this didn't happen in June 1941, but in September 1939. One night there was a banging on the door. "Open up! You've got half an hour to get ready. Take only what you need," someone yelled in Russian.

World War II arrived in Ukraine not in June 1941, but in September 1939. Western Ukrainians, at the very least, whose lands were a part of Poland at the time, would remember this date very distinctly. The Polish army was ineffectual and demoralized, so there was no point in fighting two million-strong armies, the German and the Soviet ones. "The Polish army rides around on bicycles," Ukrainians used to joke, and that was an almost wholly accurate depiction of the real situation.

The Germans were the first to start pressing down on Poland, and due to the fact that there was no particular opposition, they managed to advance pretty far—farther than had been previously agreed to with the Soviets in the Molotov-Ribbentrop Pact. However, the "valiant" Red Army appeared rather quickly, and the Germans were forced to retreat.

The claims that either the Germans or Bolsheviks were met with particular joy by some are untrue. Their respective appearances were generally received as that of an ordinary change of occupier, no more. It's possible that some Ukrainians greeted some with the traditional welcome of bread and salt, but these were sooner exceptions than the rule. Uncertainty and alarm reigned in society. People knew perfectly well who the Bolsheviks were; they remembered the recent Holodomor in Central and Eastern Ukraine and the thousands of swollen Ukrainians from beyond the Zbruch River, who were lucky enough to make it to Halychyna (Galicia) for a hunk of bread. They had no delusions. The attitude toward the Germans was somewhat better. After all, European Germany and the tattered Bolsheviks weren't quite on the same level. Nonetheless, an overall bad premonition of impending grave events hung in the air, and people simply focused on surviving. Very quickly that which had been foreboded would surpass all fears and expectations ...

My Grandma Vira's family was living in Ternopil. The war encountered them in their new house, which her parents had just built after many years of moving from one village in Halychyna to another. Prior to that my great-grandfather — a man who knew seven languages fluently — had been a teacher, but he had been unable to find a job in Ternopil because he didn't want to switch to using Polish and become a Pole.

At the time my grandma was in the lower gymnasium, and her brother Rodio (Rodion) was close to graduating. But when the Bolsheviks arrived, the gymnasium was immediately turned into an ordinary ten-year school, and the former gymnasium students were given the opportunity to study there for an additional year — probably to firmly master the new lessons of Soviet life.

At first the Soviets' arrival didn't bring any particular changes, and people even began to think that their apprehension had been in vain. There were, of course, certain misunderstandings and occasionally even bizarre behavior on the part of the foreign Soviet occupiers, but people didn't attach any particular significance to any of this. They didn't marvel at the ragged-looking Soviet soldiers, who, against the backdrop of German and Polish ones, looked like beggars: the officers' wives would attend the theater in the nightgowns of Polish ladies that they had found in their abandoned estates, they would use chamber pots as vases for flowers ... There were all kinds of strange things going on, but none of it was life-threatening. Yet the reality of life changed very rapidly. The nuts and bolts were slowly being tightened. Rumors were already spreading about people disappearing and being deported to Siberia.

Sometime in the spring of 1941, after the annual school celebration of Taras Shevchenko's birthday, weird things started occurring with the students. One student was summoned to the director's office and didn't return; another was shoved into a black car out in the street and disappeared; yet another simply vanished without a trace. A boy with the last name of Hrynkiv, whose family lodged at my great-grandfather's farmstead, went similarly missing. Agitated parents searched for their children, but no one at either the prison or the police station could offer any advice. Little by little, fear crept under people's skins.

One morning Rodio refused to go to school. "Something's wrong. I don't feel all that well." His mother — that is, my great-grandmother — was empathetic toward her son and let him stay at home. Then at lunchtime a flustered classmate came running over and shared the news that Rodio and some other boys had been called to the director's office. Those of the summoned boys that had been in school never returned to class from the director's office. They were put in a black car and driven off to who knows where. Understandably, after that news no one was about to send anyone else off to school anymore. Rodio stayed at home for a little while longer and then one evening went to our relatives' house in a neighboring town, to hide. I don't know for a fact whether Great-Grandma Maria suspected that she was seeing her son for the last time that night, but she probably did suspect it.

A few weeks passed, then one night, on May 21, there was a banging on the door: "Open up! You've got half an hour to get ready. Take only what you need." Great-Grandpa Prokip, the one that spoke seven languages — a refined intellectual very well versed in law and legal matters, who addressed every last one of his students with the formal You — on principle couldn't believe that something like that could be happening to him. As if nailed to the ground, he stood with two brushes in his hands and kept repeating, "But this can't be ... We're not guilty of anything ..." If not for my great-grandma, who, having soberly assessed the situation, set about quickly packing up, they would've ended up heading to Siberia in the clothes they had slept in, with two fabric brushes as an added bonus.

Grandma Vira was supposed to have stayed behind. She had been sleeping in the attic alongside the family's student lodger, and no one was even looking for her. Great-Grandma, as she packed, consciously spoke loudly so that Vira would hear what was going on in the house — that they were being deported — and would stay quiet. She didn't even take Vira's things, expecting that Vira would stay behind. But my grandma couldn't stay put. At the last moment, as the car was already pulling out, she leapt down from her hid-

The Tkachuk family. Parents Prokip and Mariia (née Korduba), their son Rodio (Rodion), and their daughter Vira. Ternopil, 1929 or 1930

ing place and rushed to her parents. The soldiers didn't want to let her in because they thought she was someone else's child, but she nonetheless managed to clamber into the vehicle and grasped her mother's hand. There was horrible lamentation in the street: several families were being taken off at the same time. People were wailing as if at a funeral. Those who weren't being taken came out of their homes and escorted their neighbors off to the unknown.

The deportees were brought to the train station in Ternopil and locked into boxcars designated for cattle transport. They kept them there for a few days until a whole train-full had been rounded up, then drove them off.

It was spring of 1941. The endpoint of my grandma's, great-grandma's, and great-grandpa's land travels became Salekhard. Then came a journey by barge somewhere in the Gulf of Ob, an existence marked by cold and hunger, long years of felling two cubic meters of forest a day (my grandma was thirteen at the time), my great-grandma's imprisonment for stealing a single fish (in order to not starve to death), and many other things—all of it for the sake of the heroic victory of the "great Stalin" and the no less "great Soviet people" over the evil fascists.

In the meantime, Germany attacked the USSR. The Germans entered Ternopil and opened up the prison. Neither the residents of Ternopil, nor even the Germans themselves had ever experienced such horror before. The prison was literally chock-full of corpses. Congealed blood pooled on the floor. Here and there the corpses had been sprinkled with lime, but for the most part they had simply been dumped in heaps. The "valiant" Soviet apparatus, not wanting to bother deporting prisoners, had simply shot them down in packs in the prison. More accurately, they didn't simply shoot them down but did so with a particular method. They tortured them, abused them, cut off pieces of their bodies, and only after all that finished them off. Among the thousands of bodies, the remains of some of Rodio's friends, fellow students from the Ternopil Gymnasium, were also found. Today a plaque hangs on the wall of the gymnasium with their last names and the date of their deaths: June 21 – 26, 1941.

Relatives of the disappeared and arrested came flocking from throughout the Ternopil region in order to identify and humanely bury the remains. There was no limit to the curses and tears. The same thing was transpiring in all the cities and towns of Western Ukraine. This region hadn't sustained such anguish since the time of the Tatar invasion.

Immediately after the German attack and the announcement of the restoration of the Ukrainian State in Lviv on June 30, 1941, Grandma's brother Rodio traveled to Lviv and, already as a member of the Organization of Ukrainian Nationals (OUN), volunteered into the administration of the Ukrainian government. But a Ukrainian state didn't figure into Hitler's plans, so everyone involved in its formation very soon started getting arrested. Rodio too was arrested. The fate of many Ukrainian patriots could have befallen him and he would've gotten his bullet back in the first days of the war, but Providence had prepared a different mission for him. The young man somehow managed to escape from custody and return to Ternopil. Unfortunately, the details of his escape will continue to remain a mystery because there's no one left to tell them today. In Ternopil, Rodio settled semi-legally in his parents' house, which had been looted by Soviet police, and set about building up an organizational network. His mother's sister, Aunt Stefa, who lived not far away, helped him considerably in this endeavor. She had no children of her own, so Rodio was like a son to her. Her house was constantly being frequented by someone or other. These people would eat, rest or spend the night, then leave. The woman prepared meals for them and, as the need arose, carried out the duties of a courier, obtaining information, purchasing train tickets, and fetching parcels from drop-off points. According to family lore, Rodio was the organization's district leader for the Skalat area. Even people who crossed paths with him during the war period confirm this information, but, unfortunately, nothing resembling documents from that time has been located: the underground movement barely pretended to bureaucracy and through the end of 1943—namely, the time of the Ukrainian Insurgent Army's emergence—few matters went documented.

Sometime in late 1942 the Gestapo publicly hanged several OUN members in Ternopil. The organization decided to avenge their members' deaths and planned a bold operation. At the time there was a

Rodion Tkachuk. Ternopil, 1942

restaurant named Polonia in the center of Ternopil, frequented mostly by senior German officials and Volksdeutsche. An "Only for Germans" plaque hung proudly on the door of the establishment, so mere mortals were prohibited from setting foot in there.

One beautiful day two Wehrmacht officers entered the Polonia restaurant. Glancing around the dining hall, they wordlessly discharged a few magazines and—leaving in their wake a true mishmash of posh dishes, drinks, and soldiers of the Führer—exited out into the street just as calmly. To say that such a brazen stunt was a complete shock for the occupiers is to say nothing. A manhunt was immediately orchestrated in the city: all the entrances and exits were blocked off, and all the nooks and crannies were searched, but the two subversives in Wehrmacht officer uniforms were never found. Meanwhile, the two "officers" were having a leisurely repose a few blocks away at my great-grandmother's house. One of them was Rodio, but the name of the second, unfortunately, will remain unknown.

Active subversive involvement right under the Gestapo's nose couldn't remain unnoticed, and not long after Rodio was declared a wanted man.

He was forced to leave the city and switched jobs to one in the district he supervised. One night, as he was walking from one village to another, he came across a German patrol. The Germans were riding in the back of a wagon driven by a Pole he knew from Ternopil and, upon spotting the man out on the road at night, demanded his documents. The man seemed to resemble the one the Gestapo had been fruitlessly hunting for several months already. Rodio reached into his pocket for his documents, but in lieu of them pulled out a pistol and knocked the Germans off on the spot. The Polish driver he left untouched. After exchanging a few words with him, Rodio bid the man goodnight and went about his business. However, the Pole turned out to be less amicable and magnanimous. He picked up his rifle and shot Rodio in the back.

Back in Ternopil, Aunt Stefa was immediately arrested and taken off for further interrogation. Interestingly, they didn't even permit Rodio's body to be cleared off the road. They just placed a guard next to it. When the on-site investigation was completed, the body was left lying on the side of the road, and Aunt Stefa was locked up in a Gestapo jail. Somehow the OUN boys managed to get her out of there, and a few weeks later she returned home, where she resumed her old activities assisting the underground.

Meanwhile, some villagers from a neighboring village orchestrated a solemn nighttime burial for Rodion in their local cemetery. Per the organization's orders, the following day, in all the churches throughout the Ternopil region, memorial services were held for Rodio's soul and bells tolled dolefully.

When my grandmother, great-grandmother, and great-grandfather returned from Siberia, a Soviet civil servant was already living in their house with his family, so they were forced to seek shelter among their kin. Thankfully, Aunt Stefa was still alive, and she described to them what had happened with Rodio. My great-grandmother spent a long time walking from village to village, asking people where her son's grave was. People were scared to talk about that sort of thing: those were frightening times. But my great-grandmother kept searching nonetheless. One day fate brought her together with a woman whose father had organized the funeral back then, and the woman showed her where Rodio's grave was. My great-grandmother had a cross placed for her son, but up until the collapse of the Soviet Union no one ever did find the courage to write his name on the headstone.

And that's the whole story. It would be nice to fill in some more of the details, but, unfortunately, there's no one left to do so.

Oleh Kotsarev

How My Great-Grandfather Helped Establish the Third Reich in Kharkiv

Of course, like many of this book's readers, I have a grandfather who was a veteran, and he marched with the Workers' and Peasants' Red Army from Stalingrad to Vienna (which I'll talk about some other time). Similarly, it's probable that many of you also had a grandfather who dodged the draft. It's also no surprise that some of my great-uncles became members of the *Hilfspolizei*, the Ukrainian auxiliary police service set up by the Nazis in occupied Ukraine. But we have an exclusive story in our family history: my great-grandfather was the mayor of Kharkiv during the German occupation. He was Mayor Oleksii Kramarenko, the one whose order banning the Russian language in the city's state institutions is quoted from time to time in pro-Russian publications.

Oleksii Ivanovych Kramarenko was born on March 17, 1882 in Yelysavethrad (present-day Kropyvnytskyi) as the son of a railway worker. He studied to be a chemist at the Kharkiv Technological Institute (now the Polytechnic) and then worked as chief engineer in many factories across Ukraine; for example, he helped launch production at the Budiansk faience pottery factory and the Chasivoiarsk refractory plant.

He was highly regarded as a specialist and was given the equivalent of a knighthood. He was constantly travelling abroad, even under Soviet rule. He taught at universities in Kamianets-Podilskyi and Kharkiv, and served as head of the glass materials department at Kharkiv's Technological Institute.

Oleksii Kramarenko did not take part in any fighting in the Civil War between 1917 and 1920, and only vague information about his political sympathies remains: there are hints about his commitment to the Ukrainian People's Republic, his declarative Russophobia, and his contempt toward Lenin combined with an admiration for Trotsky.

His descendants claim that the two armies — the Red and the White — both wanted to expropriate Oleksii's and his wife Mariia Leonidivna's beautiful Art Nouveau-style piano (which my mother now plays), but both times Kramarenko managed to get it back.

My great-grandfather (second on the left) with some acquaintances, 1930s

He declared to the Whites as they departed that he "did not sympathize with their movement," and only the intervention of his wife's influential relatives could save him after that remark.

Kramarenko had an "Englishman's disposition," and his tastes were typical of the old-guard intelligentsia of the time: the authors Hoffman, Blok, and Vynnychenko (he also wrote poetry himself, and on occasion could even quote the poet Vasyl Chumak), as well as reciting poetry to music, the theatre, cards, alcohol, and adultery.

This latter passion resulted in a divorce between him and my great-grandmother and a subsequent marriage to fellow chemist Nataliia Bershadskyi. Perhaps this is what later saved our family.

The Nazis occupied Kharkiv on October 21, 1941. Out of Ukraine's major cities, life in Kharkiv was perhaps the hardest. The Nazis deliberately restricted access to supplies and introduced extremely brutal repressions for the city's residents.

However, they had to form a local Ukrainian self-governing body for show. As historian Anatolii Skorobohatov recounts, the Germans appointed Oleksii Kramarenko as mayor after consultations with teachers at the Technological Institute—which may have been where the Nazis' residence was.

What were the functions and capabilities of the then "mayor" of Kharkiv (considering that Kharkiv didn't belong to the civil administration of *Reichskommissariat Ukraine* but to frontline territory)?

Oleksii Kramarenko

They were quite limited.

In theory, he should have been organizing the regeneration of the city's industry, which had been destroyed by the Bolsheviks during their retreat, as well as ensuring the provision of supplies for the population. He also should have been monitoring the proper execution of the German authorities' orders.

There was no opportunity to perform these tasks, however, as the real power was in the hands of the Germans. Kramarenko was left to "shake up" his cumbersome and corrupt administrative apparatus and record the number of residential spaces "liberated from the Jews" (in fact, he offered to give one of these "liberated" apartments to his ex-wife, my great-grandmother; had she agreed, one can only imagine the Bolsheviks' reaction to this when they arrived back in Kharkiv in 1943). He also had to create soup kitchens for "his people," and take care of humanitarian activity.

This humanitarian work was the only place where Kramarenko left a noticeable mark. He contributed to restoring Kharkiv's churches. Before the war, there was only one functioning cathedral left in Kharkiv, but with the mayor's assistance many were returned to the city's faithful. Churches belonging to the Ukrainian Autocephalous Orthodox Church and the Autonomous Church — the analogue of today's Moscow Patriarchate — were restored (but both churches were forced to run services in honour of the "liberator" Hitler).

Oleksii Ivanonovych was not religious, but he assisted in the restoration of Kharkiv's churches and was very happy to hear the sound of church bells once again ringing over the city.

Kramarenko's most famous "act" was his decree on language:

> This is the fifth month that our native, yellow-and-blue Ukrainian flag has been flying over the free city next to the victorious German flag as a symbol of our new life, of the revival of our Motherland.
> But, to all us Ukrainians' great misfortune and disgrace, our shameful Bolshevik legacy remains in some places.
> A source of great disgrace to all of us and of quite understandable anger to the Ukrainian people, conversations in Russian, held by government officials who are apparently ashamed of their native language, can be heard in some institutions and even in local district administrations.
> This is a disgrace for those who have become free citizens of their liberated homeland. Those who shun their native language will only meet shame and they have no place among us. We cannot accept this, for this cannot go on. That is why I order a categorical ban for any government official to speak in Russian during office hours at their institution.

It is precisely thanks to this order that, even today, my great-grandfather's surname can be found from time to time in all sorts of propaganda articles by pro-Russian trolls.

The mayor helped his former family, and at times came by for a visit.

At that time, his new wife had fallen pregnant, and in August 1942 Oleksii Kramarenko was arrested by the Gestapo.

They say that as he was walking along the street with the Gestapo officers, he saw an acquaintance.

"Where are you off to, Oleksii Ivanovych?"

"Well, I'm rather like Dickens' parrot."

For litterateurs of the time, it was a rather simple allusion; the quote was: "I suppose I'll go then, as the parrot said when the cat got his tail."

One version of the story claims that my great-grandfather was arrested for selling food and other supplies illicitly. According to another, he was too active in helping to free prisoners of the Kholodna Hora concentration camp, which counted partisan fighters and Jews among its captives.

In addition, a family friend named Ivantsova passed him a proposal for cooperation with the Soviet intelligence services, which Kramarenko refused. It's possiblethat because of this the Reds may have "slipped" information about him to their Nazi colleagues. Or, to the contrary, perhaps he really did collaborate with the Soviet intelligence or with the Resistance.

In any case, we only know that the Gestapo told my grandmother, Valeriia: "Your father will be detained until the end of the war".

Oleksii Kramarenko on a business trip to the United States

While he was in prison, his second wife gave birth to a son, Oleksii, who only survived for a few years and died of meningitis. The subsequent fate of Kramarenko himself is shrouded in mystery.

Some said that the Germans shot him; others said that he was freed and taken to Poland during the German retreat. Another acquaintance in our family allegedly saw Oleksii Kramarenko in London after the war, where he was living under a different name. Then again, these are probably just whimsical fabrications ...

After the Soviets' return to power, my grandmother, Kramarenko's daughter, was interrogated several times before being left in peace. Nataliia Bershadska also escaped severe persecution by the looks of it. Mariia Leonidivna, his ex-wife, died.

For a long time, my family avoided spreading this story about, although they didn't hide it either. After all, it is a very symbolic one that shows that collaboration during the twentieth century's most disastrous war in Europe was not reserved for the great powers.

It fell upon some to partition Czechoslovakia, others to arm and teach the Reich, and others still to claim "national independence" or a "people's democracy," while ordinary people "took notes" from the geopolitics of the time, from which they could only rarely deviate completely.

Pavlo Solodko

Over the Course of Their Wartime Separation, My Grandma and Grandpa Wrote Two Hundred and Fifty Letters to One Another

My paternal grandma, Nadiia Oleksiivna Neizzhala, met my grandpa, Pavlo Andriiovych Solodko, during the occupation. I asked her to tell me about this romantic story that unfolded against the backdrop of a bloody World War in greater detail. When he passed, my late grandpa left behind memoirs from the front: I've interwoven them with my grandma's story.

Grandma Nadia finished school in June 1941 in Bakhmach in the Chernihiv region. Grandpa Pavlo finished school then as well, in Kurin, a village outside Bakhmach, and his graduation was on June 22. They hadn't met yet, and in August Grandpa was drafted into the army. He was nineteen.

* * *

In September 1941 we were retreating from the Luhansk region to Stalingrad Oblast (present-day Volgograd Oblast in the Russian Federation).

We moved mainly at night and on foot. Sometimes we covered up to sixty kilometers a night, sleeping on the move. We were carrying duffel bags on our backs. It was pouring rain and our field cloaks, which doubled as tents, did little to help. When daybreak brought with it frost, the cloak served as a shell.

Our cannons were horse drawn. You could barely put one foot ahead of the other, when, as luck would have it, a cannon would get stuck. We'd cluster around it, some pulling it by the wheels, others by its traces.

We made it to a village, and the staff sergeant with the wagons and food was nowhere to be seen. But the potatoes hadn't been harvested in all of the collective farms: that saved us.

We traveled close to seven hundred and fifty kilometers like that — though we rode back later by train. On May 12, 1942 we went on the offensive: that was the Kharkiv Offensive Operation. To my soldier's mind, our command didn't organize it in the best way possible.

No one talked about the fact that we were under threat of being encircled by the enemy. When on May 22 we were issued four days' worth

In the years 1941 and 1943, over 1500 people left Kurin for the front. Of those, 867 did not return.

of food rations and were immediately warned to stretch it out over eight days, we started to surmise that we had been cut off into a pocket.

On one of the final days of May, at noon, I noticed a flight unit of Junkers coming in on our position. I dropped into a ditch. The Germans had even turned on their sirens to mess with our heads. Suddenly there was a terrible explosion; the air was squeezed out of my lungs. I thought to myself, "Maybe I've been killed. That's the end of that."

What happened next and how long it lasted – I don't remember. My consciousness returned for a brief time: I was lying in the body of a vehicle, it was night, there were flames, crossfire ... I couldn't hear any shots: I had lost my hearing and my ability to speak.

I was probably in an ambulance. How many nights I rode in it – I don't know, even till this day. I finally came to. I opened my eyes: it was a bright, sunny day. There was a horrible pain and noise in my head and ears. I turned my head: alongside me, on top of some sort of rags, wounded men were lying and moaning. All around me were carts, vehicles, a lot of wounded, bloodstained bandages ... Germans were walking around with machine guns.

I pulled my duffel bag out from under my back: it was covered in bits of shrapnel. Sometime later I found holes in my overcoat too, made by shrapnel.

In early June I ended up in Uman, in a POW camp – the well-known "Uman pit." Later we were transferred to a camp in the village of Ivanhorod, not far from Khrystynivka. There I ran into Ivan Tsybulka, who I had once fought with.

Ivan and I got to know two other young men of about our age, from Siberia, who had been taken into captivity outside Kerch. The four of us started to prepare for escape.

The place was surrounded by two rows of barbed wire, with more barbed wire crisscrossed over the ground and watchtowers in the corners. Some prisoners tried to run away while on work details, but they'd leave tracks in the field: the guard would get on his horse and chase them down. In the evening the poor wretches would be shot near the camp. They'd bury them outside the wire fence and, without fail, would put up a birch cross (the Germans required this). There were already a good many such crosses surrounding the camp.

Our pit-house was located in the far row. At night we dug out an opening up to the barbed wire. We took off our shoes and left behind our overcoats. I crawled through the fencing last.

After I made it through the first row of fencing, I heard footsteps. There were three meters between the two rows of barbed wire. A guard was walking the length of the fence, and my heart was pounding as if ready to leap out of my chest. My hair was standing on end, and I thought to myself: "Pavlo, you're nineteen, but it's time to say goodbye to life." I flattened myself against the ground as the guard's footsteps grew closer and closer. He would be alongside me at any moment, he would fire off a round from his machine gun ... That minute felt like an eternity.

And then the guard walked up alongside me – and walked right past. Maybe he didn't notice me, or maybe a good man was walking past me (we were guarded by Latvians) and took pity on me.

* * *

The war began with horrible bombardments. A host of troop trains had crammed into the Bakhmach-Kyivskyi Railway Station (they later said that it was a diversion), and on July 14 they were bombed so hard that scraps of metal, charred wood, and military overcoats had ended up all the way over where we lived, which was several kilometers away.

There were awful fires: on the street that leads to the Bakhmach-Homelskyi Station, ten houses were blazing at once.

The Germans dropped these types of cluster bombs – two metal casings closed together, with a load of incendiary bombs inside. People later used these receptacles as water troughs for cattle. And after the war, it was fashionable to feed dogs out of German helmets.

In 1941, in place of the collective farm, the Germans created a commune. They didn't pay people anything for work and would take away their grain and livestock. There was no school.

Then in 1942 they began building a new railway turntable for locomotives and sent all the young people there. Old Germans, who were no longer of use at the front, were in charge there. And then one day these Germans rounded up all the young men and women that had come to work into a shop—to get sent off to Germany. But our boys that were serving in the railway guard—they wore these black uniforms—went and unlocked that shop. And they yelled, "Run!" The Germans didn't look for us: they didn't know who had let us out and were themselves scared that our boys might punish them.

* * *

Where to go? I knew my geography. We headed northeast, orienting ourselves by the North Star. We decided to split up: Vasko and I ran straight, and Tsybulko and Vasyl went left.

There were decrees from the German authorities posted everywhere that forbade giving food and shelter to POWs, partisans, and "Bolshevik agents." If you violated this, you'd be executed, whereas if you handed someone over to the Germans, you'd be allotted a plot of land. But there were few amoral people around: over the course of our long journey, no one gave us away.

We fell into the hands of the police a few times. I ordered Vasko to stay quiet with his Russian accent; I did the talking myself. I'd show them a photograph of my family and explain what had happened. They'd let us go, sometimes even suggesting the best way to go.

At the end of August 1942, Vasko and I made it to Kurin. The village elder refused to register him and sent him to the commandant for permission. But Vasko was a fearless guy: "If they lock me up," he said, "I'll run away again." He survived the war: in 1946 he sent me a letter from Donbas.

During the occupation people generally engaged in subsistence farming. Stores were closed, and the post office wasn't working. People told stories about how initially there were Hungarian troops on our territory. They were crueler than the Germans. Sometimes a person walking from the village to the bazaar in the district center would be detained and shot without so much as an explanation.

At the end of February 1943, a punitive expedition was conducted in the district. Thousands of people were shot and burned to death. Thirty-four were killed in Kurin, among them the headmaster of our school

Ivana Zhyhyliia, the teachers Anatolii Ivanenko and Lukiia Sukhodolska, and my friends Pavlo Makarenko and Andrii Nechyporenko.

Vasyl Tsyban, a Polizei, told me that he had been tasked with picking me up as well but had weaseled his way out of it, claiming he couldn't find me.

The Germans were brutal. Though it wasn't even the Germans, but the Hungarians and Asians that served in the German army that were the most brutal: they were the ones that burned down houses with people inside them and murdered them. They murdered people everywhere — in Bakhmach and in Kurin.

* * *

Children were still being sent to Germany, but only the ones on lists now. The village elder compiled them. I didn't make it onto a list: my father somehow settled that issue. He hadn't gone to the front because he had an exemption as a railroader (like most Bakhmach residents, he spent his whole life working on the railroad — under the Soviets, under the Germans, under the Denikinites, and under the Petliurites).

In October 1942 there was an announcement that an agricultural technical college was being opened and that students enrolled there supposedly wouldn't be taken to Germany. All the young people from the surrounding villages who had a secondary education enrolled in that technical college. Pavlo enrolled too.

He noticed me and sent over a friend of his to meet me. The guy sat down next to me and said, "Nadiia, there's a boy that wants to meet you." And I asked, "What's his last name?" "Solodko," he replied. Meanwhile, your grandpa was sitting a few rows away and watching the expression on my face.

And we started meeting up in the evenings outside the dormitory. I liked him because he was interesting to talk to. Obviously, we didn't get to kissing right away [*she giggles*]. We were school friends. We talked about our acquaintances, about literature ... Everyone who'd finished high school read a lot because there was no other form of entertainment.

The Germans bombed the district library, and my girlfriend and I gathered up half a bag each of books — and not the best ones anymore either.

At the time, Ukrainian classics and contemporary Ukrainian literature were considered the "best" literature among school-aged young people. Ivan Le, Oleksa Desniak, Oleksandr Kopylenko, Yanovsky's and Smolych's adventure novels, Zinaida Tulub's *The Manhunters* ... I found *War and Peace* and Gogol's *Dead Souls* — even an illustrated edition.

When Pavlo learned that I had visited the bombed-out library, he was overjoyed. "Let's trade!" he said. So, I'd bring him books from Bakhmach, and he'd bring me ones from Kurin.

The technical college lasted until about December, and then the building was turned into a hospital. Then in May 1943 all the students were summoned, supposedly for some hands-on experience but, in reality, for some kind of farm work. Pavlo and I would meet up there too, and we'd get along well. And then in June we up and had an argument.

Pavlo and a friend of his had come to visit us at our dormitory, and someone needed to fetch a bucket of water. But he didn't help. I fetched that bucket of water, and then I no longer went for a rendezvous with him. It's not that he didn't notice; he didn't realize that he should've helped. He was accustomed to girls fetching water themselves in Kurin.

His village was called Kurin because of the Cossacks of the Bakhmach Regiment that had been sent to the guardhouse there, and those roughnecks lived in makeshift huts there called *kurins*. People from Kurin are still called "arsonists" in the area because of the cruel revenge the Cossacks used to carry out for everyday wrongdoings: setting someone's house on fire. Obviously, though,

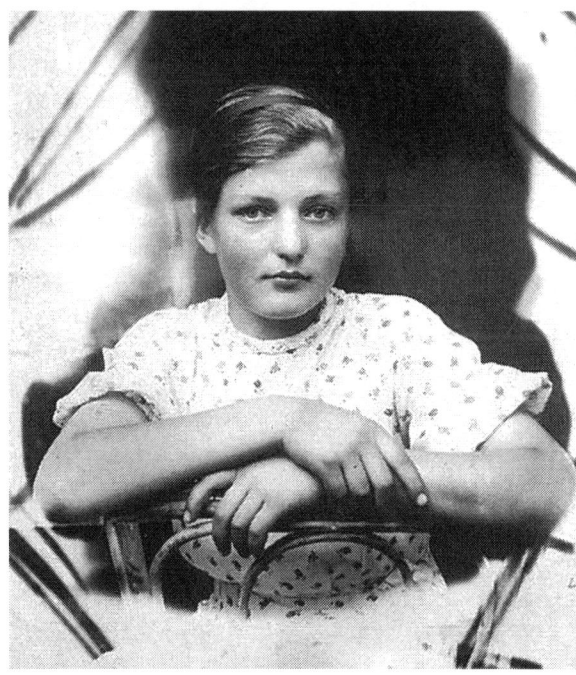

My grandmother, Nadia, in tenth grade. My grandfather refused to give this photograph back to her when he was suddenly called to the front. 1941

My grandmother wrote one hundred and thirty letters to my grandfather when he was in the army ...

people are the same in Kurin as everywhere — good and not so good.

But in Bakhmach, where I'm from, that wasn't the case — because it's a city [*she laughs*].

So, he and I didn't meet up anymore. Pavlo tried, but I showed him my female pride. Well, and then he decided to show his. I gave him back his photograph of him and asked him to give me back mine. But he didn't return it.

On the back of my photograph, I had written in Russian, "May it help you, may my young love protect you from bullets." Later your grandfather would write to me in Ukrainian, "The words that you wrote on the photograph really do seem to protect me."

Everyone wrote that sort of thing at the time — in Russian on top of it because in Ukrainian it didn't seem as fancy, though everyone, at home and at school, spoke our language. Incidentally, Grandpa's division published a newspaper in Ukrainian called *For the Fatherland!*, and his commander, a Russian, was constantly asking that someone translate it for him. "So what are they writing about the Fatherland?" he'd ask in Ukrainian, but pronouncing the word "fatherland" in Russian — *batkOvshchyna*.

I had gifted him the photograph back in May, then in July already rumors started spreading that the front was approaching. And the Germans weren't that sprightly anymore; they had gone quiet.

So why did I write that? Because Pavlo had said to me on more than one occasion, "The front will be back soon, I'll go to war yet …" But I didn't think about it that much: I was eighteen and Pavlo was twenty, and he was a soldier already.

We parted ways and didn't see each other at all until 1946. I remember his first letter from the front by heart: "Write to me as a friend, Cupid's business is worth nothing here." I felt so sorry for him, he was going through so much …

We wrote to each other a lot, but in this formal tone. We had had a fight, after all, so we wouldn't admit to loving one another. Everything was very prim.

I was convinced for some reason that Pavlo would come back. I wrote that in one of my letters, and this was his dashing reply: "If your words come true, you deserve a kiss for them and then some."

I don't believe in fate, but sometimes I felt the urge to.

* * *

When after the occupation we were being lined up at the enlistment center, the officer said, "Whoever has served in the artillery, take two steps forward." I stepped out of the line. And of those who were left in it, many died two months later, during the assault-crossing of the Dnipro River. There were rumors going round that they hadn't even been issued uniforms.

… and my grandfather wrote her one hundred and twenty letters back. My grandmother has kept them all to this day.

An extract from my grandmother's letter: "For some reason, I'm absolutely convinced you're still alive ... The times we spent together were the best times of my life."

In November 1943 the battalion commander sent me with the commander of the intelligence section to the front line to observe the enemy. That was the Lyutizh Bridgehead, near Yasnohorodka. We jumped into a trench and caught our breaths. I didn't like the trench. I proposed to the sergeant that we dig a new one.

The soil was sandy, and we dug it out in no time — and as we're digging a mine fell into the old trench.

A small shard got lodged in my head but didn't damage my skull.

Or there was the incident on December 7, 1943 near Rosa Luxemburg's hamlet outside Korosten: Our artillery battery was supporting a battalion, and the German infantry was being supported by twelve tanks. Our cannons were laid for direct fire. The battery commander, Senior Lieutenant Rozumovskyi, was giving orders, and I was relaying them to the battery.

We noticed a tank, and I ran over to the first cannon and showed the gunner where it was moving from. Then I ran back. During this time a shell exploded on the building where the battery commander was. Rozumovskyi and the signalman Shevchenko were killed.

On December 28, 1943 the new battery commander sent me to the front line to collect a captured German cannon and shells. Five of us climbed up onto a limber (a horse-drawn wagon that cannons would be attached to for transport). We had almost reached our target already when carts from the mortar battery appeared. Dmytro Tkachenko, who was driving, asked that some of us move over to their cart because their drawbar kept rising. All of us had warmed up by then; no one wanted to get off.

For some reason I decided to jump off and ran over to the cart, and Oleksii Zhyla followed me. And then out of nowhere we heard an explosion: the limber had run onto an anti-tank mine. The three soldiers on it were killed, and the others were seriously wounded.

* * *

I think that one other reason your grandpa survived was because he loved education and was smart. When, after the occupation, the men were recalled for service, they were lined up and the commander said, "Whoever has served in the artillery, take two steps forward." Pavlo stepped out of the line, and that saved him — because the artillery, after all, is not as bad as the infantry.

He wrote to me in a letter: "I sometimes try to remember what we learned in algebra in tenth grade. Nothing comes back to me. Some sort of progressions, inequalities, bases with negative exponents, etc. appear in my mind, and that's all. But I have a feeling that if I looked it over twice, I'd remember it." That's what he wrote. And while he was at war, he used a logarithm table and some sort

My grandfather describes the military victories in Poland and hints at the beauty of the local Polish girls: "Then we beat those German dogs in Halychyna, and now we are beating them back through Poland beyond the Vistula ... There are a lot of interesting things here, but there's no time to find out more about them. And the Polish girls are mostly very beautiful."

My grandfather Pavlo: the insignia on his shoulder shows his rank of artillery sergeant. He has among his medals an Order of Glory and a Medal "For Courage." 1945

of mathematical instruments.

After the war Pavlo was still finishing his service, then wrote that he was in Kurin already. I was studying in Kyiv at the time, at the agricultural academy, and wrote back: "Pavlo dearest, I'm begging you, I'll come home during the school break, and you come visit me in Bakhmach."

And he came. And I asked for his forgiveness. We embraced, cried a bit, and then started dating seriously.

He couldn't be a full-time student because his father had died in 1944 and Pavlo was taking care of the family (only two of the four brothers returned from the front). We didn't get married until February 1949.

I didn't even have a dress for the wedding, so Pavlo gave me some crepe back satin that he had found during the war. I had the dress made at a tailor's in Holosiiv, on Dobryi Shliakh Street. I remember it as if it were yesterday — because there was nothing available to buy then. Once in a while my father would bring fabric home from Minsk when he was working as a train maintenance technician on the Kremenchuk-Minsk line, and that was it.

But that crepe back satin Pavlo had sent by mail from the front. He sent a few parcels like that home. This is what would happen: after a battle somewhere in Germany, a store would be burning, and some soldier would walk in, grab a roll of fabric, and then give it out to family and friends ...

I once said, "You could've at least brought me back a gold ring." And Pavlo replied, "If you only knew how those rings were gotten ... A soldier would chop off a dead soldier's finger and remove a ring." I didn't bring it up anymore.

Then one time ten years later we were in Kyiv, and Pavlo said, "Let's go into this store." It turned out to be a jewelry store. We picked out a wedding band for me, but Pavlo never ended up wearing one.

For the first five years, he screamed in his sleep. He was moving on the enemy, and shooting, and calling out to someone—"Throw a grenade!", "Hurrah!", and whatever else it is soldiers yell—until I'd poke him in the side. But otherwise, he didn't like to talk about the war, unless it was somewhere with other men. Most soldiers who made it through alive didn't like to bring it up.

My grandfather and grandmother after their wedding. 1949

He'd describe how he had wounded his knee. He also had shrapnel in the back of his head. It had grown over and didn't bother him: he ended up dying with that shrapnel still in him. He'd describe how he had refused to shoot two POWs. He

The Solodko family. Below: Pavlo (my grandfather), Nadiia (my grandmother), and Volodia (my father and future car engineer). Top: Vira (future professor at the Kyiv-Mohyla Academy), and Yura (future doctor). 1966

said to the commanding officer, "In battle—sure, no problem, but otherwise I can't."

He'd also talk about an incident similar to the one that had happened to him when he was escaping the camp. He was walking after a battle and pretended not to notice a wounded German, but the German decided to shoot him in the back. But Pavlo heard the click of the lock and managed to turn around in time and get a shot off first.

About May 9, 1945 he wrote the following in a letter to me: "Everyone was a drunkard, except for me." He didn't drink or smoke, even while at war. That too attracted me to your grandfather.

* * *

From 1953 to 1984 Grandpa worked as the director of the Bakhmach-1 Village School. Grandma taught at the same school. Grandpa died in 2008. Grandma wanted to put their wartime correspondence into his coffin, but her children wouldn't let her.

Dmytro Krapyvenko

"The Infantry Had Deserted Us, but We Had Already Taken Our Positions, So We Weren't about to Retreat."

Even half a century later, Ivan Serhiiovych Mikhieiev, my maternal grandfather and a former frontline driver, could recall every last town on the road to Uman as if he were there yesterday. As for my paternal grandfather, Petro Fedorovych Krapyvenko, he left behind a few medals, an Order of the Great Patriotic War, and a family story grown hazy with time.

"I remember when the Krauts bombed this station. It was like something out of a book: both heaven and earth were in flames," my grandfather remembers when we stop in Popilnia. It's 1995 and we are travelling from Korosten to Uman to attend my older sister Maryna's wedding.

Over half a century has passed, but he, a former frontline driver, can recall every last town as if he were there yesterday.

"The woman who put us up in Skvyra treated us to some homebrew. It was the first time I ever tried it. Man, was it tough getting up the next morning!" he laughs. "And in Bila Tserkva we had a fight with the police; they'd gotten a bit sharp with us."

My maternal grandfather, Ivan Serhiiovych Mikhieiev, was always a witty man, even when recounting stories about the war. It wasn't because he found the war funny as such; that was just his nature. I think that's precisely what helped him make it through tough times at the front.

Like many young men of his time, Ivan Mikhieiev wanted to join a flying club and become a pilot, but instead he ended up training to become a driver.

"It worked out better that way," Grandpa Ivan says now. "I would've crashed and burned in the bushes in the very first days of the war."

In June 1941 an artillery division was formed in his home district of Yuryev-Polsky in Vladimir Oblast, Russia, and nearly the whole unit fell while defending Smolensk. But instead of joining them, Grandpa Ivan, the smart and literate young Komsomol member that he was, managed to get taken to a political academy that

Ivan feels young and is still driving at the age of eighty-six.

had been evacuated from Leningrad. Who knows how many red stars the new political instructor Mikhieiev would have gotten on his collar tabs if not for the rapid German offensive?

After a few months of cadet life, of the barracks' internal struggles between the "townies" and the "country boys," and of being punished "in the dark" (when someone would be covered with an army overcoat and beaten by everyone at the behest of a vicious petty officer), the rank and file were sent as infantry to the front.

"Lenin's city is in danger," the political commissioner said in his farewell speech.

January 1942 was the time of my grandfather's worst memories are from January 1942. He was on the Volkhov front. They were starving, and there were weapons and ammunition shortages. It was below zero, and the swamps around Novgorod were impassable.

"There were corpses piled up: young lads with dark features—Spaniards from the Blue Division. They didn't even fight, it seems. They just froze to death," Grandpa Ivan remembers. "And it was rare for any of our soldiers to make it to their third offensive."

During one of these attacks, a German mine exploded somewhere right next to him, and shrapnel got lodged in his leg. The doctors in the hospital couldn't remove all the fragments. He was wounded in February, and by April the unit my grandfather was fighting in had found itself surrounded in a location with the horrible and gruesome name of Myasnoy Bor, namely, "Butcher's Wood."

They were the Second Shock Army, the remnants of which were taken prisoner under the command of General Vlasov, who would later cooperate with the Nazis and lead the infamous Russian Liberation Army. Only a small group of the unit's soldiers managed to escape after being surrounded, and they joined the defenders of Leningrad.

His memories of the field hospital involve "constant millet soup" and showings of pre-war comedies in lieu of dinner. They reorganized and were redeployed, with Ivan Mikhieiev becoming a driver for the artillery brigade of Katyusha rocket launchers on the Kursk Bulge.

He earned his first Order of Glory in the Battle of Prokhorovka and received a second one for his time in the Battle of Okhtyrka.

"The infantry deserted us without providing cover, but we'd already taken our positions, so we weren't about to retreat," my grandfather explained after a few jabs at me for "pestering him for war stories."

He shared memories of the abandoned German equipment in the spring mud near Shepetivka, of being on the steppe with nowhere to hide from the bombers, the intense suffering of his platoon leader who was wounded in the stomach near Proskurov, the fierce battles for Zhytomyr, the tears of the terrified Volkssturm POWs, wounds sustained in the last days of the war, and hundreds of long, long miles on the front.

At the same time he reminisced about his cheerful brothers-in-arms: lads from Podillia, former sailors called up to the navy before the war and sent off to fight as infantry on dry land, the comical Polish lads in their cropped trousers, and seeing a restaurant with his own eyes for the first time in Kraków.

Grandpa Ivan's stories intertwined wit and tragedy in a way that not every talented screenwriter could pull off. Then again, he hadn't seen the war on a screen.

The medals are the only thing I have left of my Grandfather Petro, who was from the Kuban region. Among his service medals is his Order of the Great Patriotic War, which wasn't given out to just anybody.

I barely remember my paternal grandfather, Petro Fedorovych Krapyvenko: he died when I was eight years old. He left behind a handful of medals, an Order of the Great Patriotic War, and his story, preserved in dusty family annals.

Petro Krapyvenko, a lad from the Kuban region in eastern Ukraine, found himself on the front at the beginning of the war. Like Grandpa Ivan, he was a driver. He was wounded in the Caucasus Campaign and was then taken prisoner. He escaped, then fought in either a Slovak or Czech partisan detachment before joining the Red Army.

After the war the "relevant authorities" didn't forget his spell in captivity and exiled him to the Urals for this. I don't know whether it was as a result of his exile or because of collectivization and repressions, both of which caused terrible suffering for the poor Kuban Krapyvenko family, but Grandpa Petro sincerely hated Stalin.

After his time in the Urals, he moved to Tbilisi, where he worked as a bus driver for a long time. It was a trend among Georgian drivers at the time to hang a picture of Koba — that is, Stalin — in their cabs. Petro Krapyvenko's bus bypassed this trend: once he even came to blows with his new colleagues for trying to hang up a picture of Stalin in his vehicle.

Taras Shamaida

A German Tried Persuading My Grandfather to Marry His Daughter—So That the Red Army Wouldn't Touch Her.

My grandfather, Mykola Vasylovych Kutko, lived in Lysychansk in the Luhansk region. He was born in 1921 in the village of Vilshana in the Dvorichanskyi District of Kharkiv Oblast. He was a witness to collectivization, and the Holodomor, and all the horrors of World War II. My grandfather died in 2013.

Prewar Life

Prior to collectivization, the Kutko family belonged to the class of financially comfortable middle peasants. "They had land, cattle, and a large orchard. They worked a lot but also lived well," my grandfather recalls. "But in 1929 the communists began to take everything away from the people. They took a wonderful plough from us, oxen, horses—everything."

My grandpa, Mykola Vasylovich Kutko, can't mention the Holodomor without tears till this day: "The commissars were taking away everything they could—bread, any and all food, every last apple they could find. People were digging up frozen beets in the fields in desperation. There were corpses everywhere out on the roads. The communists would scour yards with dogs in search of hidden food.

"In Russia, right next door to us, there was none of that, and people would go there to exchange gold and little crucifixes for bread. But at the border they would be stopped, pulled off trains and carts, stripped of everything they had, and sent back to die."

Mykola lost an aunt, an uncle, a grandfather, and a grandmother. His father's and mother's health declined, and they too died within a few years.

In 1937 another aunt took the boy away to Lysychansk and persuaded a mining secondary school to accept him as an orphan. He ended up staying in Donbas to live, and in 1939 he went to work at the Melnykov Mine, to which he returned after the war as well, spending nearly half a century working as a miner.

Retreat

Mykola was drafted into the army in May 1941, and in June the war began. He served at that time in the training unit of an aviation regiment near Kolomyia.

One day there was a shortage of drivers for the retreat of a large quantity of military equipment, and Mykola was brought on as an assistant truck driver.

We drove off to Kyiv for tanks," my grandfather recalls. "Our aviation unit was in Kamianka: all of it was destroyed in the first days of the war, and then they started bombarding us too. All of a sudden Messerschmitts show up and start shooting at our vehicles. The roads are smoking, everything's destroyed, loads of killed soldiers are being hauled off on carts ..."

As they retreated to the east, they burned down a refueling station in Zhytomyr so that it wouldn't fall into German hands.

"Our motor battalion, which was upward of eight vehicles, fell behind and was trying to catch up with our unit in this turmoil. We had fuel and ammunition but no food. In order to avoid being noticed by German aircraft, we drove only by night; turning on headlights meant we would be shot.

"But driving without headlights was very difficult. At the Desna River one of our cars turned over in the rain, and we barely managed to pull it out. We finally caught up with our unit by Bila Tserkva, where they had returned to from the Chernihiv region."

In Captivity

In September 1941 their column came under heavy bombardment in the Kharkiv region. Many people died, and my grandfather was wounded in the head. He didn't regain consciousness until he was already in captivity.

"We were lined up in a long, long column of five men across. People were flanked on either side of us, crying and looking for their loved ones in the column. Whoever rushed out of formation in response to a mother's cries would get shot by the Germans or beaten with the butts of their guns. The weather was dry: a ton of dust hung over the column. At first they herded us on foot westward. Then they piled us into wagons and drove us off to Zhytomyr, and a few days later to Kholm."

Mykola Kutko met the winter of 1941 – 42 in Kholm (now Polish territory). He and the other prisoners wintered in pits dug into the ground. A lot of people would approach them, wanting to take in the POWs.

My grandfather, Mykola Kutko. 1945

The Germans would release captive Polish citizens to their homes, and sometimes Ukrainians from the USSR as well, particularly when relatives arrived with their documents, but they didn't release the Russians. From Kholm my grandfather was taken with other POWs to a concentration camp one hundred twenty kilometers from Berlin, and then on to another camp near Fürstenberg, where they were held till the end of winter.

"Then in the spring of 1942, they used fire hoses with fog nozzles to 'bathe' us and drove us into town. In Fürstenberg German farmers 'divvied up' the POWs. Everyone who took captives to work on their farm assumed a personal responsibility for the prisoners. Our master turned out to be fairly generous: he lodged us in his granary, and let us help ourselves to food and cook for ourselves. He had a dozen or so of us, mostly Ukrainians."

And since my grandfather was familiar with German electrical equipment from his time in Donbas and had picked up some German there as well, he found himself in a "privileged position": he barely worked in the field, but instead stayed behind at the farm and fixed the equipment.

A Miraculous Rescue

In 1942 Mykola fell ill with typhus. A lot of people were dying from typhus then, and this same fate seemed to await him as well. While laid up in the Guben city hospital for POWs, Mykola lost consciousness, and by the time he opened his eyes, he was already being transported to the morgue as beyond help.

He was saved by a meeting that can be described as nothing short of a miracle. "As I was being taken to the morgue, a police

major—a Ukrainian—noticed me and asked, 'Where are you taking him? Why, he's still alive!' And then he leaned in over me and asked, 'Where are you from?'
"'From the Kharkiv region,' I say.
"'And from what district?'
"'From the Dvorichanskyi District.'
"'And from which village?'
"'From Vilshany.'
"'And whose son are you?!'
"I answered.
"'Head back immediately!' the policeman commanded. I was carried back to the medical unit, where the stranger ordered, 'This man must be saved!' Then to me he said, 'I'm Hrytsko Chubenko, remember my name.'

"Later I figured out that that had been my uncle. This miraculous encounter saved my life. I convalesced on cod liver oil, and Chubenko checked on me a number of times to see how I was recovering. Later the Germans accused him of being up to no good and shot him."

In the Medical Unit

After regaining his health, Mykola Kutko became a steward in that same medical unit and lived there for two years. He acquired even better German, which would come in handy in many a situation.

The captives were malnourished, especially the Soviet ones, and so the French prisoners would share their food. With time generically addressed parcels began arriving from the United States for the Soviet captives.

Mykola befriended the Germans in the kitchen and, owing to this, was able to take away leftovers—a few liters of soup that he would always distribute to the POWs in the hospital. He would even supplement the food of the doctors, who were also Soviet POWs.

"Everyone knew me in the hospital and would let me go wherever I wanted. I became friends with French and Yugoslav captives, who were also in our hospital," my grandfather narrates. "The French POWs were even allowed to walk around the city freely. I remember a doctor who was a French major forever consulting in German with our Dr. Raiskyi, a Ukrainian from Melitopol, about how to perform certain operations."

In the meantime, the front was nearing Germany. "American aircraft were bombing the neighboring city of Cottbus so hard that the ground was shaking. I look up, and twenty bombers are flying at us, and they're surrounded by even more fighter jets keeping watch."

The captives weren't kept under that close a watch in the hospital, and one day Mykola Kutko, together with a wounded Soviet pilot, decided to escape. They got ready, then left the hospital at night. But almost immediately they ran into a policeman driving down the street.

"The pilot scuttled off to the side, but I lingered and the policeman noticed me. 'Stop! Where are you from?' he asked. I said that I had been in the workroom and fallen asleep, but now needed to go to Hospital No. 104. The policeman gave me a ride to the hospital. 'Take him, he's one of yours,' he said. The guards knew me, so they didn't suspect anything."

My grandfather is eighty-nine years old, but his memory is still perfect.

An Unexpected Proposition

In the spring of 1945, a guard at the hospital named Michael invited Mykola to his house out of the blue.

"We arrived, and his wife brought us something to eat. Then Michael says to me, 'I have an eighteen-year-old daughter and no one else. Let's go ahead and register you as her husband.'

"He thought that as a relative of a Red Army soldier, Soviet authorities would leave him alone. Germans were very afraid for their families because our people really did do all kinds of unsavory things in Germany: I would see that later with my own eyes.

"'Why, the Soviets will shoot me immediately!' I replied to his proposition. 'And you too.'"

But Michael didn't believe it and was always trying to persuade me to marry his daughter, promising me both clothing and money. The man simply refused to understand that for the Soviet government all captives were traitors, and whoever married into an enemy soldier's family definitely wouldn't remain alive—for just that reason.

Liberation

In April 1945 my grandfather's hospital was seized by the Red Army. No one knew what fate awaited them. Many POWs and *Ostarbeiters* were attempting to escape to the West. Meanwhile, special subunits were poking around everywhere and snatching up citizens of the USSR.

Rumors reached the hospital that in other parts of the front POWs were often being arrested as enemies of the people and even being shot. But my grandfather and his friends proved lucky. Each of them was interrogated quickly and somewhat carelessly, taken off to the bathhouse, and issued a uniform. Even a portion of the police officers that were deemed inculpable in the crimes of the Nazis were being taken into the Red Army. Mykola Kutko was immediately appointed as a senior sergeant. He served in Germany until 1946.

In March 1946 my grandfather was demobilized along with other miners. They were needed to restore the Donbas mines that the Red Army had blasted or flooded as it retreated.

It's interesting to note that over the course of the entire war, he never did take the oath of enlistment for the Red Army: the war caught him in "boot camp," and later on commanding officers had other things to worry about.

Serhii Taran

"One Grandfather Went to Fight in Bessarabia in 1940, While the Other Joined Stepan Bandera's Insurgent Army."

Both of my grandfathers are from the same village of Pavlysh in Kirovohrad Oblast. For one grandfather the war ended while he was in Prague; it ended for the other while "in the woods" among the "Banderites."

My paternal grandfather, Vasyl Vasylovych Taran (1908 – 1983), was a regular soldier. The war began for him in the town of Bolhrad, Bessarabia, where he had joined the 25th Artillery Division back in 1940.

On the morning of June 22, my grandfather was called up to his unit, and Grandma Mania—Mariia Hnativna Taran (née Shvachka) (1908 – 1985)—was left all alone with her six-year-old daughter, while expecting her son to be born at any moment.

Straightaway the outskirts of Bolhrad became a front, and my grandmother grabbed a few satchels and boarded the train back to her native Pavlysh that very day. It took her and her daughter ten days to reach there because their train was bombarded twice.

"The first time they sat us in the back and the front of the train got bombed, and the second time we were sitting at the front and the rear of the train got bombed," my grandmother described.

Back in her home village, everyone was waiting to be evacuated. They had already learned how to tell the different planes apart, even by their sound: if it was a bomber, everyone would go hide in their cellars. But the evacuation was as poorly organized as the concurrent mobilization: the army conscripts were held at the enlistment office for three days but were never taken to the front. This ended up proving fatal for many of the village boys: left behind on "enemy territory" because of delays in mobilization, they were labeled as traitors upon the Red Army's arrival and were passed through the meat grinder of penal battalions and "test units," where, as some of the Pavlysh veterans recall, they were issued one rifle to share among four soldiers.

When the German troops were approaching, Grandma Mania and some of the other families from the village decided to flee across the Dnipro River. Her son, my father, was just five days old at the time. But they were too late.

On the approach to the crossing, near the village of Dereviivka, they were overtaken by German motorcyclists. The Germans put all of their belongings into one pile and began to frisk the villagers to see what pickings were on offer. They found some gray cloth and red braid trim in my grandmother's suitcase, which were handed over to the officers as material for trousers.

The Germans turned out to have their wits about them and worked out that the refugees included some relatives of Soviet officers, so they set about interrogating them in order to find out who they were. No one said anything, however, and after being held till morning, the fugitives were all released and ordered to return home.

Life during the first year of occupation was very difficult for my grandma and her two small children. The worst part was that no one had sown anything in the spring, and there were no jobs whatsoever. My grandfather's brother, Danylo, saved them. He worked in agricultural product procurement and secretly brought them grain hidden in his boots.

My grandmother used a wild foal she had found outside the village for the heavy work around her smallholding, but when "our side" arrived later, it was confiscated for the needs of the Red Army.

From time to time, German soldiers would stop by my grandmother's house. There were no partisan activities in the vicinity of the village, and there were no particular conflicts between the local population and its occupiers in Pavlysh itself. The German officers paid no attention to the locals whatsoever, while the rank-and-file soldiers would sometimes give the children some of their army rations.

To avoid what could be called "unintended consequences," my grandmother—who, before the war, had been a real glamour gal—deliberately tried to dress as scruffily as possible, "accidentally" smearing her face with soot, since she knew that German soldiers "didn't like dirty women."

At one point the Germans set up a bakery in her house. My grandmother received a little on the side for it, of course. They brought flour and, more importantly, firewood to the house, the latter of which was for some reason a highly valuable commodity in the village at the time. Her neighbor Dunka was so envious of this firewood that she went to the local council and denounced my grandmother as the wife of a political commissar in a supervisory military position, a fact they should know because they "hang all the commissars."

Families of commissars were indeed being executed by the Germans, so the next morning the Gestapo came to her house ("in black

Grandpa Vasyl, Grandma Mania, and Auntie Larysa. This is the same photograph that saved the family's life. 1940

uniform," as she would later describe) and in a bureaucratic manner calmly explained to her that, seeing as she was the wife of a political commissar, she and her children would all be hanged the following day.

There was no sense in persuading them otherwise, and my grandmother distinctly recalls how much she wanted to be hanged first so she wouldn't see her children being hanged. And they definitely would have been hanged had it not occurred to Grandma Mania to show the Gestapo officers a picture from before the war in which the insignia on his collar tabs visibly proved that her husband was not a commissar at all but "just" a Red Army officer. The execution was cancelled.

Dunka, the neighbor, was flogged in public for lying. It's worth adding that back then village people didn't wear undergarments, so the whole village saw quite vividly what it meant to lie to the new regime.

At the time my grandfather was fighting on the front, defending Odesa and Sevastopol. While heavily wounded, he and his comrades-in-arms were surrounded at Sevastopol. They held their defense for a long time in the catacombs, but when their ammunition ran out, he was taken prisoner. During the fighting, he hid his officer insignia and mixed in with the other rank-and-file soldiers, thus increasing his chances of survival.

The POW camp was near Mykolaiv. The conditions were so terrible there that within a few months my grandfather had become very ill, but he still had to go out and perform hard labor. The prisoners were particularly beleaguered by hunger as all they were given was half-cooked bran still in its husk.

One of the camp guards happened to be from the same area as my grandfather and recognized him. Rather than telling his superiors about my grandfather's officer status, he warned my grandfather that the Germans had noticed him because he couldn't march at all and concluded he must be an officer. It was this guard who let Grandma Mania know that my grandfather had been taken prisoner and warned her that he was sure to die if no one got him out of there.

My grandmother realized straightaway that my grandfather had to be rescued somehow. There was a similar POW camp near Pavlysh, and hundreds of ex-Red Army soldiers had already perished in it. As they prepared to retreat, the Germans allowed the people of Pavlysh to take any prisoners home if they were their relatives.

Many of her fellow villagers took home Red Army prisoners that were complete strangers to them, claiming them to be relatives and most likely saving their lives.

Inspired by these events, my grandmother bundled up two pieces of cloth, a kerchief, trousers, and some other things, and went off to organize her husband's escape. All the "wealth" she had on her she gave to the guard from their area, and while that guard was on the lookout, my grandfather and some of his comrades escaped. They travelled by night to Pavlysh. A manhunt ensued, and my grandfather remembers sitting in a swamp for a long time in order to throw the dogs off their scent. In the end they escaped their pursuers after muscling a cart off a local peasant.

For multiple weeks my grandfather lived in an old well by his own house while Fedot Illo, the village elder and my grandfather's stepbrother, made him some certificate—a ludicrous one, what with today's knowledge of the war—confirming that he had allegedly been released from the POW camp "on account of his poor health."

As it later turned out, Fedot was connected to the underground resistance, which explained why the Ukrainian Hilfspolizei were mostly on the villagers' side: for instance, they would warn people when to hide their children to avoid being kidnapped and "taken off to Germany".

In the winter my grandfather would fashion shoes for people out of old car tires, and in the summer he would work in his vegetable patch.

Children weren't the only ones being taken to Germany. When my grandfather was going to be sent there, his brother Danylo went in his place under my grandfather's name. As he himself explained it, he did it because he had no children, whereas Vasyl already had two.

Later my grandfather did in fact get taken off to Germany, but he managed to break through the boards in the freight train that was transporting him and fled. When he returned to his village, he hid in a cellar that had a pit dug in it. People had covered the pit with boards and scattered hay, and put a goat on top—so yes, you could say that my grandfather waited for the Reds "under a goat."

After the Germans fled and before the Reds arrived, the women of the village grabbed their pitchforks and went off looting, taking with them anything and everything left behind by the enemy.

Years later, local children were still wearing coats sewn from German woolen blankets with soft suede collars. The women took pitchforks with them, thinking that were they to stumble on a mine or a grenade, this would spare them from having to fling it away with their bare hands. Grandpa Vasyl couldn't stop laughing when he heard about the pitchforks, aware that they would be useless against the mines.

My grandparents waited for the Red Army to arrive, but naturally they were afraid that my grandfather might be shot because of his time spent imprisoned. As it turned out, the Battle for Sevastopol was one of the few instances where being captured wasn't viewed as treason, and so my grandfather was "pardoned." He was even ordered to help organize the collective farm, since there were no other men left in the village and the front needed provisions.

My grandfather endured two months on the collective farm, setting up the "Grain Procurement Bureau." But by spring 1944 he had been called to the front and subsequently fought all over Eastern Europe. As a member of the 9th Guards Division, he distinguished himself by shooting down a Messerschmitt-109 with his rifle as it flew over his unit's position. Bringing down an aircraft with light arms fire was extremely unusual, and my grandfather received an Order of the Great Patriotic War First Class.

The war ended for him in the Czech capital and with the rank of guards captain. Higher command offered that he continue his service and promised him an important military career. He would have stayed in the military had my grandmother not explicitly told him that she hated war so much that she would never again be a soldier's wife. And so, Grandpa Vasyl once more returned to Pavlysh.

Little is known about my other grandfather, Ivan Zakharovych Skoryk (1906 – ?), although some of his story did emerge finally after the fall of the Soviet Union.

Before the war his family had been one of the hubs of local cultural life and all its manifestations. As other villagers used to describe it, my grandfather was very "convivial," meanwhile his cousin Vasyl Sukhomlynskyi, who later became a well-known education specialist, was "well-read" but "very stern" My grandmother, Tetiana Yalyseiivna Skoryk (1906 – 1993), would talk about how before the war their home was always "packed" with people and they would host all sorts of fun get-togethers.

However, after Grandpa Ivan went off to war in 1941, no one heard anything about him until 1947. Grandma Tania, who was left with an infant born in 1941 (my mother), survived the occupation, and as soon as the Red Army arrived, she tried to find out what had happened to my grandfather.

She only learned what had happened after the war, when she went to see my Uncle Dymyd in Kyiv. He said that Ivan was fighting "in the forest." Back then nobody used the name "Ukrainian Insurgent Army" in reference to Stepan Bandera's men; instead, they'd say someone was fighting "in the forest" or "with the Banderites." But Uncle Dymyd had worse news as well: after eight years of separation, Grandpa Ivan had found himself another woman, a "Banderite woman."

I know nothing about where Grandpa Ivan fought, what he did, or what fate awaited him after the 1940s. No one in Pavlyshyn knew anything either since no one had seen him. It was only in the 1960s that people found out he was still alive and living with a family either in Kirovohrad (present-day Kropyvnytskyi) or Znamianka.

His adult children were tracked down in the 1970s, but, unfortunately, my grandmother didn't want to see them. It had nothing to do with them being "Banderites,"

Grandpa Ivan during the district consumer union accountants' course at the Kharkiv Regional Consumer Union. 1936

of course. Grandma Tania intensely disliked the communists too. She hung up portraits of the communist leaders above the stove in the kitchen shed outside—"So we don't stain the white wall," she used to say, or so that when the hot oil spits out of the pan, "It'll squirt onto their dirty mugs". When the first elections came along in, first, the Ukrainian SSR and then independent Ukraine, she always voted for the nationalist Rukh party and dissident leader Viacheslav Chornovil.

My grandmother had long forgiven my grandfather for going off with the "Banderites," but she simply couldn't forgive him for going off with a Banderite woman.

Taras Antypovych

A Life Bought with Milk and Cheese

Thanks are owed to three people for the salvation of my grandfather, Ivan Tymofiiovych Denysko: an Estonian captain, who didn't make his soldiers take up their arms in a senseless shootout against German machine gunners; the farmstead owner Mr. Latsis, who freed him from the Germans with bribes of eggs, milk, and cheese; and an unknown man, who noted in a hospital certificate that my grandfather had served in the army as a clerk at headquarters and was therefore trustworthy.

My grandfather, Ivan Tymofiiovych Denysko (1922 – 1992) from the Poltava region, learned about the start of World War II on a troop train. This train was carrying conscripts from Ukraine to the Workers' and Peasants' Red Army in a territory newly occupied by the Communist Russian Empire — the Baltics.

The conscripts were hurriedly given out prehistoric rifles, shown how to pull the trigger, and tossed into battle with the Germans. The battles on the territory of Latvia ended in encirclement for my grandfather and his comrades-in-arms (or rather, lack-of-arms). They tried to escape, making their way eastward through forests and swamps.

One night they fell asleep exhausted in a small wood. My grandfather was awoken by the sound of motorcycles. He leaps to his feet and sees that their commander, an Estonian captain, is standing at the edge of the wood with a white flag and that the entire wood has been surrounded by German machine gunners on motorcycles. Resistance was futile. I'd like to extend my thanks to the Estonian captain for not making his boys take up arms for a senseless shootout against a motorized armada of machine gunners.

My grandfather had a lump of sugar in his pocket. That lump plus water were his only nourishment for several days in a POW camp.

Meanwhile, the Germans were parceling out captives to Latvian farmsteads, whose owners were supposed to supply the Reich with food and were being given a supplemental labor force for this reason.

My grandfather got lucky. His master Mr. Latsis, from a farmstead bearing the same name near Daugavplis, turned out to be an upright and fair man. Seeing that my grandfather was able to do any sort of farmwork and that he was conscientious and honest, Latsis treated him like an equal. They ate meals at the same table and worked together in the field.

However, it was possible that my grandfather's Cossack roots, which most likely stretched back centuries to Kremenets, would not allow him to reconcile with captivity, even one as seemingly comfortable as this experience was. As such, one day my grandfather, together with another war prisoner from a neighboring farmstead, naively ran away eastward, to Ukraine.

Needless to say, the Germans caught them very quickly. They beat them profusely. And they would've killed my grandfather had that same Master Latsis not come to his aid. He loaded up a cart with eggs, milk, cheese, and butter — whatever he had on hand — and rode off to buy Ivan Denysko off the Germans. And he bought him out of captivity. Meanwhile, his friend, in all likelihood, was killed, since my grandfather never did find him after the war.

My grandfather, Ivan Denysko, with my Grandma Mariia, by then his bride.

When the Germans skedaddled out of Latvia, the captives were rounded up from the farmsteads and remobilized by the Soviet army. My grandfather ended up taking part in the battles on the advance on Königsberg.

Later he would always recall with indignation how the former POWs were treated: weapons would be distributed in the morning and taken back in the evening. Apparently, when it came to dying on the battlefield, everyone was equal, but when it was time for a rest break, you became a second-class citizen.

On October 9, 1944 my grandfather was wounded in the leg. He lost a section of the bone and calf to a shell fragment. The driver that was transporting him to the field hospital said, "Thank that shrapnel because you're both alive and done fighting."

But my grandfather never uttered thank you to the shrapnel because later that wound would open every summer and, with each year, heal more painfully and slowly until it finally took him from this world.

After the war my grandfather worked as a combine operator. In his native village of Zahrunivka in the Poltava region, he taught all of his fellow villagers to rake hay onto tripods, as the Latvians did, and not leave it on the ground where it was susceptible to moisture and rot.

He would tell his relatives about the horrific deeds committed by the Muscovite "liberators" of the Latvian people in the summer of 1941. They shot the political prisoners dead, but were in such a rush to get away from the Germans that they didn't make time to bury them. And while the fighting was in progress, the corpses decomposed in the scorching sun.

But the third person that deserves thanks for saving my grandfather's life, alongside the Estonian captain and Mr. Latsis, is the unknown man who, while writing up a certificate of discharge from the hospital for my grandfather, noted that he had held the position of clerk at headquarters, rather than being a POW. My grandfather was never a clerk: his handwriting wasn't even remotely suitable for such a position. Evidently, the man was filled with sympathy toward the young man, who was so eager to go home and didn't know what awaited former POWs that had worked on Latvian farms there. My grandfather was "assigned" a position that was supposed to serve as a "lightning deterrent": he had served at headquarters and was therefore trustworthy.

And indeed, my grandfather didn't get persecuted upon his return.

Incidentally, while my grandfather was in the hospital, they issued a killed in action letter for him and sent it to his mother, my Great-Grandmother Oleksandra Karpivna Denysko. If my grandfather's letter from the hospital had not arrived ahead of his KIA notice, then my great-grandmother would have likely gone mad from grief. This was because a total of three killed in action letters arrived at her door at the same time: for her sons Ivan and Petro and for their father Tymofii Yosypovych Denysko, her husband. The wording on all three was identical: "While at the front, he disappeared without a trace in December 1943."

In reality, my grandfather's brother Petro (a teacher by profession), who was drafted into the Border Troops near Brest in 1940, had died in the first days of the war.

My Great-Grandfather Tymofii had an even more tragic story. He and those like him — Zahrunivka men getting on in their years — were conscripted into the rear troops. My great-grandfather ended up serving as a groom for the Narymanovsky Rural Consumer Society in Astrakhan Oblast. He delivered goods to shops. With the kopecks that he saved up, he bought calfskin to have boots made for his family after his return. They say that local bandits killed him for that boot leather. Despite evading German bullets, he died at the hands of some riffraff from the Volga.

Oleh Pokalchuk

"The Officer Showed My Mother How Germany Planned to Expand Its *Lebensraum*."

The war began for my parents in the same way as it did for most Ukrainians—with German planes flying above, the Soviets deserting the city, and the local population panic stricken.

My mother, Oksana Tushkan, was born in the Katerynoslav region (present-day Dnipropetrovsk Oblast) to Pavlo Tushkan, an agronomy professor and state adviser. She moved to Kyiv when her father joined the government of the Ukrainian People's Republic as a bureaucrat in charge of land cadaster.

My father, Volodymyr Pokalchuk, was born in the Zhytomyr region. He graduated from secondary school and then the Lutsk Gymnasium, and subsequently fought in the Ukrainian People's Army under the command of Captain Omelianovych-Pavlenko. He was a graduate student under Professor Mykola Zerov in Kyiv, which is when he met my mother.

After his interment in Lukianivska Prison after the Union for the Freedom of Ukraine show trial (he was denounced by a classmate, who would later become the Soviet playwright Oleksandr Korniichuk), my father was banned from having anything to do with the Ukrainian language or literature. No one was willing to employ him, and he only found a position as a Russian teacher in the newly annexed Ternopil region in 1939. That's where my parents were when the war began—in the town of Kremenets.

The war began for them in the same way as it did for most Ukrainians—with German planes in the sky flying eastward, the Soviets quietly deserting the city, a panic-stricken local population, and an attempt at evacuation. My parents hastily grabbed some essential household things and a few family items of sentimental value, threw them onto a cart, and tried to move east with a few others. They hoped to reach Kharkiv, where my mother's father was a professor.

But en route they met other people coming from the opposite direction, who said that there had long been a front out that way. Battles had broken out there, and they wouldn't be able to get through. My parents could hear the bombing ahead of them. Meanwhile, German trucks with soldiers were overtaking them from be-

My father and mother. Beginning of the 1950s

hind, and the German soldiers were shouting at the civilians to not go any further because it was too dangerous. My parents understood German: back then it was as popular as English is today, and most people learned it in school.

They turned back towards Kremenets, where a temporary Ukrainian-German administration was already in operation. At one point my mother decided to take a shortcut: as it turned out, she had gone through a minefield, yet she passed through unharmed.

In Kremenets their papers were checked in search of Soviet affiliation. Initially, my father was detained because he wasn't a local, but he was soon released. He was queried about his plans. My father responded that he was going to stay with his father and sister in Lutsk, so he was given an *Ausweis*, an identity card, and an accompanying note outlining where he was heading with his family and why.

The German bureaucracy worked with lightning speed: within a day the postal service was working, the police had arrived, and so on. My father received a letter from Volyn (Volhynia), informing him that everything there was all right and he could come. My grandfather, Feofan Karpovych Pokalchuk, lived on a farm outside Lutsk. The Germans had secured all the locals' property rights, and my grandfather was issued a piece of paper written in both German and Ukrainian, confirming which land and farm were his. The document was typed on a typewriter in red lettering, with red stamps on each separate text. I have seen this paper myself.

My father arrived in Lutsk after the Germans had already opened the gates of the Lutsk prison and carried away the dead — several thousand people in total from all over Volyn. The horrific thing about it wasn't even that they had been shot or blown up by grenades, or that the NKVD agents had just thrown them into cells and left them there because they were in a hurry. What was truly horrific was how brutally the Reds had tortured the prisoners. For several days, people came from all over the region to try and find their relatives, and many did find them. Bells were rung in the churches in mourning (the Germans reopened all the churches and chapels closed by the Soviets).

This happened across all of Western Ukraine. I mention it only to demonstrate why, quite understandably after something like this, the local population didn't just see the Germans as saviors and liberators: people were asking to somehow enlist in the German army or be given arms.

People were so enraged that they were ready to themselves travel east in search of revenge. They even envied the residents of Halychyna at first, whom the Germans had allowed to create their own Ukrainian army division. All the historians have attested that Hitler's first mistake was ignoring this mass impulse.

Regarding the national question, after the war began all the Polish "colonists" fled en masse to the west, whereas the Jewish communists fled to the east. My grandfather said that when the Reds came in 1939, the Jews and the Poles informed on the Ukrainians to the Soviets, and when the Germans came, then the Ukrainians informed on the Jews and the Poles to the Nazis.

These weren't ethnic conflicts but quarrels, shootings, and denunciations over property and land because each government — be it Soviet, Polish, or German — creamed off assets from its opponents for its own supporters, and this automatically went along ethnic lines. Wherever there were no property disputes, everyone got along like they had before the war since there was nothing to be divided. They exchanged food and shared extra earnings or whatever else with one another.

Until about 1943 the situation in Lutsk was quite calm, and it would make no sense whatsoever to describe the area as "occupied" in the modern sense of the term. Order was established immediately. Thieves were shot on the spot or publicly hanged, and people could be flogged (which was a form of punishment then) for their third time arriving late to work, with the police seemingly authorized for this level of enforcement. My father wasn't allowed to stay on the farm. Instead, it was "emphatically suggested" that he become a Ukrainian teacher in a Ukrainian gymnasium, whose headmaster was the linguist Professor Biletskyi. But when relations between the Ukrainians and the Germans worsened because of the activities of Stepan Bandera's faction, the gymnasium was closed, with the exception of the final year diploma courses (which were, in essence, the start of higher education), and my father took over as head of these courses. From the point of view of the OUN's history, Volyn had been loyal to one of Bandera's political rivals, Andrii Melnyk. As such, the Volyn nationalists—and there were enough of them around after the Ukrainian People's Republic—viewed the Banderites as a "band of beggars from Halychyna" and as "schismatics," but they underestimated their persistence. When the Germans put Bandera in a concentration camp, in one night the whole Ukrainian Hilfspolizei in Volyn disappeared from the former Polish barracks where they had been stationed. They deserted with their weapons in hand and joined Bandera's Ukrainian People's Army (UPA). The armed Banderites often made the *Melnykivtsi* or Melnikites, as Melnyk's followers were called, join the UPA under duress: they would surround them and remonstrate with them, and if any of the latter refused, they were shot.

In Lutsk's Ukrainian circles—like elsewhere—there were two opposing ideas: either fight the Germans, or collaborate with them in the hope they would grant Ukraine its independence. The Abwehr and Wehrmacht officers believed this themselves and would persuade Ukrainians of it, parroting the ideas of Wilhelm Canaris and Alfred Rosenberg.

But the Gestapo and the SS couldn't care less about the Ukrainian people, and their actions gave the Ukrainians a whole load of reasons as to why the Germans should be expelled from Ukraine just like the Soviets had been.

At the time, there were no more Moscow sympathizers in Volyn. The Soviets had shot the entire Communist Party of Western Ukraine back in 1939, and the survivors turned over to the nationalists and overwhelmingly became radical Banderites.

My mother told me how a German officer once showed her on a map how the Third Reich was planning to expand its Lebensraum, and from this she realized that the Reich treated people as little more than garbage. From the way he explained it—prudently, carefully, and even in a benevolent tone—it was clear that he didn't even conceive that the "Frau" with whom he had been billeted could count herself among this surplus population.

The Ukrainian partisans hiding out in the forests gradually began to beat the Germans back, and this resulted in Ukrainian life in Lutsk being turned almost completely upside down. Things were getting increasingly worse for the Germans at the front, and they saw the interior as a mere resource base, without any of the cultural frills of a real country. It was approximately then that my father started working in something like a district consumer union—a kind of procurement office for mushrooms, berries, and various medicinal flowers.

People remembered the Wehrmacht servicemen as being very neat, extraordinarily punctual, and even rather naive people, who always kept their word in their daily dealings.

There were few SS officers in Lutsk, but everyone was afraid of the "men in black" since they strived to teach the ordinary troops how important they were: they could shoot a man down in the middle of the street over a trifle just to demonstrate their importance.

The German soldiers did not revere the SS. They considered them arrogant, upstart "desk commandos."

From his new job, my father would send part of his procured food "to the forest." Terms like "the Ukrainian People's Army" and other political jargon used today weren't around back then. People called them "partisans," "our lads," and so on. This is how my parents got the food to them: they made a hideout with brick shelves in the loess under the stone stairs in their house, big enough for a few people to be able to crouch down and hide in. In addition to food "procured" by my father, they also hid a radio receiver there—a retro Grundig. Bricks that were the same color as the wall lay on the floor, and one could quickly hole up the hiding place with them, plastering over the joints with earth. The door to the house was left unlocked, and the "lads" came and went at night on their own. To convey that food was available, my parents would signal with a lit candle in the window that overlooked a field, beyond which lay the forest.

Our neighbor—the village priest with the surname of Tkach, who was affiliated with the Ukrainian Autocephalous Orthodox Church—was also involved in this network. He had a son about my age who once unearthed a gun in his garden accidentally—a Walter PPK or something similar, I remember—for which he was thrashed to a pulp, and the gun was then thrown in a cesspool.

I tried digging up my own yard in search of loot, but I wasn't as lucky. I didn't know then that my dad hadn't been involved in that particular business. Instead, he had edited insurgent leaflets. I found out about this by chance as a teenager when I decided to remove a pile of dirty bricks from the basement, at which point my mom and dad had to have a conversation about whether that hiding place was still needed.

When the Germans retreated, they invited my father to go with them. He consulted with my grandfather and then declined. They shrugged, shared some words of pity, and left. I still don't know whether he made the right decision because in the early 1990s some of his former students arrived in Lutsk from the West, where they had gone with the Germans. They thought that my father was still alive and wanted to thank him—that's how wonderfully their lives had turned out.

The Red Army's offensive moved very swiftly, and this haste actually saved my father's life. During the second Red occupation—under the "second Soviets," as they would say in Lutsk—he was interrogated by army intelligence. When he was asked about his collaboration with the Germans, my father answered that he had merely been "going with the flow" by teaching people how to read and write, and that if he had refused to count dried mushrooms at the procurement office, he would have been shot, which wasn't worth it. Witnesses confirmed this. The captain who interrogated him was from Poltava. He sighed and quietly reminded my father what to say and how when the NKVD came. He wrote him a document stating that my father had been very diligently interrogated by military intelligence—and no crime could be charged against him.

When the Chekists came for my father a week later, he calmly said something like, "Put me in jail. I've already been to jail because of you, and I'm not particularly scared of it. But the fact that you're creating an interdepartmental conflict isn't earning you any brownie points because the army already interrogated me. Here's my certificate: it's all written down there."

"So what, you don't believe the victorious Red Army?" he added. "What if Comrade Stalin finds out?"

To the accompaniment of swears and curses, the NKVD agents kicked him out.

In the 1960s—when the true war veterans and frontline soldiers were all almost gone, having finally succumbed to their wounds or died from other wartime trauma—the communists enlisted almost all people of a more or less appropriate age to spin yarns about the war in "memory classes" in schools, even if they took their stories from a book or textbook. There were instructions to talk about: a) the inhumanity of the German occupiers and the horrors of occupation, b) the heroism of the communists and the crimes of the nationalist partisans; and c) the victorious teachings of Lenin. My father was not a member of the party, so he wasn't ordered to do it, though he did get "emphatically asked," rather like the Gestapo had done. They said that if he didn't agree, they would cut off the light to his house and take away his vegetable patch.

A big family meeting was held behind drawn curtains. What should he do? They found an ingenious way to get out of it. My father said that he wouldn't have time to study all the necessary material, and it would be worse if he got confused with the "testimonies" he was supposed to recount on Victory Day on May 9.

However, he'd be happy to tell the children about the civil war on October Revolution Day ...

My classmates, as usual, asked him if he had ever seen Lenin. My father, who had served in the army of the Ukrainian People's Republic, coughed for a long time and did his best to hide his laughter. He told them that he had never seen Lenin but had heard a lot about him. He struggled to resist the urge to note that he had, however, seen President of the UPR Symon Petliura.

Iryna Slavinska

They Used Girls to Help "Get the German Tongues" or Obtain Information.

I would like to tell the story of my grandparents, Ivan Serhiiovych Korniienko and Yevdokiia Vasylivna Korniienko (née Holovko). This narrative is based on what was told to me by my father, Ivan Ivanovych Korniienko.

My grandfather fought in the war. The war encountered him at the border, where he had been serving in the army as a border guard. He was a good shooter: when he was still serving at the border outpost, he was responsible for adjusting gun sights on rifles.

There ended up being no battle: the Germans bypassed the outpost. In order to not be taken prisoner, the border guards set about chasing after the front line. But the Germans were moving at such a pace that they weren't able to catch up with them. That's how Grandpa ended up in captivity. He spent three days there, then ran away.

After some time, the former border guards found one another (there were only five of them at first) and organized themselves into their own partisan detachment—in Belarus. They established contact with military command, who began to give them assignments and send them arms from the "great land" — namely, the Soviet rear units. Later they were joined by others, also escaped POWs.

Initially Grandpa served as a scout, but then he was noticed by his superiors and offered the position of unit commander. He needed an officer's rank for this, but he was only a sergeant, so an exception was made to entrust him with the command. That's how my grandfather became a platoon commander and later a company commander with the Voroshilov Partisan Brigade in the Kopyl District of Minsk Oblast. In 1944 he himself organized the Patriot of the Homeland partisan unit within that same brigade. The weapons supplied from the "great land" were issued to partisans as needed. Their unit was poorly armed: they didn't have enough grenades, machine guns, and the like. But my grandfather managed to make do.

One time his detachment attacked and defeated a small German convoy transporting goods, where they stumbled on a brand-new German accordion, decorated with mother-of-pearl and even

> My grandfather's biography, handwritten by him. 1945

in a carrying case. It was obviously a concert instrument. No one in the detachment knew how to play it, so when Grandpa was going to fetch weapons, he took it with him and gifted it to the supervisor of the arms depot. The supervisor then allowed Grandpa and his men to take as many weapons as they could carry. The boys from my grandfather's detachment filled up a whole sleigh with ammunition. I guess you could call it an example of the "corrupt dealings" that went on at the time.

In Belarus he'd cross paths with soldiers from the Ukrainian Insurgent Army (UPA). The partisans and the UPA soldiers didn't bother one another; they existed and worked in parallel. My grandfather never said anything negative about the UPA.

During the war Grandpa was wounded twice — once in the leg and once in the arm, both times with exploding bullets. The bullets exploded and fragments scattered throughout his body, though it was a good thing that the bones remained intact on both occasions. All the medical treatment at the time was happening in a clearing in the woods. In order to collect the fragments, a needle would be inserted into the body. The fragments would make a ringing sound, and the doctor would know where to look for them in order to pull them out.

My grandfather would sometimes describe how hard it was to command people. When he was first introduced to his two or three hundred subordinates, he took a quick look at them and grew frightened because the people were all very different. Not all of them had weapons. And all of them needed to be fed and clothed, and discipline needed to be maintained. He saw that his job wouldn't be that simple, but he managed.

Grandpa was friends with the partisan formation commander Pylyp Pylypovych Kapusta, one of the original five men that had united into a detachment with him. My grandfather and the future General Kapusta became friends by courting two sisters from the same family. Later they also befriended the chief of staff, Vasyl Hryhorovych Yeremenko. These friendships proved very helpful: it became a little easier to obtain weapons or get a little extra ammunition for his detachment. Generally speaking, these were very unusual friendships because my grandfather was much lower in rank than the other men, and higher-ranking officers as a rule didn't socialize with lower-ranking ones. His friendship with General Kapusta continued after the war as well: the general and his wife would often travel from Kyiv to the village of Besidka (Stavyshche District, Kyiv Oblast), where my grandfather headed a collective farm.

Grandpa would also tell stories about "getting the Germans' tongues." A *yazyk*, or "tongue," was a German that you could suss information out of. Usually they'd look to "get" this so-called tongue with the help of some girls. They'd make an agreement with one of the local girls that she'd invite the German over to her house after the dance at the village club. Meanwhile, they'd be waiting there to "get the tongue."

When asked if he would kill those taken in this way, my grandfather said that they tried not to kill them because the Germans could go so far as to burn down the village in retaliation for

The roster for the brigade where Ivan Korniienko began his partisan "career." You can see here how his fellow fighters' lives turned out: Volodymyr Korban, for instance, became the chief editor of the magazine *Vozhyk* ("Hedgehog"), a Belarusian equivalent to the Ukrainian satire magazine *Perets* ("Pepper").

My maternal grandfather and partisan border guard Ivan Korniienko. Extract from a post-war newspaper

the killing of a soldier. Those taken captive would be sent off by plane to the "great land"—and it was there that they were interrogated and their subsequent fate "taken care of."

One time my grandfather was almost shot dead. He was serving in a reconnaissance detachment at the time. His assignment was to scout the enemy while remaining in hiding, but not shoot so as not to draw attention to himself. In particular, his detachment was forbidden from shooting at motorcyclists. They said that the Germans had armored motorcycles, so there was no point in shooting at them: it was just a waste of ammunition and an unnecessary risk.

One day, from his hiding spot, my grandfather saw two motorcyclists driving through a completely empty clearing—as empty as a clean plate. He fired his machine gun, and it turned out that the motorcycles weren't armored. The bullets pierced them like a sieve. No one could believe that the Germans had motorcycles as flimsy as tin cans—that is, you could shoot them.

But my grandfather was court-martialed because he disobeyed a direct order. He was spared execution only by the fact that this violation of a direct order buoyed up the partisan detachment's fighting spirit and dispelled the myth of the German motorized infantry's invulnerability and invincibility.

Fate brought my grandfather together with good people, and he finished the remainder of his service normally. He had a Medal "For Courage," which he received in 1943 (they were still rarely given at the time, though toward the end of the war this award was devalued because they started giving it to everyone). He also had an Order of the Red Star, an Order of the Red Banner, and other, less notable awards. More can be learned about his service and wartime activities at the Belarusian State Museum of the History of the Great Patriotic War.

Ivan Serhiiovych Korniienko was the father of five children and the head of the collective farm in the village of Besidka in the Stavyshchenskyi District in Kyiv Oblast. He organized the construction of dams in the village to create ponds for breeding fish. He also came up with the idea of partitioning off a separate melon field for growing watermelons. And every summer he'd invite over his former comrades-in-arms for watermelons—"to wage battle on kidney stones," as he used to joke.

My grandmother, Yevdokiia Vasylivna Holovka, was also affected by the war. At the time she was living with her parents and brothers in the suburbs of Mariupol (they were originally from the port city of Berdyansk in Zaporizhia Oblast and moved to Mariupol during the Holodomor). It was in Mariupol that an incredible story of them being saved from famine occurred. It's interesting that two different legends about this miracle exist in our family: both describe a fortuitous event that brought salvation, but each is adorned with slightly different details.

Their partisan unit. My grandfather is center-back, the taller of the two figures.

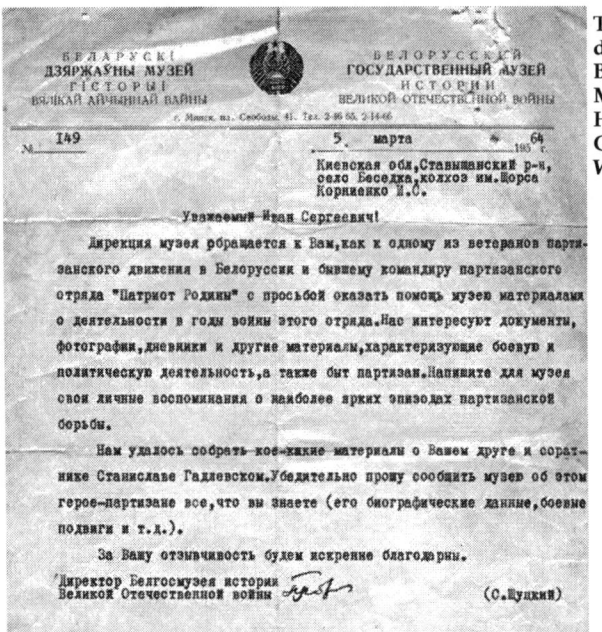

This letter is on display at the Belarusian State Museum of the History of the Great Patriotic War.

This is how my dad tells the story: During the Holodomor, Grandma Ahafiia (that is, my great-grandmother) had a dream about a woman in white. In her dream, this woman said that it wasn't worth crying over hunger because Ahafiia had a lot of bread at home. My great-grandma told her husband, my Great-Grandfather Vasyl, about the dream. He struck his ax where the woman from the dream had indicated—and that's how they found a secret stash of grain in the house that saved the family.

This is my aunt's version: In the winter Grandma Ahafiia gathered up a few items and some clothing and went off to the bazaar in town to exchange them for food. She cut straight through a field, as the crow flies, where she tripped against something covered lightly with snow. It was a sack of wheat grain, about fifty kilos' worth. My grandma was short and of rather delicate stature, but she managed to sling the sack over her shoulder and make it back home with it. She was carrying the sack and, in addition to it, the things she had gathered that she was getting ready to exchange. Halfway home a man on a horse-drawn cart caught up with her and offered to give her a lift. More precisely, he offered to place the heavy sack on the cart while she walked alongside, because she had broken a sweat and could catch a draft and fall sick: it was winter, after all. Grandma placed her sack in the cart and was walking alongside it, with one hand on the cart, thinking to herself that all that man needed was one switch of his whip, and she would never manage to catch up with him and would be left with nothing. But he turned out to be a decent man. Once at home, she put the sack in the shed because she heard that Roma kids from the neighborhood had stopped by to play with her children. She walked into the house with the things that she had taken to barter, which everyone took to mean that she hadn't exchanged anything and there'd be no food. But after the neighbors went home, she cheered up the family with her find. We still don't know who lost that sack of wheat in the middle of the field.

According to my dad, his mother, my Grandma Yevdokiia, used to talk about the occupation of Mariupol often. When the Germans had not yet entered the city, but the Soviet authorities had already fled, the local residents rushed to plunder the stores, saying that they didn't want anything to be left for the Germans. Her family, as Grandma would describe it, didn't immediately spring into action, and all they managed to get was a container of lollipops. They drank tea with lollipops the entire war because there was no sugar. She reminisced about those lollipops for a long time after.

My dad once told me, "Here's a story that happened to my mom. She was supposed to be taken to Germany for hard labor as an *Ostarbeiter*. Before her departure, a medical commission was appointed. She started mulling over how to weasel her way out of going by failing her medical exam. Someone sold her some kind

Graduation from the eighth grade. My grandmother is in the second row from the bottom, fourth from the left.

Yevdokiia Holovko, my grandmother and my father's mother. 1940s

of cigarette and told her to smoke that cigarette the day before going in to see the medical commission. My mom smoked that cigarette and the following day went for her medical exam. They listened to her lungs there and declared her unfit for work. People always came up with all sorts of tricks to get out of things."

Here's another story from my dad: "My mom's older brother, Volodymyr Vasylovych Holovko, fought in the war and was in a tank crew. He had a lot of thank you letters from Stalin. When a tank regiment would first enter a city, all the soldiers would receive letters of thanks on behalf of Stalin. Mom's younger brother, Dmytro, was still a child during the war. One time he was grazing cows outside Mariupol and found a grenade. The grenade exploded, and the boy was very seriously injured. All the Soviet doctors had been conscripted and were at the front, and the only hospital that was available in the city was a German one. Grandma Ahafiia ran over there in hopes of saving her son. She took everything that she could find with her: milk and eggs and *salo* (salt pork). They saved the child. So, this is how things worked out: one brother was fighting Germans at the front while a German doctor was saving the other brother's life. Mom always said that there was no black and white when it came to war."

Elina Slobodianiuk

A Wartime Fairytale: "Cinderella? That's My Grandma."

My parents were lucky enough to catch a train out of Riga when it was invaded. Their train was bombed along the way. They escaped almost unscathed, save for the piece of shrapnel lodged in my mother's shoulder blade; she was still a child. When I was as old as she had been then, I was allowed to wash my mom's back, and I tried to wash and scrub the scar off her shoulder. I know and have touched what war is.

I've always believed in the fairytale about Cinderella. That's because Cinderella is my grandma. It's *her* magical size-one-and-a-half shoes that are still lying in my closet today.

Her prince? That's my grandpa. His photograph showing the little "flashes" on his collar confirms this as historical fact: only a prince could be as handsome as my grandpa in that photo.

It's just that the storyteller has gotten it all mixed up. It wasn't the shoe that brought the prince to Cinderella; it was the prince who fell in love with a Cinderella all covered with cinders and dung, and gave her a pair of magical shoes and two children.

This is what really happened: My grandfather was an occupier, and my grandmother was an occupier, as were my then-three-year-old mother and my future uncle, who'd just learned to walk and talk. The young regimental commissar and his family arrived in Riga in the summer of 1940, where his infantry regiment had been posted.

My grandfather didn't have blue blood. He was a bright lad "from peasant stock" that had diligently studied and served in the army. The only thing that he brought with him to the army was a proper book collection.

The young lad was noticed by the party, and since 1937 he had been rapidly climbing the career ladder.

By the age of thirty he had already become his regiment's political commissar, and he brought his family with him to Latvia's magical capital.

They were housed in the magical house of a pharmacist. The pharmacist was a childless woman who was very kind, which is why the children never guessed they were occupiers.

My grandfather, Hryhorii Klymovych Kolomiiets. Prewar photo

My grandma enjoyed her magical life. Every month she'd go to the theater with her prince, and she would order not just one, but two (!) pairs of shoes from a skilled craftsman at a shop at Marijas iela 21.

The only photo taken in that magical year is of my mother and uncle—two angelic infants.

When war broke out the pharmacist found herself housing refugees instead of occupiers. As such, she was no longer happy with them and prudently escorted them to the train station.

As if by magic, my family was lucky enough to catch a train from Riga after war was declared. Well, they were sort of lucky: my grandpa pulled out all the stops to get them out.

With his political commissar's metal "flashes" sparkling on his collar, he bundled his wife, children, and suitcase full of books into the wagon of the train. As was customary at the time, they were bombed along the way. They escaped almost unscathed, with just a piece of shrapnel lodged in my four-year-old mother's shoulder. When I was as old as she had been then, I was allowed to wash my mom's back, and I tried to wash and scrub the scar off her shoulder. I know and have touched what war is.

Bundling his family onto the train was the first time that my grandfather took advantage of his position. The second and last time he did so was near Kaliningrad in early 1942.

One of his comrades-in-arms said that after the death of the regiment commander, my grandfather, who was a senior officer, took over command and mounted an attack, and then died heroically as well. I don't know if that's the real story. But that's exactly how things go in a fairytale.

After that ... What happened after that? Their story was just like everyone else's. You have widows with two children in fairytales too. There are thousands of them in this tale.

My grandpa's book collection happened to be a saving grace: they were fortunate enough to exchange the books for food. My grandma said that, generally, they didn't go hungry during the war. She had another period of her life to compare things to: she had lived through the famine of 1933.

After that my mother was never shot at by anyone again. But later it did happen to my father. How? People tried to shoot him.

In the early 1950s my father, a twenty-year-old primary school principal, was a part-time party organizer at a collective farm in the north Carpathian foothills. Some Banderite fighters came to the house one night. His landlady hid her tenant in the attic and begged the armed shadows to take pity on the lad and not to cart her off to prison. When I heard this story as a child, before I knew anything about the Banderites, I was convinced that they had been following the law. I felt that they had the right to wish death on a collective farm party organizer while simultaneously taking pity on an old lady and a young lad. For some reason, I never thought that the word "Banderite" came from the word "band" or "gang," as my classmates said it did. I was convinced that the Banderites were fairytale warriors from the forest. I still don't know where I picked up this notion. But that's a fairytale from a completely different war ...

My mother, Nelia (right), and Uncle Tolia Kolomiiets. Taken in the winter of 1940 – 1941

Sevhil Musaieva

My Crimea: "They Can't Really Want to Take Our Homeland Again, Can They?"

Over 180,000 Crimean Tatars left Crimea in the mass emigration of 1854 – 1862 that followed the Crimean War. The emigration process lasted until 1920. By the early twentieth century, Crimean Tatars comprised only about twenty percent of the peninsula's population. Later followed the Soviet deportation during World War II. The Crimean Tatars were only able to return to their homeland in 1989. What is transpiring in Crimea today pains them in their very hearts.

I remember the day very well. I had just turned ten, and my parents and I had come to Feodosia to visit my great-aunt.
I knock on the green gate, trying to get a look at the yard through the small cracks between the gate's slats.
"Who is it?" a timid child's voice responds.
I have nothing to say, so I answer with silence.
"My parents aren't home," says the little girl without opening the gate. "Come back later."
"Why did you have to go and knock?" my mother reproaches me. "And what would you have said if they had opened the gate?"
I feel a little ashamed. My first cousins and I take pictures of ourselves against the backdrop of the house.
Prior to the deportation of 1944, my grandmother's large family had lived on these premises.
When I was five years old, I liked to climb up and join her under her comforter and listen to stories about how they used to run through the winding streets of Feodosia as children. About how their mother would scold them when they would sneak away to go swimming in the sea in May. About how my grandma saw a big airplane for the first time. About how my great-grandfather, who owned his own barber shop, would hand out sweets to his and the neighborhood children every evening after work.
I've told stories about the Crimean Tatars on so many occasions to my classmates, to fellow travelers I met by chance on trains, to my colleagues. My arsenal contains a dozen stories retold to me by my grandmothers and grandfathers, as well as heaps of books I've read and reread about the Crimean Khanate and pre-

war Crimea. This arsenal of mine also holds one lingering question that I've been searching for an answer to for a long time: how has this tiny nation managed to survive after all the vicissitudes of its history?

The regional ethnographer Feoktist Khartakhai drew a definitive dot in the history of my people back in the nineteenth century in his article "The Historical Fate of the Crimean Tatars."

The article was published not long after the mass emigration of 1854 – 1862 that followed the Crimean War.

According to official figures alone, more than 180,000 Tatars left Crimea over the course of less than ten years. The process of emigration continued into the next half century as well: by 1920 the Tatars comprised only about twenty percent of the peninsula's population.

Noman Çelebicihan, head of the Crimean government, 1914 – 1918

Then came the war for independence. In the spring of 1917, the first Qurultay (Congress) of the Crimean Tatar People announced a course for the creation of an independent and multi-national Crimea. "Our task is to create a state like Switzerland," Noman Çelebicihan, one of the most authoritative leaders of the Crimean Tatar people, used to say.

Not long after, Çelebicihan was shot to death by the Bolsheviks, and his body was dumped in the Black Sea.

It is to this person that we owe our national anthem: Çelebicihan wrote the lyrics and melody of the song "*Ant Etkenmen*" ("I Have Promised"). It includes the following lines:

> I pledged, I gave my word to die for my nation!
> What is death to me, if I cannot wipe away its tears.

When the Tatars were deported from Crimea, my grandma was just eighteen years old: a shack without windows or doors somewhere in the Urals, passage by rail to Uzbekistan, relatives returning from the front and searching Crimea's towns and villages for their families, the mandatory curfew ...

Old Kaffa

There was one attempt to return and get registered: they bought a house in Crimea, but one wintry day people from the village council arrived, tossed all of the family's belongings into a truck, and drove them off to Vadym Station—beyond the boundary of the peninsula.

Every summer Grandma would visit her native Feodosia, in whose honor her parents had named her Kaffie (the city's long-standing Crimean Tatar name was Kaffa).

My family, like thousands of other Crimean Tatar families, returned to Crimea in 1989. My parents gave up jobs, a new house, and stability in a foreign land in exchange for the opportunity to live in their forefathers' homeland.

The first years after our return were very difficult for us. My father couldn't get hired anywhere, so my mother, who had a degree in economics, ended up having to clean the floors at Kerch Airport.

When I was sixteen years old, all of a sudden I stopped understanding my parents. How could they abandon everything—paid jobs, a home, relationships—to return to their historical homeland, where they had nothing?

I know my parents well. They aren't people prone to wild adventures. When I cautiously posed my mother the question of what had impelled them to do it, she answered without a second thought, "Grandma really wanted to come back. We too felt like we were out of place there."

"There's nothing left anymore, everything's been destroyed":

My Crimea 79

Theodosia waterfront, beginning of the twentieth century

that's how my grandma would conclude all of her stories about pre-war Crimea and her childhood.

Crimean Tatars really did return to a different peninsula. The gardens were overgrown, many villages had simply been destroyed and renamed, no mosques remained, and hundreds of manuscripts had vanished from the libraries of the Khan's Palace.

On the spot of my great-grandfather's barber shop, there's now a grocery store. Tourists that come to Crimea can obtain a sense of our culture only from the preserved Bakhchisaray Palace.

Despite all their deprivations, our people—my fellow countrymen—managed to preserve that which was left. Owing to them, we have our own musical theater, artists' studios and workshops, and musical ensembles. Owing to them, our traditions are being restored bit by bit, and neglected mosques—used until recently as warehouses or, at best, as libraries—are being rebuilt.

It's this unconscious love for our native land that has helped us to survive. Ask any Crimean Tatar: no matter where he may live and work, Crimea will always remain his homeland. My friends—also Crimean Tatars—study in various cities throughout Ukraine and the world, but practically all of them dream of returning home in their old age.

What's transpiring in Crimea right now pains our very hearts. The wounds of deportation and the humiliation we underwent at

> СОВЕТ НАРОДНЫХ КОМИССАРОВ
> Крымской АССР
>
> РАСПОРЯЖЕНИЕ № 592
> г. Симферополь   23 июня   1944 г.
>
> В целях сохранения картин, посуды и другого инвентаря, имеющих художественно-музейное значение, обязать городские и районные Советы депутатов трудящихся произвести, из числа вещей спецпереселенцев, отбор картин, посуды и другого инвентаря, имеющего художественно-музейное значение, и впредь до особого распоряжения отобранные вещи хранить под контролем.
>
> Зам. Председателя Совета
> Народных Комиссаров Крымской
> АССР   /С.ГРАЧЕВ/

A fabulously cynical document showing how the Soviet authorities confiscated any items of "artistic or historical significance." We are unlikely to ever know the number of families who were robbed like this.

the time haven't yet fully healed in these same hearts of ours. It's not just our grandmothers who remember this: this pain passes down from generation to generation.

Every day I console my crying mother over the phone. "Who can protect us if the need arises?" she asks me. I don't know how to answer her.

"They can't really want to take our homeland again, can they?" asks a Crimean Tatar friend of mine. He's twenty-eight years old, lives in Kyiv, and works for a prestigious company. He said that he'd take leave and go home to Crimea — to defend it and to help, should anything happen. For three months he stood in the protests on the Maidan, kept watch at the barricades, and helped in any way he could.

"We'll defend our homeland without fail," he says. "Don't you worry. We managed to survive the deportation and come back, didn't we? We'll manage this time around too."

Ihor Shchupak

Why a Nazi Officer's Daughter Would Visit Ukraine to Investigate Her Father's past Crimes

Lilo Bhatia is the daughter of a former Nazi officer, who killed many people in occupied Dnipropetrovsk. She came to visit Ukraine after she happened across her father's personnel file, from which she learned about his war crimes. Lilo insists on the importance of preserving the memory of the past, no matter what form it takes.

The daughter of a Nazi officer that shot and killed many people in occupied Dnipropetrovsk came to visit the city, now known as Dnipro.

She was accompanied by German historians, journalists, and civil activists. During the trip, which was organized by the International Foundation of Mutual Understanding and Tolerance, they visited Kyiv and Babyn Yar. Then we hosted the group of Germans.

They had an excursion to the Jewish Memory and Holocaust in Ukraine Museum, where they met the head rabbi of Dnipro city and its surrounding oblast, Shmuel Kaminetsky. They visited a monument in Ihren to the patients and doctors of a psychiatric hospital, as well as the Soviet POWs and Jews that had been tortured and killed there.

This was followed by a meeting between the German delegation and some veterans of the Second World War, and then a meeting at the Tkuma Ukrainian Institute for Holocaust Studies with some historians. Through all this, many questions, emotions, and thoughts were shared.

The group of German visitors next to the monument in Ihren dedicated to the patients, doctors, and POWs, who had been murdered by the Nazis on the site of Ihren Psychiatric Hospital on the outskirts of Dnipro. Taken in 2016

Document:

> 31.12.1943. To the chairman of the Extraordinary State Commission for the Establishment and Investigation of the Atrocities of the German Fascist Invaders, Comrade Shvernik.
> During the German occupation of the small town of Ihren in the Dnipropetrovsk suburban area, the German occupying authorities, alongside the participation of a group of medical workers who counted as Soviet citizens, carried out the mass execution of 1300 people who were patients undergoing treatment at the Ihren Psychiatric Hospital ...
> ... At the beginning of October 1941, 4 Gestapo officers came to Ihren Hospital, where they suggested to the hospital director, Goncharov, that all the patients undergoing treatment should be put to death. The latter gave his consent ...

The German woman's name is Lilo Bhatia (she took her husband's surname, who is of Indian heritage). Her father, the German officer of the C6 Einsatzkommando, which annihilated the Jews and all "enemies of the Reich" in occupied Dnipropetrovsk, was named Wilhelm Ober.

Document:

> In mid-October 1941 the hospital department heads, with the involvement of their subordinate medical personnel, began the medical destruction of patients by injection of doses of narcotic substances into the body ...
> ... In connection with a lack of morphine for the destruction of these patients, lethal doses of ammonia, strychnine, insulin and other poisons were also administered into the body, which caused painful death.
> The corpses of those poisoned to death were buried in pits that were prepared in advance.
> In the summer of 1943, with Goncharov's consent, the eighty remaining patients were shot by Gestapo officers on hospital territory.

"This disabled man costs the people 60,000 Reichsmarks over his lifetime. Citizens, this is your money too!" Nazi poster, c. 1938

Document:

> From the testimony of witness Sofia Nadel:
> "There were also Jews among the hospital staff: the first head of the department of psychiatry, D.B. Frank, who led the department from 1921 to 1937; the head pharmacist Shymon Volfovych and his family, and the head of the personnel department, Ostrovskyi. They were shot by a Hilfspolizei by the name of Berg (one of the local German colonizers)."

A street in occupied Dnipropetrovsk

Document:

> From the account of Volodymyr Serhiiovych Ostashko, previously a 13-year-old prisoner of the No.956 Ihren concentration camp, and later a prisoner in Dachau and Mauthausen:
> "The Ihren concentration camp was a holding camp for the Mittelbau-Dora concentration camp, which was located in Germany. We heard from our senior comrades that there were two rabbis in the camp. The Nazis promised to spare their lives if they agreed to work for them.
> "The rabbis refused and were exterminated. As I recall, thousands of prisoners were stripped naked in the −30 °C cold and shot in this concentration camp."

I told Lilo that I couldn't imagine what I would feel like in her place. I asked what her motives were in investigating her father's terrible crimes and what she was feeling about her discoveries.

Lilo shared her story. Her father, Wilhelm Ober, served in the Nazi Third Reich and fought on the Eastern Front. After the war, in 1947, he was convicted in a German court for crimes committed in German territory. Lilo thought that that was where the terrible story of crime and punishment ended.

Her father did not want to tell her about what he did on the territory of occupied Ukraine, mentioning only that he was in the "investigation services." He spoke a little about the rich land, about the huge sunflowers growing on it, and about the "naive people" who, in his description, by the time of Hitler's arrival in the country didn't even know they no longer had a Tsar.

Lilo Bhatia (middle) in Dnipro

Wilhelm died in 1996. By some miracle Lilo managed to find some documents—namely, her father's personnel file (although, at first, the archive's official answer was that no such file existed). From these documents it emerged that Wilhelm Ober was in occupied Dnipropetrovsk between 1941 and 1943, serving in the C6 Einsatzkommando. Lilo learned from these German documents (which she will eventually, with the permission of the archives, be able to entrust to the Tkuma Institute and the Holocaust Museum) that the victims who were shot included both old and sick people, and women dressed in nightgowns, all screaming in terror.

The members of the Einsatzkommando asserted that, though they did not believe that these people were saboteurs or enemy collaborators, they were still just "doing their job".

Lilo was amazed by the way the German soldiers "consciously" followed orders. They shot their victims one by one in the back of the head with their rifles and pistols.

Lilo was scared to visit Dnipro. She was scared to discover even worse things about her father.

"What could be worse than that?" she was asked.

At a meeting between historians, Pavlo Polliul, an employee at the Holocaust Museum, said that one of the victims of the massacre at Ihren was his uncle, Serhii Polliul. He was of German descent and was murdered alongside the other hospital patients.

Historians know that the Nazis were killing tens of thousands of people suffering from psychiatric or other illnesses on German territory from the 1930s onward. If Hitler's followers could kill "wrong Germans" who were citizens of their own state, then it was obvious what fate awaited the inhabitants of territories occupied by the Wehrmacht.

Among the victims of these Nazi crimes were Jews who were shot for being Jews. One of the Jews murdered there was Reb Dov Ber Schneerson, the brother of the Lubavitcher Rebbe Menachem Mendel Schneerson.

In 2008, after the monument to Dov Ber was unveiled, Rabbi Shmuel Kaminetsky said: "In the same ward as Dov Ber, there was a man who the Germans didn't shoot because he was so strong. He was taken to a concentration camp. This man survived the war; he remembered these events and told us about them."

Lilo Bhatia laid flowers at these monuments and talked about the documents she had found and about the importance of preserving the memory of the past, no matter what form it takes.

She said that she saw viewed passing on that memory to the younger generation of Germans, who know very little about the terrible war and the Holocaust, as her calling. Lilo already knew which German schools she would visit to share her father's stories.

Oleksandr Zinchenko

Petro Movchan, a Man Who Won Us the War

I would like to tell the story of a man named Petro Movchan. He died seventy-one years ago, in the fall of 1943, during the Battle of the Dnipro. He had just turned thirty-one.

In 1939 Petro Movchan was enlisted and deployed to Finland to fight in a war that Ukrainians did not need to fight for land that Ukraine did not need. That time he was lucky enough to return home, but in 1941 he was remobilized. This time, Petro was taken captive by the Germans, but again he proved lucky: he was released and returned to his native village of Strokova.

In 1943 the Hitlerites were driven out of his village, and within a few days all of the village's male residents were mobilized. They weren't even given uniforms to change into and were just sent off to war as they were, in their own peasant jackets and overcoats. They were even nicknamed accordingly: *chornopidzhachnyky* ("the black jackets"), *chornosvytnyky* ("the black overcoats"), *chorna pikhota* ("the black infantry").

Chorna pikhota, chornosvytnyky, and the Russian equivalent *chornorubashechnyky*—these terms didn't make it into the Soviet history books. But the people these terms denoted were remembered in the villages surrounding the Bukrin Bridgehead, as well as on the opposite bank of the Dnipro River—in those villages from which they were mobilized.

Ukrainians that had survived the occupation were often treated as traitors—even though the sole wrongdoing of, for instance, sixteen-to-eighteen-year-old boys lay in their being aged fourteen or fifteen in 1941. The so-called "field enlistment offices" sometimes didn't even include them in their registers, which is why they weren't issued uniforms or weapons.

General Zhukov clearly treated them like cannon fodder. The task of the black infantry was sometimes quite simple: to draw enemy fire onto itself so that the regular army could adjust its fire to and destroy the opponent's now-revealed firing positions. This was a disposable infantry.

There's a little village to the south of the capital—Balyko-Shchuchynka, the former ancient Rus settlement of Chuchyn. It was at this location that the Soviet military command tried to establish the Bukrin Bridgehead in 1943. It was there in Balyko-Shchuchynka that

I met an elderly woman, who described seeing liberators in the fall of 1943 — but not soldiers. Walking along the stream were boys and men in ordinary peasant clothing, in traditional embroidered shirts, and practically unarmed. Within a few hours the Germans would mow them down right by the village, on the hill overlooking the stream — and the water in the stream would turn red.

The story of Petro Movchan's death is very similar.

A few years ago, I witnessed an entire village come out to escort a fellow villager on his final journey. The interment was incredibly moving. Petro Movchan had died in the fall of 1943, and only sixty-five years later was he finally buried.

Petro Movchan. Prewar photo

There were still women alive that had gone to school with Petro Movchan, and they were crying and mourning him as if he had just passed the day beforehand or even earlier that day. Alongside them stood his two sons: Oleksii, the eldest, and Mykola, the youngest.

Oleksii later shared how when his father was heading off to war, Oleksii grabbed his leg at the last moment and didn't want to let go. It was a case of childish hysterics: he was screaming, "Father, don't go! Father, take me with you! I'm going to help you!"

His father went nonetheless. Several dozen men from Strokova went off to war that day. In fact, nearly the entire male population of this village in the Pereiaslav region did. Only two of three of them returned. One of them saw Petro Movchan die.

In the fall of 1943, Petro Movchan was one of the few black infantrymen that had not only military experience, but also a weapon in his hands. He provided cover for his fellow soldiers' retreat when the enemy's tank attack began.

Witnesses of that battle recall how Petro Movchanko's weapon fell silent only when a German tank drove over his trench. The tank drove onto Petro, spun a little in place, embedding him into the *chornozem* — the rich, black soil — then drove off.

When a search team found his remains in 2008, they discovered a piece of paper among the decomposing remnants of his jack-

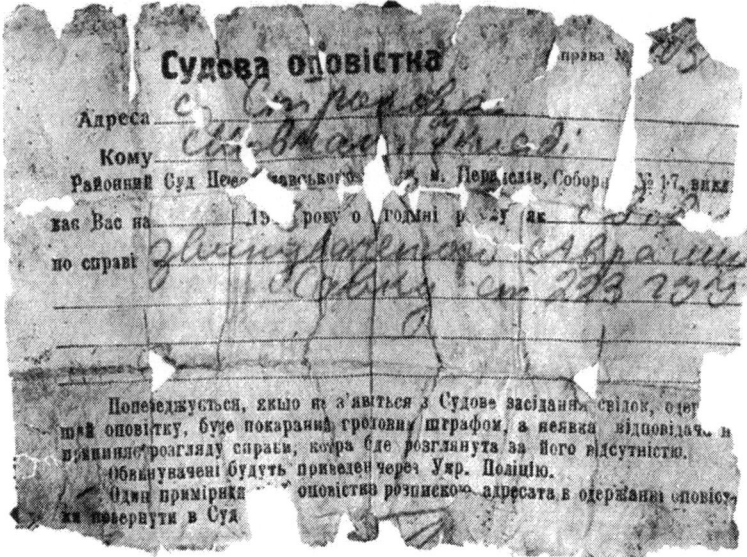

A court notice issued before the war, with Movchan's name on it. 2008

et. It turned out to be a court summons. The last name Movchan and the village Strokova were noted on it. And so, this little piece of paper returned a father to his sons.

Petro Movchan was fortunate: he died with a weapon in his hands. Most of the chornosvytnyky went into battle empty handed. They were supposed to "procure weapons during combat": that's what the enlistment officers told them to do. The enemy mowed them down in hundreds and thousands — on the approaches to the Dnipro and in the Dnipro's waters.

By the end of that fall, the bodies of those killed in the battle for Kyiv began to form "dams" near Kaniv: the stories about this are told to this day in the surrounding villages.

Eight to ten million Ukrainians and other natives of Ukraine's lands — Russians, Jews, Poles, and Georgians — perished in that war. "8 – 10 million": two million human lives subsumed by a small dash.

We'll never know the exact number of people that actually died — whether it was eight million or ten million. We'll never know because the USSR never bothered reckoning human lives and wasn't particularly concerned with death tolls.

The black infantry is just one of the symbols of the price at which the expulsion of the Nazis from Ukraine's territory took place.

This wasn't a liberation: Ukraine was not liberated at the end of the autumn of 1944.

All that occurred was that one monstrous bloodsucker was replaced by another as our ruler. Neither Hitler nor Stalin were liberators of Ukraine. As soon as the Nazis were expelled from Ukrainian lands, new communist repressions began here.

In the spring of 1944, the Crimean Tatar people were deported. That's almost two hundred thousand human souls that were loaded into cramped freight cars.

The communist authorities immediately began a battle against the Ukrainian liberation movement. For the communist regime, the struggle for Ukraine's independence was a crime. For participation in or connections to the insurrectional movement, half a million people were subjected to repressions. Many of the members of this movement received sentences of twenty-five-years in the labor camps.

And that's not all: a significant portion of those who came back from German POW camps or forced labor after the end of the war immediately ended up in Soviet camps, in the GULAG.

This was no liberation. A country where so much space is fenced with barbed wire cannot possibly be free.

The real liberation of Ukraine is only beginning now because only now are we beginning to square up to our communist totalitarian past. The USSR was lying when it talked about the liberation of Ukraine and the "heroic feats of the Soviet people." Yes, there were heroic feats, but these were the feats of heroes that the communist regime tossed unarmed under Hitler's tanks.

The memory of these heroic feats was inconvenient for the communist regime. That is why in the USSR they talked about the "feat of the Soviet people" and not the heroism of specific Ukrainians, Russians, and Georgians. Because people's real fates demonstrated how little the life of one person mattered to the Soviet state. It is for this reason that Ukraine's losses in that war amounted to more than the combined losses of Great Britain, Canada, Poland, the United States, and France.

That's why today we cannot talk about a "Liberation Day." This wasn't the liberation of Ukraine; it was the expulsion of the Nazis from our lands. This isn't a holiday at all; it's just a day of remembrance for those who, with weapons in hand, fought for our land.

This is a day of remembrance for those like Petro Movchan from Strokova near Kyiv.

The Soviet state forgot about this hero's feat. He was remembered by those who, by some miracle, escaped death in that battle; he was remembered by his fellow villagers and by his sons Mykola and Oleksii, and that was it. He received no medals, no salutes, and no tombstone ...

Many years passed. The Soviet Union ceased to exist. Yet, the black infantryman Petro Movchan remained unburied the entire time.

The hero's remains were found by chance at the Bukrin Bridgehead, only a few years ago. Petro Movchan was buried under the Ukrainian flag—in an independent Ukraine for whose freedom he fought.

Today, we remember men like him.

Sviatoslav Lypovetskyi

"The Most Terrifying Moment Was When They Bombed Their Own Artillery"

My grandfather, Vasyl Ivanovych Sydorchuk (1926 – 1989), was born and lived his whole life in the village of Klekotiv in the Brody District of Lviv Oblast. Today, the boundary between the Lviv and Rivne Oblasts runs through there and, about a dozen kilometers away, of Volyn Oblast as well. Before World War I this place marked the border between Austria-Hungary and Russia. Even today, one can study the ethnographic variations between Halychyna and Volyn in Klekotiv and the surrounding villages.

The lands of Halychyna and Volyn (Galicia and Volhynia) in the former Austro-Hungarian and Russian Empires became part of the Second Polish Republic after World War I, but even eighty years later, in the 2000s, local boys would say, "We're going to the Muscovites'" when they were heading to the disco in the neighboring village in Rivne Oblast.

The arrival in 1939 of the *pershi sovity*, or the "first Soviets," as they're referred to here, put an end to social and civic development in the region. The cultural society Prosvita, the educational society Ridna Shkola, the sports association Luh, the brass band, and the local branch of the most popular parliamentary party — the Ukrainian National Democratic Alliance (UNDO), of which my great-grandfathers were members — all ceased to operate in Klekotiv and the surrounding villages.

According to my grandmother, as a teenager my grandfather transported underground literature by night with his friends — an activity in which wider circles of young people were probably involved.

Community life was partially revived during the German occupation: young people organized theatrical performances, which played a role in allowing my grandmother and grandfather to grow close to each other. During this period my grandfather was able to continue his studies at the trade school in Brody. In the village, the community constructed the largest burial mound in the surrounding area and placed a cross on it in memory of the victims of the first Soviets.

In early 1944 my grandfather turned eighteen and was enlisted in the Red Army and deployed to the front. As part of the 1st Belorussian Front, his task was to liberate Warsaw and capture Berlin.

Grandma Nastia, Grandpa Vasyl, and his sister Yelysaveta. End of the 1940s

However, there is a little-known part to that story. When, in the second half of the 1980s, my grandfather was applying for his pension, an interesting fact emerged: the unit in which he had served had ties to the Stavka, the Red Army's general command headquarters. According to the testimony of officials, that's an almost unbelievable fact because conscripts from Western Ukraine generally weren't assigned to units like these.

Nevertheless, after his return from the war, and till the end of his life, my grandfather lived by the principle of "taking nothing from the state." He categorically refused veteran benefits and various other forms of preferential treatment. His first and final postwar photograph with military decorations was with my grandmother, his then-new wife.

Incidentally, his collection of military decorations doesn't include an Order of the Patriotic War medal, which all veterans received. When it was being presented, my grandfather simply didn't go to collect it.

Grandma Nastia would recall how after his return from Germany he once said, "Nastia, my love, Ukraine will be free." This statement was the only thing from which I was able to glean some idea of his attitude toward Ukraine, since my grandfather died in 1989, when I was only ten. However, I recently came across some case materials regarding the village's underground network. The network was made public in 1948. Vasyl Sydorchuk, it turned out, headed *Yunatstvo OUN*, the youth branch of the Organization of

Ukrainian Nationalists. He managed to avoid arrest, since he remained serving in Germany, where he was enrolled in a school for non-commissioned officers.

Skimming the list of those OUN youths, I came across the names of two others that were mobilized for the war. After all, the most famous OUN member to serve in the Red Army was a native of a nearby village, my distant relative Petro Fedun. He was older than my grandfather, and as such ended up in the army under the "first Soviets." He fought and was taken prisoner, and upon his release he joined the partisans. There, under the nom de guerre of "Poltava," he became one of the OUN's political theorists, the deputy commander-in-chief of the Ukrainian Insurgent Army (UPA), and the deputy head of the General Secretariat of the Ukrainian Supreme Liberation Council (UHVR).

Eventually I had the opportunity to meet other men of that generation, born in 1926, like my grandfather and his friends. Generally, this was among the diaspora, and their fates turned out somewhat differently. They too passed through the ranks of the Yunatstvo OUN, then in 1944 the Germans mobilized them for anti-aircraft defense. Such was the price of statelessness: young men from Halychyna, who believed in the ideals of the OUN — namely, an independent and unified Ukrainian state — were mobilized into the artillery units of both the Bolsheviks and the Nazis.

Pages from a soldier's notebook

The most horrible wartime memory I've heard was about the battles in Poland. Over a brief period, confusion broke out several times in the radio communications with the aviation units, and aircraft would attack their own artillery units. People were losing their sanity right there in the field. In one of these instances, while everyone was hiding behind the artillery guns during a blitz, one of the soldiers set out running around the military equipment and yelling, "Guys, all is lost!" A moment or two later, his head was blown off. What they lived through and saw in those moments perturbed them for the rest of their lives. After that my grandfather couldn't attend funerals or see a dead person ever again.

Another instance that could've cost him his life occurred, I believe, in Germany. My grandfather was at a river filling his mess tin with water when a German soldier showed up on the other bank to draw water. The war had a human face too: the soldiers of the Red Army and the Wehrmacht just exchanged glances and went their separate ways.

After the war my grandfather was assigned to the forces stationed in Germany. He'd send my grandmother photographs and would in turn receive photographs from the boys in the village, who would pose in front of the church. The photographs bore notes beginning with "To our dear friend Vasyl!"

Even though my grandfather came back from the war in 1951 and began working in the district financial department, everything didn't definitively return to its rightful place until a year later, when my grandparents were married in 1952.

My grandfather was warned at work that a frontline veteran and employee of the financial department should not get married in a church. My grandparents chose faith and tradition. His career was ended by this, but they were left with a life rooted in their own principles and convictions.

Valentyn Stetsiuk

War, Occupation, and Evacuation

People evacuated during the war made every effort to return home as soon as they could, but they would retain some very pleasant memories about Central Asia and, after their return, often reminisced about its exoticism. However, I noticed that the locals in Uzbekistan did not share the same interest toward us: as I observed during my postwar visits, the evacuees had almost been forgotten in these places. Perhaps Europeans have a different mentality, which is characterized by an openness to what is foreign to them.

The Beginning of the War

I remember June 22, 1941 well, partly because it coincided with my brother's birthday. He was the one who told me about the beginning of the war and encouraged me to listen to Vyacheslav Molotov's speech with our parents, which had already been announced on the radio. Aside from the fact that war had been declared, I didn't understand any of it. It was only years later that I learned that in his speech, Molotov, the People's Commissar for Foreign Affairs (who until May of that year had also been the Chairman of the Council of People's Commissars), announced that Germany, without first having put forth any grievances to the Soviet Union, had invaded the country with no declaration of war. Soviet propaganda did not cease to remind us about this German treachery, although it should be noted that the German ambassador, Schulenburg, had handed Molotov a note on the night of the German attack that declared war. In response, the People's Commissar asked him in despair, "What have we done to deserve this?"

My granny was supposed to come visit us from Kirovohrad Oblast at the start of June, something we had been waiting for for a long time, but she didn't come as planned. Later I found out why: in early June rumours started circulating about an impending war with Germany. However, on June 14 a TASS announcement was issued describing any talk of war as "false and provocative". Believing this statement, my granny decided to make the trip, and a day later the war began. She was no longer able to return home because all passenger transport heading west had been cancelled:

only troops and military equipment were being transported in that direction. I remember military equipment passing by our building from time to time in a steady stream. I don't recall anymore what type of equipment it was exactly, but I remember the quadruple-barrel anti-aircraft guns being carried on cars. They looked very powerful and probably helped instill faith in a rapid victory in the populace. This faith was formed by instilling in the people a distinct military and patriotic spirit, which was reflected particularly in marching songs like "If War Arrives Tomorrow." Other songs would involve lyrics like:

> If new wars will flood
> this peaceful land of ours
> with a heavy rain of bullets,
> We will ride our war horses
> along familiar roads
> for our beloved People's Commissar.

But things didn't go according to plan. Soon endless swaths of refugees heading east stretched along the highway as clear proof that we weren't destined to beat the enemy on our own territory. It gradually became obvious that the Germans could soon reach Donbas, and the whole civilian population was soon engaged in constructing fortifications. Old mining wagons were used to build barricades in anticipation of potential street fighting, which never did take place. A deep anti-tank trench with an embankment was dug around the city, and the old quarry was filled with earth so that a westward road could be laid, to be used for communication with the defensive positions located around the quarry. Problems with food distribution started almost immediately after the war began: I remember how happy I was when my mom brought home a pea pasty from work one time. As it later turned out, the fortifications the people had built were of almost no use as the Red Army didn't defend the

New Year's, 1941

city and deserted it three days after the Germans arrived. The local population there took advantage of the power vacuum to loot shops and warehouses storing food and industrial goods. Though it may seem surprising, on July 14, 1942 the enemy was represented by a single scout on a bicycle, who arrived on the newly built dirt road. Finding no trace of the Red Army, he turned back, and a few hours later the invaders entered the city in much larger numbers.

Our family had already left by then, however. In November 1941 all of us, with the exception of my dad, were evacuated to an unknown location. As I understand it, only the families of critical workers and communists were evacuated. My father was a specialist in what was then a new field of automatic electrical engineering and also a party member, which is how we found ourselves among the "elect." There was a terrible panic before the evacuation because the Krauts were just a few kilometers away from our city already. We hastily gathered our belongings. We weren't allowed to take much with us, only the essentials, since there was very little space in the train carriages. We were loaded onto a truck and taken to a train station, while those left behind watched after the evacuees with reproach, envy, and, for many of them, anger. There were eight families to each of the small freight cars, or "cattle cars" as we called them. Each was equipped with four two-tiered bunks, and they would be attached to any train heading east at the first opportunity.

Alongside other key workers, my father stayed behind in the city in order to complete the evacuation of a power station to the Urals. He was later assigned to a group of demolition workers tasked with blowing up factories, mines, power stations, and substations before the Germans' arrival. When I was an adult, he told me a story from that time about an incident in one of the coal shafts:

The local population, comprising mostly women and children, were vehemently protesting the mine's destruction. "The mine is our only employer," they said. Miners weren't being taken to the front; they were exempted from service. People knew from their past experience of the civil war that no matter what government was in charge, it needed coal, be it the Reds, the Whites, Petliura's forces, or Nestor Makhno's forces. The Germans would surely need coal too. Everyone paid good money for coal, which is why the local population wanted to keep the mine in working condition. This protest was reported via the appropriate government channels, and a day later an NKVD detachment appeared. All the inhabitants of the mine were lined up and then decimated: every tenth person was shot, regardless of gender or age. There were no more demonstrations of the sort again. However, at the end of November, the Germans halted their advance just before reaching the city, so the scheduled demolition of public facilities was stopped. Moreover, in the spring the authorities set out to rebuild what they had succeeded in blowing up. Apparently, the Kremlin had decided that after being defeated by the Germans at Moscow, there would be no further offensives. Zhymerin, the People's Commissar for Power Stations, traveled to Donbas to oversee the reconstruction of the power grid in person.

The Evacuation

My mother and I were already in Central Asia by then, in the small town of Quvasoy in Ferghana Oblast, Uzbekistan. Some department or other would approve the evacuees' destination while they were on their journey east. Only carriages transporting technical equipment, such as automatic workstations, turbines, and generators, were directed to the Urals, accompanied by specialist workers. The families of these workers were sent to either the Urals or Central Asia. Everything depended on which route was free of traffic because the whole railway network was clogged up with transport that had a strategic destination. In addition, the Germans would routinely bomb the railway lines.

It took us exactly a month to reach Quvasoy since we would periodically get stuck at train stations, sometimes for three days at a time. In Quvasoy, all the evacuated were initially housed in the auditorium of the town club where we could watch movies for free almost every day. The club didn't have a toilet, so for the month and a half before we were settled in the barracks, the whole outside area adjacent to the club was turned into one large toilet. Gradually, the evacuees were rehoused wherever possible, with some lucky enough to be settled in decent semi-detached houses. Our family was assigned the last housing left—namely, the barracks. At first, while we still had money, things weren't that bad because the market prices for food were relatively low. I remember once having a whole bag of dried apricots, which we clearly hadn't bought at a premium. But after we ran out of money, my mom would go to villages near and far—even as far away as Kyrgyzstan—to exchange various items for food. Life in a foreign land was particularly hard for my grandmother; she pined after her homeland and died in February 1942. She was only sixty-six. Later, my mom found a job as a security guard at a power station. One time when she was on night watch, a detachment of armed horsemen in typical Central Asian attire approached the facilities from the nearest hollow between the mountains. They turned out to not have any bad intentions and peacefully passed by the station, heading somewhere else. In the morning, my mother told the chief of security about the incident, and he explained that they were Central Asian resistance fighters known as Basmachi.

As a whole, Central Asia made a very strong impression on the evacuees. For me, it was a place of pure exoticism: its people were entirely different, with very different languages and customs, and in different national dress. We were struck most by the fact that the men wore daggers tucked into their belts and the women wore full-veil *paranjas* and light, flowing trousers. Some women didn't wear a paranja, and then you could see that their brows were painted in a single line with a special dark pigment. Their ability to carry things on their head without the help of their hands was also remarkable, as they could balance various loads, even jugs of water, on their heads. The differing types of braids on the young girls were also fascinating.

My mother and I on my birthday on March 13

One thing in particular that was exotic for that time of deficit was the fruit, some of which I had never seen before: peaches, apricots, pomegranates. The fruit and vegetables that I already knew of were equally impressive in their size. For instance, the watermelons were bigger than me, and the apples were almost the size of a child's head. Beyond the river that flowed beneath the mountain lay the Muyan State Farm's fruit orchard, and my brother often went there to see what treats he could glean from there. The place had guards, but they were quite lenient with teenagers, and occasionally they even let them pick some fruit.

The evacuation was also a good practical education in interethnic relations and respect for other peoples since there was a mixed population in these parts: Uzbeks, Kyrgyz, Tajiks, and Russians. Naturally, there were cases of hostility toward foreigners on the part of the local population, but, in general, there was no interethnic animosity. For example, our family often received help from an elderly Uzbek lady, whom we simply called *Apa* (a term of respect for an older woman, sister, aunt, or other relative). Some of the hostility to evacuees probably resulted from theft, encouraged by the local custom of leaving the doors of houses unlocked. This practice was swiftly brought to an end.

There was another custom that also made an impression on me. A wandering circus once came to our town. Anyone who wished could watch the performance, sitting right on the ground in an improvised arena. No tickets were being sold, but the Uzbeks willingly paid money for the event, however much they were able. That being said, each of them would walk around the arena so that everyone could see how much money they were putting in the basket. The evacuees, obviously, didn't donate any money, but nobody scolded us for it. Of all the performances, I only remember the tightrope walkers, who moved down the rope blindfolded, holding a balance weight and with a dagger strapped to their feet.

Despite the fact that the evacuees wanted to return home as quickly as possible, people retained very pleasant memories of Central Asia. They often recalled these memories when talking to other former evacuees after their return to Donbas and often shared stories of the wonders they had seen with others. When I was back at school, I became the general expert on all countries east of Ukraine, and my teacher often consulted me on the East, even when the discussion had moved to somewhere more distant like Japan. In my adult years, I visited the places from my early childhood several times, and the people I had gotten to know in the distant years of the war were eager to hear about my new experiences of their home country. But I noticed that the locals in Uzbekistan did not share the same interest toward us. As I observed during my postwar visits, the evacuees had almost been forgotten in these places — a fact that I confirmed during my later travels. Perhaps Europeans have a different mentality, which is characterized by an openness to what is foreign to them, to what is exotic. These traits were recorded by the chronicler Fulcher of Chartres in the twelfth century, who wrote: "Those of us who were Europeans have now become inhabitants of the East ... He who was once a foreigner has now become one of them".

Malaria left many of us with unpleasant memories, partly because almost all us who came to Uzbekistan contracted it. When I fell sick with malaria, I was so feverish that I felt freezing, despite the heat outside. Patients were treated with acridine, which we referred to as *khina*. This drug caused liver complications and negatively affected people's hearing. This is probably why I have been deaf in one ear my whole life, though I know one woman who went almost completely deaf as a result. The hot sun there was another source of discomfort. One day I escaped from my kindergarten and went on an all-day adventure with some of the older boys. I only had little shorts on, and I got so sunburnt that the next day my whole body was covered in blisters and my skin was literally peeling off in sheets. Another time I was blackmailed by those same boys, who said they would go to the village soviet and report my brother for allegedly committing some crime—murder, perhaps. To keep them from doing this, I had to steal something from home for them to eat.

That summer my father joined us. After blowing up the substation he had been commanded to before the Germans advanced, he had to flee immediately because the Germans began a sudden and rapid attack on Stalingrad. During the demolition, a tragedy was narrowly avoided. The explosives they used had been improvised, that is, they weren't standard issue. According to the instructions they were given for the explosion, the fuse was supposed to burn for twelve minutes. The moment my father lit it, a one-and-a-half-ton truck full of soldiers flew up the road nearby at great speed. My father halted them with a red flag designed for this purpose. The truck stopped, and the indignant commander—a senior one, with three "patches" on his collar—stepped out. My father explained that there was about to be a powerful explosion and that they had to wait. When the twelve minutes had passed and the explosion still hadn't occurred, the commander, clearly very afraid of the advancing Germans, grew furious. They waited a little longer—still no explosion. My bewildered father decided that the explosive was defective and it would no longer go off, so he let the truck through. However, the moment it passed the substation building, the explosives detonated. The truck bounced up into the air with all four wheels, but then landed and flew on. And so, the demolition man, content with how the situation had ended, put on his rucksack filled with dried bread crusts, slung his three-line rifle over his shoulder, and made his way east to find his superiors and ask for further instructions. That was in July 1942.

I don't know how it was that my father was sent to work in Central Asia. Clearly, he had received some kind of documents that allowed him to reach his family via Tikhoretsk, Baku, and Krasnovodsk without any major obstacles, although he did encounter a few minor hiccups along the way. Upon his arrival in Tashkent, he was assigned to the city of Ferghana and was hired at a local thermal power station. It wasn't far from Quvasoy, and we soon moved to Ferghana, where we were given a room to share. My mother started working as a kindergarten teacher, and my older brother entered the factory apprenticeship school and completed an apprenticeship at a textile factory.

Despite the fact that my sister and I were the only dependents, we were very short on food. I remember that the portions at the kindergarten were so stingy that the children licked their plates clean till they shone. We were hungry all the time. We would suck with great pleasure on light-blue clay found locally, which tasted a bit like milk and probably contained some sort of nutrients necessary for a growing child's body. On holidays, though, we would get some sort of treats in school, the origin of which I am not sure of to this day: cubes of colored sugar, nut brittle, and tidbits made of some sort of nut. When I tried coconut for the first time as an adult, I was surprised to find that I recognized the taste. Confused for a while, I finally remembered the nuts we would get in the kindergarten. Considering that coconut palms don't grow in Central Asia, I decided that they, possibly along with some other products, must have been imported from Iran, which had been occupied by the Soviet Union and America during the war.

As a whole, fresh and dried fruits came to the evacuees' rescue since they were very cheap and plentiful in those parts. It was even possible to buy press cake at the bazaar, the solid remnants left over from pressing sunflower seeds for oil. You could suck on it, or add it to dishes, or even make little patties out of it. I was very fond of the local *shurpa* soup and of the onion pies, but I was only able to enjoy those delicacies a few times. Our vegetable patch also saved us. My father received a small plot of land from his employer, and we sowed it with corn, sorghum, and mung beans. The type of sorghum that they had there, called *dzhugara*, was a tall plant similar to corn, with a sweet-tasting stem. But it only contained grains inside the panicle, the plant's "head." We made porridge out of it without any additional processing, and we ground the corn in a mill and made *mamaliga*—cornmeal porridge—out of it. The mung beans were our favorite. They're a type of green bean that makes a very tasty soup. We tried growing this plant after we returned to Donbas, but it didn't yield a crop. My father explained that it was unable to pollinate. That was my first lesson in botany. However, our vegetable patch was only small and needed watering, which wasn't easy to ensure. There is no rain in Central Asia during the summer, and locals rely on a system of special canals adapted for irrigation, but use of these is assigned by a specific person, a *mirab*. The water guardian would only let water flow through to people's land for an allotted amount of time. The water flowed on a downward incline via grooves that meandered round the allotments, but there often wasn't enough to reach the lowest parcels of land. As such, there wasn't much growing on that patch.

Although we were able to resolve the problem of feeding ourselves using various methods, it was hard to find clothing and shoes. We mostly wore the clothing we had brought with us from Donbas. My mother repaired and darned these old clothes, and even managed to sew me some new short trousers out of some fabric scraps. I even wore these shorts in winter—though, to be fair, I also had stockings on (I don't recall where those came from). The winters in Central Asia were relatively warm. Temperatures fell below zero at night, and sometimes it snowed, but the snow would melt during the day. If the ice on some big puddle in one of the yards lasted for a few days, the children considered themselves very lucky and went skating in homemade wooden ice-skates. We all had to wear homemade bast shoes, which my mother wove out of fibrous tree bark and sewed up with whatever she could find. My brother would bring home the necessary webbing and thread from work (having stolen it, obviously). The guards at the gates turned a blind eye to trifles like these, but they detained those who tried to take away any finished goods. Cases like these didn't make it to court, however, because management understood how needy people were at the time.

I underwent a bizarre evolution in my sense of national consciousness in Ferghana. The children in my kindergarten were nurtured with a patriotic attitude toward the Motherland and had a hatred toward the German invaders instilled in them. We sang adult songs almost exclusively, ones about the war, and the few children's ones we sang were rather serious, in the spirit of the times. I remember how in one children's singing game we had to sing the line, "We raise our daggers thus!" and jab the air with our pretend daggers. I was very worried the Germans were overcoming the Red Army, and I was overjoyed when we started beating them back. This patriotic education of the children was closely bound to the importance placed on Russian national consciousness, and I became convinced that I was Russian. I was utterly shocked when I found out from the older children that Stalin wasn't Russian but Georgian. I couldn't come to terms with the notion that we Russians were being led by a Georgian. In my eyes, this was a great humiliation for the Russians, and I simply couldn't believe it. When my father confirmed this inconvenient truth, I, quite understandably, expressed my utter despair, to which he responded, "What are you worrying about? You're not Russian!"

Unable to believe my ears, I asked, "Who am I then?"

"You're Ukrainian," was his answer.

This was a great relief: I could apply my sense of nationalism to a completely different ethnicity—one I hadn't heard anything bad about. I realized that the slight discrepancy between the Donbas dialect I spoke at home and the Russian language I heard in school was the result of another language, Ukrainian, that I had never been aware of before. I decided to learn Ukrainian and would ask my parents to tell me Ukrainian fairy tales. But they didn't know very many Ukrainian stories, and, to tell the truth, my childhood self had other things to care about.

A year later, in August 1943, when the Germans retreated after the Battle of Kursk, my father was called back to Donbas. Donbas was still in the hands of the enemy, but it was already clear that the Germans would lose the war. Party workers were called back first, and specialist workers were to remain in place for the time being, but the local regional committee didn't understand the difference between the two, so the director of the Ferghana thermal power station was given the order to release the Ukrainian specialists back home. He resisted fiercely due to the fact there was nobody to replace them, but the regional committee explained to him, "This is not your labor force. It's Ukraine's!"

Three of them returned together. They were advised to buy melons en route, in Shymkent, which they could sell at a profit later on their journey. And that is what they did. They sold melons for twenty rubles apiece in Sol-Iletsk and bought lots of salt with the money they made. Someone else had advised them to do the latter. When they arrived in Kupiansk, where the Ukrainian SSR government was then based and where they were to be directed to their next place of work, they exchanged the salt for oil and eggs, according to the "a knuckle of salt for a knuckle of oil" exchange rate. They brought some salt back to Donbas, but they weren't as lucky with that: Donbas had its own salt. My father asked to be sent back to where he had worked before the evacuation and returned to our hometown of Sergo three days after his release, arriving by foot from Luhansk (then Voroshilovgrad). But some of his management had returned before he had, together with the military units. The local population enthusiastically greeted their liberators, and everyone actively participated in rebuilding the Donbasenergo power station. At the same time they established a haphazard food supply and, subsequently, shops, cafeterias, and a kindergarten were reopened. Curiously, there were two cafeterias at Donbasenergo: one for the engineering and technical specialists, and another for the ordinary workers. There was no real difference between them, although at the time this was commonplace. Our town of Sergo was then renamed Kadiivka, making it sound like some sort of village.

Childhood Impressions of the Occupation Years

The rest of the family returned home in April 1944 when the enemy had already retreated far away. From my brother I know that the return took twenty days. The tracks were busy at all the railway stations, just like during the evacuation. Open flatcars carried a lot of military equipment that had been taken off the enemy. The older children would scurry around them and bring back caliber conversion adapters or whatever else they had looted. Our train's last stop was Luhansk, and from there we took a truck to Sergo. Although we arrived late at night, our nextdoor neighbors had stayed up waiting for us impatiently, probably as atonement for the sins they had committed while under occupation. A curious child, I asked the other children about the Germans, who, in my imagination influenced by my Soviet kindergarten education, must have been cruel oppressors. To my great surprise, the children had nothing bad to say about the German soldiers, even insisting that they had been nice to them and sometimes treated them to chocolate. The latter was what surprised me the most, as I hadn't seen chocolate since before the war. I found it interesting that the Germans taught people to address them as *Pan,* or "Sir" in Ukrainian. Perhaps the Germans had appropriated this form of address during their last occupation, at the time of the civil war. The use of this word turned out to be so widespread that even after the war people addressed the German POWs as Pan. Generally, when conversing with the local population, the Germans relied on Polish, comfortably using at least the most common Polish words like *matka* ("mother"), *mleko* ("milk"), *kura* ("chicken"), *jajka* ("eggs"), and so on.

I was very surprised that the Germans never touched the grave of a Red Army officer who had died just before their arrival in town and was buried in the small town square. I imagined at the time that the Germans would have necessarily destroyed the tomb of their enemy, razing the memorial to the ground. I couldn't understand why they had not done so. The children who had known the real, live Germans saw nothing strange in this. Though this may seem strange, I have often met people that had no complaints about their occupiers. When asked directly about how the Nazis treated the local population, most of them would answer that there were all sorts of different Germans. When I was an adult already, I was fascinated by a story I heard from someone from Konotop. I believe this boy's story, but when I retell it, most people do not believe me. Nevertheless, I'll retell what I heard:

A German officer had spent several days living in a woman's apartment. When it was time for his unit to advance further east, the German wanted to take the bed he had been sleeping on with him. But the bed was the only valuable thing that the woman owned. Nowadays there are none left like it: it was a small work of art, made of iron. The bed had springs, of course, and beyond that it was decorated with various ornaments—shining baubles and rings. Older generations might remember what a bed like that looks like. The woman was prepared to defend her treasure. She literally clung to the bed and would not let him take it away: "I won't give it away for anything!" But the officer promised her that he would bring it back. The woman didn't believe his promise, but she had to give it up.

Time passed, and the Germans were driven back westward. One fine day, against a backdrop of artillery shelling and gunfire, a German truck raced up to the woman's house. Two Germans hurriedly jumped out, pulled the bed out of the back of it, ran it over the yard, and dropped it on the ground, before scarpering off.

I believe this is based on actual events. It's a hard story to make up.

The same boy also told me that a German car once stopped in front of his family's house, and a soldier with a bucket jumped out of it. Without saying anything to anyone, he ran across the yard toward the plot of land the family used for growing vegetables. He soon returned, but with an empty bucket. The car moved off, and though the residents were surprised at first by the German's behavior, they eventually understood what he had wanted. There used to be a well just on the edge of the plot of land, but it had dried up. Apparently, the German maps were so detailed that the wells were even marked on them. These maps must have been compiled by the German cartographic service during the occupation of Ukraine in 1918.

I have never heard of any particular oppression at the hands of the Germans in our area. In my opinion, they weren't occupying the place en masse, particularly when it came to areas with no partisan resistance. To be fair, I did hear that some of the local children were beaten by the Germans for stealing because theft wasn't tolerated. The only person who was hanged on the market square during their occupation was a thief they had caught, meanwhile the temptation to steal was always there because people were living in times of great need.

As during the occupation, we were saved by exchanging our possessions for food. The most valuable things were industrial products: cameras, gramophones, and sewing machines in particular. You could get a whole sack of potatoes for one sewing machine out in the villages. Some rural people had accumulated more than ten such machines. After the war they resold them at great profit. People would go to exchange these sewing machines with homemade two-wheeled wheelbarrows, which they had crafted from materials found on the grounds of abandoned industrial enterprises. Alongside this particular invention, it's worth remembering the original homemade grain mills people made, which testified to the natural ingenuity of people forced to adapt under difficult circumstances. People had the materials for these mills on hand. A hexagonal rod would be put on a metal plate, and a pipe of a larger diameter would be placed over the rod. Coarse pieces of wire would be laid inside this second rod, then bent at the pipe's edges, keeping them in place. This ribbed surface inside the pipe, which rolled around the rod, thus allowed the grain—usually corn—to be ground. The grain would be poured into the top hole of the pipe. A hook-shaped handle attached to the pipe was used to turn it, and the milled grain would gather in the lower part of the pipe. For it to fall out, the pipe had to be lifted from time to time and the flour shoveled out by hand. These mills were used for some time after the war. I myself had to use one of the mills on an almost daily basis and can attest that it is a very tedious activity.

Grain, like other products, was exchanged in remote rural areas during the war, somewhere in Starobilsk District, where agricultural production increased during the period of occupation. This was because the Germans, it seemed, did not try to destroy the collective farm system. According to people's personal recollections, the Germans did not seize food by force, but paid in German marks, which they introduced during the occupation at a fixed exchange rate. These marks were not in demand, however, and it was almost impossible to buy anything with them. Why people didn't have confidence in them, I don't know; perhaps people believed in victory.

Aside from the Germans, troops from satellite states—namely, Hungarians, Romanians, and Italians—also passed through Donbas as they advanced onto Stalingrad. I remember the following descriptions of these other nationalities: the Hungarians treated the local population the worst, taking whatever they could by force; the Italians tended to be honest and ask people for whatever they needed; and the Romanians mostly stole things, for which they were punished not only by the German gendarmerie, but also by feisty Ukrainian women who would chase after them and whip them with pieces of wet cloth.

As soon as we returned home, neighbors of ours who had stayed behind during the occupation started approaching us one by one and denouncing each other for cooperating with the Germans. In particular, many of them complained about the behavior of young women who had fallen in love with German servicemen. The women, in turn, would often justify themselves by claiming they had been in the underground resistance and were using their close relations with these men to extract military secrets from them. There was a lot of talk about the members of the underground resistance that stayed behind in the city to fight their occupiers. The headquarters of the underground was based at the abode of a teach-

My mother, my sister (born 1939) and I, as well as the neighbor's son, who walked into the shot to see what we were doing

er named Tina Dmytrivna Synetska, in a two-apartment building in our neighborhood that was typical for Donbas at the time—the same one where Oleh Koshovyi, one of the leaders of the Krasnodon Young Guard, lived in one just like it. From what I recall, at first these underground activists were allegedly awarded military orders, then a year or two later they were tried for unknown crimes. There was talk that the partisans had lynched one of their own comrades for some unknown reason. He had either betrayed them to the Germans, or they were avenging someone: nobody could say for sure. The underground had no courts and had no laws. It's unclear whether the Soviet Court ever discerned the truth, but Tina Dmytrivna would say nothing to her neighbors about those events. There was a mass grave in the center of the town that had always been a mystery to me, but I never heard any official references to who was buried in it. There were names on memorial plaques there at one point, but they later disappeared.

Before he had to flee from the Germans, my father buried all of the family's valuables beneath the flooring in our house. He hoped to dig them up again after we returned because he believed we would win the war. All these valuables were stolen by our neighbors to exchange for food. This was a rather common phenomenon, but the authorities were indifferent to those who found their belongings in other people's possession, to the original owners' chagrin. Orders had come from above not to investigate these cases: people had had to survive somehow during the occupation, and so their theft was justified by necessity. Similarly, the mass looting that occurred during the Soviet retreat was never investigated by the authorities.

I probably ought to write something about May 9, 1945. It had already been long since clear that the war was coming to an end, and the fall of Berlin on May 2 was taken as a de facto victory. That is why I didn't note any special elation or great joy in people on Victory Day. Now I realize that people understood that they should have been rejoicing, but not a single joyous moment would come to mind to remind them why they should be rejoicing. Many of the women simply wept. How could people feel joy when someone from nearly every single family had died on the front, and there was no victory on earth that could bring them back alive? To be fair, no one in my immediate family had served on the front. My brother, born in 1927, was not called up to war because, like my father, he was protected as part of a quota: he worked as an electrician in an electrics enterprise. However, three of my maternal uncles, a paternal uncle, and my cousin were all on the front, and two of those men died. Most of my childhood friends grew up without a father.

After victory, nothing changed in our daily lives. We only felt a real change in December 1947, after the monetary reform and the food tokens being abolished. But before then we children, when reminiscing about better times, would always say, "Ah, but during peacetime …" It didn't even cross our minds that peacetime had been around for a long while already. For twenty years there was no mention of victory, not until the twentieth anniversary of the end of the war, when many of its victims had gradually been forgotten. Then, all of a sudden, a crop of people appeared who would boast about what they had done in the war, without any particular grounds for their boasting.

At the end of my twenty-five years of service, the military wouldn't give me my release documents until I had worked a month in an enlistment office. The fortieth anniversary of the victory was approaching, and in honor of the occasion anyone who had taken part in the war was supposed to receive an Order of the Great Patriotic War. Those who had been wounded were to receive an Order of the First Class, while the rest received an Order of the Second Class. I worked alongside a lot of other demobilized soldiers like myself on the personal files of war veterans, to see who deserved which Order. We were struck by how many of the veterans were only on the front for all of a few days or a few weeks, mostly in the summer of 1941. It was obvious that they had spent the rest of the war as POWs. The entire war, or a significant proportion of it, was apparently fought mainly by headquarters staff (pencil pushers) and artillerymen (operating long-range artillery, by the looks of it). As such, far from all of these veterans had actually taken part in the fighting, and it would have been fairer to honor those who had perished instead of those who had survived. Then again, judging by my own superior officers, the people who had actively taken part in the war clearly differed — in a positive way — from those who had made themselves a military career in peacetime. I think that during wars, the Lord protects those distinguished by good and humane qualities, yet not even He has the power to save all of them. That is why this "natural selection" of sorts that we call war is nothing but a tragedy for mankind.

Eleonora Koval

A Potato on a Tree: Happy New Year 1942!

This story is about a time when a potato on top of a New Year tree became both the most magical of ornaments as well as the holiday feast. These memories are of how people welcomed in the New Year in Kyiv over seventy years ago.

My mom had calculated that our stock of firewood would suffice till the middle of January, so we were not particularly anxious about the cold.

But by early November hunger had become a common sensation. Shops would open but solely for the *Volksdeutsche* — the German families that had been living in Kyiv since before the war. My mom had a German friend who offered to help us, but Mom unequivocally declined.

We survived only off what we could barter from the peasants at the market, which was the only option. By early December all the items that had any market value had been carried out of the house and bartered, and whatever we obtained for them eaten. We even traded the new tulle curtains for a bottle of oil.

The hardest thing to obtain was kerosene, but until we had adapted to cooking in our brick oven, we were forced to use a Primus stove. I remember my mom giving away her new, very fashionable, and very beautiful dress shoes for a four-liter bottle of kerosene that barely lasted us a month.

We had an unusually beautiful, old-fashioned mirror of my grandmother's. I can't recall what we exchanged it for, but our leave-taking of it — as with every item — was dramatic, as if a corroboration of our permanent parting from our previous life.

I almost bawled when my mom carried a very pretty, old kerosene lamp with a hand-painted porcelain lampshade out of the house.

Little by little the apartment emptied, and we gained a new understanding of how survival depended on having a supply of things available. By then I was gradually comprehending that not everyone had it equally hard, because many people had plundered a variety of goods from shops and apartments whose owners had left, so they now had enough at hand to exchange. I didn't dare offend my mom with related reproaches: she condemned and forbade me from looting even though my stomach was hurting with hunger.

The nine-year-old Eleonora could not have imagined what her family would live through three years later. Summer 1939

We were already finishing our last onion, which we had portioned out over two days, when Olha Ivanivna, Mom's friend from Baryshivka, unexpectedly arrived.

Right before the war started, Olha Ivanivna had been taken off to Lukianivska Prison in Kyiv for an ambiguous anecdote she had told someone. The woman was deemed an "enemy of the people," despite the fact that her work was displayed at the Exhibition of Achievements of the National Economy in Moscow and was awarded certificates of honor. (She created portraits of political leaders out of poppy seeds of various shades and grew the poppies herself. I saw her portrait of Kliment Voroshilov with my own eyes: it's an amazingly distinct and delicate art form.) The Germans, when they arrived, released everyone from the prison.

Olha Ivanivna had stopped by our house for news. Knowing that we hadn't left, she had decided to help. Getting from Baryshivka to Kyiv wasn't at all simple because there was no organized transport, so people walked and, if they were lucky, hitched rides on horse-drawn carts, sometimes without paying a thing.

The road — the main route from Kyiv to Boryspil — was cluttered on both sides with smashed military vehicles, random military equipment, scorched car frames, and the like. But the greatest impediment was the Dnipro River: the general population wasn't always allowed through on the pontoon bridges set up by the Germans and, while the river was unfrozen, had to cross on the boats of the residents of Trukhaniv Island and Slobidka.

Olha Ivanivna brought us almost half a kilo of string beans and a tiny bottle (a hundred-milligram medicine bottle) of canola oil. She too had nothing else because while she had been away, someone else had moved into her house. Her daughter-in-law lived in Kyiv, which is who she was staying with.

December was very cold, and our hunger was particularly acute. Realistically, there was nothing left to barter, but I stubbornly kept going to the bazaar, hoping to come across something. One day I unexpectedly heard some woman inquiring about Christmas tree decorations. I was ready to hug and kiss her: I set about asking her to wait while I ran home for toys. She waited for me, and I, in return, received a little bag of potatoes that I carried home like a treasure.

I had prized the toys: before then it hadn't even crossed my mind to part with them. My father had given me a garland of electric lights as a gift (which were a rarity before the war) and also some beautiful ball ornaments. One, of a little doggie that glowed in the dark, was a particular joy: I proved unable to part with it and saved it as a keepsake. I've kept it till this day.

We were running out of firewood, but I had already learned to go to Puschcha-Vodytsia in northwestern Kyiv with a little sled and drag back branches and pinecones I found there. The excursion would take me a whole day.

The day before New Year's, while out collecting firewood, I pulled home a little pine tree I had found in the woods too (it was about a meter tall) that someone had chopped down and not taken for some reason. To be sure, the delivery of the "trophy" involved a lot of effort since there was a lot of snow, but I very much wanted to celebrate the holiday. We only had one potato left, and we decided to place it on the New Year tree, all the way at the top. We decorated the tree with scraps of cotton wool, and to me, it seemed like the most beautiful tree I had ever seen.

In the morning we boiled that potato and had ourselves a holiday breakfast.

That's how we welcomed in the year 1942.

To this day I still sneak a potato under the New Year tree.

Yurii Kolomyiets

War Has Broken Out! Alas, War Has Broken Out!

The entire population was sent out to dig deep anti-tank ditches that were later revealed to be of no defensive use: the ditches didn't stop the German tanks. However, people were not going to just sit idly by, waiting for their "liberators." To tell the truth, everyone was secretly waiting for the Germans, since the Soviet powers had haunted many of us over the previous few decades, though they did not realize the horrors the Germans would bring.

Air Raids

At first it was all a bit of a game. Dnipropetrovsk was bombed; then we were bombed (we lived in the suburbs). We were even holding out for the first nights of bombing: it was something that one might describe as exotic. It was an extraordinary spectacle, with a repertoire the likes of which nobody had seen before. When there was no bombing one night, or on the one after, or on the one after that, everyone was wholly disappointed. Everyone was afraid of the bombing, yet at the same time, somewhat oddly and impatiently, we wanted to see the German planes as soon as possible — either lit up by the long streaks of searchlights at night, or by day, when their strange insignia could be discerned. At one point people complained that Hitler hadn't kept his word, since leaflets dropped from planes the day beforehand had promised us a bombing.

The orders to construct bomb shelters came almost right at the very onset of the war, when Kyiv and our city were bombed. We dug them with our neighbors for shared use. We didn't rely on anyone else since we had enough men among us: my father, Andrii Andriiovych Mandrykin, and Tolka, and even I helped a bit. The bomb shelter was deep enough for a man to stand in, and we could even sit on a bench along the wall.

When we were bombed, everyone ran for the bomb shelter: with a newfound faith in God, people prayed prayers of their own invention, afraid of dying. When the bombing stopped, everyone complained that it was over so quickly.

By then I was arriving at the conclusion that our Ukrainian people were chronically sick with an unknown illness, but it seems that the people suffering from this illness (whatever it was) were ones whose brains were located somewhere in their lower guts, rather than in their heads: survival was what they wanted, yes, but they didn't give a fig as to how or why they should survive. Unfortunately, the entirety of our small town of Soiuz-Muka belonged to this category of the infirm. Maybe the whole of Dnipropetrovsk did as well, or maybe even the whole country: who knows? For we, as a nation, are still worms to this day. We even enjoy being trampled on by our sniggering enemies. We simply love foreign oppressors and often, when we get bored of them, we grow impatient and exchange them for another. We even fall in love with what these foreign oppressors have, even if it's a hundred times worse than what we have.

I'll give an example of how this classic inferiority complex of the "sell-out" Ukrainian may manifest itself. (I intentionally do not use the word "Janissary" here, after the Turkish sultan's loyal but enslaved convert soldiers, since we only become that later in the process, after we've been forced to adapt to the oppressor's conditions and complete this metamorphic process.) This episode took place in 1945 in Nuremberg, Germany, where my family was at the time. We had just been liberated by the Americans. There followed a period when Soviet secret police were hunting down "Soviet subjects," or *Ostivtsi*—namely, Ostarbeiters who had been sent to work in Germany—and that is exactly what we were. Our group hid in bunkers and gradually regained our strength in the American military kitchens. We were equipped with fake papers testifying that we were "Westerners" from Halychyna, since the British and Americans did not have to repatriate Ostivtsi from lands occupied by the Soviets after 1939. In our case, we became *Halychany* (Halychyna natives) from the village of Myshkovychi, just north of Terebovlia. I will give more details about this another time, but for now I shall briefly recount a case of voluntary denunciation of our own self-worth—something inherent in many Soviet people.

In the bunker where we were hiding from forced repatriation to the "Motherland," there were three people among us who shared the surname "Porokh" (I don't know precisely how they were related, but they were all distant relatives from Sukha Maiachka). This notwithstanding, there were two Ivans and one Olena, and all three of them were Porokhs. One Ivan was Olena's husband, and the other Ivan was her son-in-law—that is, this son-in-law had once been married to Olena's daughter, who wasn't the daughter of the same Ivan who was now Olena's husband, but of a third man, no longer in the picture. Olena's daughter had left her husband Ivan, the one who was Olena's son-in-law. Indeed, it resulted in a certain muddle wherein sometimes Olena Porokh didn't even know which Ivan Porokh she would spend the night with (to put it lightly), since both were called Ivan and both were Porokhs.

I witnessed the seed of this Ukrainian inferiority complex with all its classic symptoms in Ivan, the one who wasn't Olena's husband but who had been her son-in-law and the son-in-law of Ivan, Olena's second husband. And this son-in-law of Olena's, Ivan, "mutated." He said—just listen to what he said! Listen carefully to what his convulsive lips (I am talking about Ivan, Olena's son-in-law) said: "I'll even take sh*t, but only if it's American!"

That was what he said then, but now listen to what he had said before: "I'll even take sh*t, but only if it's German!"

If you're Ukrainian, you know full well how much foreign sh*t we've had, yet for some reason it has always been better than our own sh*t, so to speak. Unfortunately, even at the time of writing this, "Soviet people" in Ukraine are happy for any sh*t they can get—as long as it's not Ukrainian!

The words repeated here could not be more candid: that is what was said, that is what I heard, and that is what I am recounting. This is the whole truth and nothing but the truth. Even if somebody were to trap my fingers in the door, I would still say the same. Many "Soviet people," nurtured by the Soviet system and guided by Russian institutionalized chauvinism, take "postulates" such as Ivan's to be natural human law. That was another commie innovation: Soviet man, spiritually crushed by the totalitarian system, was worth little more in the animal kingdom than a weed.

I have deviated a little from what I started to talk about. However, I couldn't not say the above.

During my service in the American army after the war

And so, no one complained about the bombing; nobody cursed it; nobody even wagged a finger at it. Provoking those who would the following day be our masters wouldn't have helped in the slightest, even if it brought comfort to the soul. To tell the truth, everyone was secretly waiting for the Germans, since the Soviet powers had haunted many of us over the previous few decades, though they did not realize the horrors the Germans would bring. The Germans were flying overhead day and night. It wasn't as entertaining during the day: the floodlights weren't shining, there were no explosions in the night sky, and the howling of the sirens wasn't as frightening as at night.

The first raid on Dnipropetrovsk Station was short and not very impressive, but the mess they left behind was quite something. Some bombs fell on the NKVD building beside the station—or rather, they didn't fall on the building itself, but on the communal latrine in the yard, with its many stalls. It's hard to believe, but it was a real coincidence: the second bomb fell right in the twentieth hole of the communal bathroom, right by the station. As you can likely imagine, it kicked up a right stink.

This wasn't just happenstance: it meant, people said, that the Germans knew where they were dropping their bombs. The NKVD building was immediately hosed down by firefighters, but we did have enough time to admire the windows splattered with something that those buildings should have been splattered with long beforehand.

This was not the first toilet incident that the passenger station had to deal with. Once, my father told me, long before the war, several boxes of yeast were transported in a compartment refrigerated with ice, and after they had been unloaded, their customs documents were misplaced. The yeast overheated in the sun and began to ferment and expand. The boys doing the loading were unsure of what to do next. "Ivan Trokhymovych, what should we do?" they asked.

"Hide it," Ivan answered.

They went and hid it by throwing it into the latrine. Well, the yeast sure fermented then! The liquid in the latrine rose and rose until it spilled out over the platform. Passenger transport via Dnipropetrovsk Station was halted for a day and a half.

The raids were most interesting at night. Floodlights would shine—not too many, but the long trails of light running across the sky and the explosions by the anti-aircraft artillery created a remarkable, astonishing spectacle. It seemed like something out of the tales about outer space, which we had only seen thus far on movie screens and in magazines on the shelves of newspaper kiosks.

Nobody slept during these raids.

In the early stages, sentries were appointed each night, and a group of young lads would gather round the sentries to watch the spectacle. I would never miss those night watches. We would always root around for any shrapnel after the raids. Often, the bombs intended for the Lotsmanska-Kamianka Bridge fell closer to our town of Soiuz-Muka. The moment dawn fell, we would be extracting bits of shrapnel, and usually we found some right there in the grass. They were easy to spot, shining steely blue on the dewy grass. Now it's hard to fathom why we would collect those bomb fragments. Maybe we were curious to touch something foreign, as up to that point we had been hermetically sealed and isolated from the rest of the world.

The bombings did not drag on. They did not cause significant physical damage, but their psychological effect and the way they affected morale were quite significant. Leaflets appeared, ordering people not to spread gossip about how all the bridges over the Dnipro River had been blown up, and about how German aircraft had already landed on our airfields and were refueling there. On one of these leaflets, a man's dark silhouette was depicted saying to a female silhouette in Russian, "Auntie Motia, stop lying about having seen a torpedo in the well down the street!"

Raids took place very often, and the German planes flew very low. You could see the pot-bellied, triple-engine silhouettes of the bombers with your naked eye. Sometimes the torch of a floodlight would catch the aircraft and illuminate their white crosses. Two or three planes would attack for a whole hour, and then in an instant the roar of their engines would disappear behind a bend somewhere beyond the Dnipro.

We quickly got the impression that the Germans were powerful and had considerable air power since they could raid so often. An idea had taken hold that the planes were only flying so often because spies were secretly informing the German secret intelligence via Morse code signals where to drop the bombs. The authorities believed that there were local informers, spies, and secret agents among the local population. It was because of them that one of the first bombs fell in the "reflection booth" (that is, in the NKVD latrines). The spies and informers had to be caught, only how?

Hunting for Spies

Placards with the silhouettes of imaginary spies appeared, providing a sort of clue as to what your average snoop might look like. For some reason, the image was always necessarily in profile — perhaps to show off the spy's hat a little more clearly. The spies always had a cigarette between his teeth, and wore glasses and most likely a tie, indicated by the hump poking out beneath the slightly raised collar on his trench coat. Our neighbor, a man named Demchenko, immediately stopped wearing his usual tie and vest outside the house. The same thing could be observed around the Dnipropetrovsk Institute of Transport Engineers (DITE), where many lecturers and professors modified their appearance to avoid any suspicion that they resembled this silhouette, which had a caption below it of "Hush, they're listening in on you!" I don't remember exactly how the rest of the text went because it was written in Russian, but it was a kind of warning not to tell any secrets to suspicious persons since this "silhouette" might be a spy or German secret service agent and tell the Germans where they should drop their bombs. When in the company of those he trusted, my father would comment on the posters with these aforementioned captions: "Beyond their cunning disguise," he'd say, "the German intelligence services have a remarkable nose. Just look where they did the most damage — in the passenger railway station and in the NKVD's backyard!"

These posters ignited a communal desire to hunt for spies, especially among the local young louts. They started looking out for anyone who resembled those silhouettes pasted onto fences and the walls of public urinals. One of the boys reported spotting someone who was a spitting image of the picture. He saw this man puffing on the exact same brand of cigarette and looking at the radio tower behind the DITE. Everyone that the boy reported the sighting to was in agreement that it must be the same man as on the poster since he had been scouting out the radio tower. Obviously, in order to avoid looking suspicious, he was puffing on a cigarette that had been rolled with real tobacco, not the rough, strong stuff everyone else smoked. A crowd gathered and, with the boy at its helm, went off to where the boy had spotted this alleged spy. And indeed, as it turned out, there was a man wearing a hat, glasses, and a tie at that exact time and exact spot — and smoking a cigarette.

The crowd attacked him, shouting, "You! You're coming with us to the police station!"

The man attempted to fight back, yelling something like, "Me? What for?!"

"Oh, you swine!" the boy shrieked. "You're asking us why we're taking you to the police — you, a Nazi rat?! Oh, you're a nasty piece of work, you are! You're even talking back to us after what you've done! You're a bloodsucker, a turncoat!"

The man was frightened. He saw that this was not a joke and tried to defend himself properly. It was fortunate that a few people happened along who recognized him as the director of the establishment Zasolpunkt ("PicklePoint"), where pickled cabbage and salted cucumbers were made, otherwise he would have been taken to the police as a dead man. After that incident, the director of PicklePoint no longer walked along that road. He could be seen on the town's backroads, sporting a Soviet-style padded jacket and a flat cap with a broken brim that hung down and hid his glasses from view.

The Germans Approach

Soiuz-Muka lay outside the city, almost abutting the military airfield. The German bombers kept trying to hit the airfield, where a few light biplanes—*kukurudznyky*, as we now call them—were standing. When the German planes would appear overhead, the Soviet planes would scatter and land wherever they could, often in cornfields, which is where they picked up the name kukurudznyk from *kukurudza*, or corn.

After one of these bombing raids, rumors spread that the Germans were closer now. At the station where my father worked, there were hundreds of trains full of wounded and evacuated people heading somewhere east. Several times when I was at the station, I'd find myself afraid of going out from behind my father's desk for fear of getting lost in that sea of people, who didn't seem to know where they were going or even where they were at that moment. Most of them were Jewish people—whole families with lots of baggage. They could be distinguished by their expensive clothes and suitcases full of expensive things. They were fleeing from the former Polish territories, from Halychyna, where the Soviet government had set itself up. They rode in closed passenger carriages, in freight cars, and on open flatcars. It wasn't just passenger wagons arriving at the platforms: there were also mixed wagons for carrying freight and passengers, as well as just open flatcars. People tried to huddle onto these open flatcars that gathered by the platforms. Nobody checked anyone's tickets because nobody was selling any anymore. There were fewer and fewer trains carrying civilians moving west, though there were more and more carrying military servicemen in that direction.

There were rumors spreading that the Germans would not make it past the Dnipro River because Marshal Budyonny, the founder of the Red Cavalry himself, would personally hold them off at the Dnipro. There were many people who believed this and awaited it expectantly.

The line of defense ran right through our small town. Our mighty army showed up, replete with poorly dressed and even more poorly armed soldiers. Many of them had only just been mobilized and were being thrown into battle without the slightest military training or direction. The entire defense was led by Marshal Budyonny in the trenches—at least that's what was claimed in the political training classes, where the political commissars taught them in the open air. Everyone hoped to see Budyonny live and in the flesh, and there were reports that he would personally inspect the line of defense. The anti-tank trenches were excavated deeper. Young or old, everyone was sent out to defend the "Motherland," to dig deep but pointless trenches. Those who didn't have a shovel were assigned to those who did, often resulting in three people to one shovel. People engaged in the trench-digging with the conscious knowledge that they wouldn't stop the German tanks, but no one was going to simply sit and wait for their "liberators" to arrive. Beyond that, they didn't really view the Germans as "liberators."

Just before the arrival of the German frontline soldiers, German planes "sowed" our Soiuz-Muka by night with huge portraits of Hitler, with the caption "Hitler the Liberator" on a light-red background. In the corner, the portraits bore instructions that they should be hung inside houses, signifying that the household was waiting for the Germans to arrive. Nobody dared pick up these portraits or even glance at them in front of others, but by the following morning there wasn't a single leaflet left. We picked one up too, and I hid it in my dog Dunai's kennel until the Germans turned up, at which point we stuck it on a wall. When my mother found out that I'd hidden a portrait of Hitler in Dunai's doghouse, she yelled at me and tried immediately to pull it out and burn it, but my father stopped her. "Let it stay," he said. "If they come after us, we'll just say that the dog brought it in."

But later—even though the portrait of the Fuhrer was hanging on our wall and we could point a finger at and say, "Look, we've got Hitler hanging up!"—they still took our balalaika! Nothing could be done: the Hungarian pilots took away our balalaika and nearly whacked Tolka round the head with it when he protested.

As such, everyone devotedly helped "defend the Motherland" while simultaneously waiting for the Germans to arrive any day. This phenomenon was considered normal since people had already become completely indifferent to this Motherland of ours. People were accustomed to obeying every order, to carefully laying every brick of the Great Wall of China, so to speak. The authorities had managed to brainwash the populace, and we carried out the will of the powers that were without a second's thought. And so, we the people dug deep anti-tank trenches.

Later, the Germans nonchalantly drove up along the highway connecting Zaporizhia with Dnipropetrovsk, right into the city center. At first there were rumors that the Germans were in Kryvyi Rih, and then they were reportedly in Piatykhatky, one hundred or so kilometers from Dnipro). The Dnipro's defense was constantly being strengthened: the anti-tank ditches were made deeper, wider, and longer. Day and night the infantry dug long, six-foot-deep trenches right outside people's homes. All their fortifications were carefully disguised. At long last, we heard artillery fire. People sat in their bomb shelters and waited for something that couldn't possibly be worse than their current situation under the Bolshies. Oh, how wrong they were!

While people were digging the fortification lines, I lived day and night with the soldiers—the *Chervonoarmiitsi*, or "Redarmymen," as we called them back then. I, along with many of my peers—Andrii Nahai, Taras Shevchenko, the Cherkasy brothers, Ivasiuk, Vaska Antonenko, and other boys—brought them food and water. The army was terribly malnourished. In the mornings they were given boiling water poured over a lump of refined sugar, and for lunch they were hurriedly doled out food from a large field kitchen that would suddenly roll in on its two huge wheels and then clear off in an instant. The soldiers would have one ladle each poured into their canteen. We waited desperately for someone to let us try at least a spoonful of the Red Army soldiers' grub, to no avail.

Life in the Trenches

We often fed the Redarmymen corn we took from other people's gardens. By then the corn cobs had matured. The Redarmymen were forbidden from leaving the trenches, so we acted as food suppliers for our protectors—our "defenders of our Motherland," as we called them back then. Most of the time we brought them boiled corn on the cob. After a while we grew so close to the Red Armymen that we felt a part of all the chaos that grew day by day right up until the sounds of heavy gunfire grew close. The Red Army's mighty force all lay in these endless trenches and looked out over the Zaporizhian highway, where the sun's flaming disc set every evening. From dawn till dusk, all you could see was their helmets sparkling over the embankments of the camouflaged trenches. Finally, horse-drawn carts brought the Red Army soldiers wooden boxes of ammunition, with several zinc tins in each box, and their commanders dealt them out themselves along the length of the trenches. Now the sound of gunfire almost never ceased and gradually approached our Soiuz-Muka. When the Germans appeared, almost all those boxes of ammunition were left unpacked because nobody had anything to shoot them with. The Germans casually sidestepped all the anti-tank ditches and trenches along the highway, meeting no resistance. The whole garrison that was entrenched beside our house had quietly retreated the night before. People said that if Budyonny himself had appeared, they would not have retreated so easily, but since he hadn't, they all fled. The Red Army saw there was no higher command in charge of them, so they fled beyond the Dnipro themselves before the bridges were all blown up.

When the Red Army soldiers had all gone, my father explained to me what happened. "The same thing happened to a certain Ukrainian soldier in Tsarist Russia," he said. "He was homesick and sang the song, 'Wind, Carry Me Home to Ukraine.' At roll call the next morning, the officer turned to the orderly. 'Where's Petrenko?' he asked. 'Petrenko was singing the song, "Wind, Carry Me Home to Ukraine,"' the Georgian orderly answered him. 'Only there wasn't any wind, so he got up and left all by himself.' The same thing happened with the Red Army: no matter how long they waited for Budyonny, he never showed up, so they got up and left by themselves."

A joyous wedding

Anastasia Lebid

When Bolshevik Rule Was First Installed, It Was Initially Quite Benign[1]

Viacheslav Molotov announced on the radio that the "liberators" were coming, saying that Stalin was going to liberate our Western brethren from the Polish yoke. That's how the Bolshevik army came marching into our area on September 17, 1939. While there was no NKVD around, we could still manage to have some semblance of a life. But when the NKVD arrived, people started getting snatched and taken away to Siberia by night. Then on June 22 1941 Hitler struck Ukraine ...

"Back in 1939 already, all you heard from anyone was the same thing: 'war,' 'war,' 'war.' Because everyone was aware of Hitler's intentions already. So in 1939 — in August already — we came to the conclusion that we needed to leave Vorokhta.[2] Why leave? Because my husband was a serviceman and, in the event of a countrywide mobilization, was supposed to be attached to the army in Poznań.

"I didn't want to stay alone with a child in the Carpathian Mountains, where famine could break out because the land was barren, so I decided to head to Volyn to my mother's. I remember that on August 30 we packed our things and left. In Lviv we stopped by a coffee shop to have some coffee and that's when we saw the placards that war had been declared.

"From Lviv my husband escorted us to Volyn and then took another train to his duty station, per his orders. But he never made it all the way there because everything there had been bombed out already. Meanwhile, I ended up staying in Volyn with our child."

---

1 The full text of the conversation is available in the collection *The Extraordinary Fates of Ordinary Women: Oral Histories from the Twentieth Century* (Lviv: Publishing House of the Lviv Polytechnic National University, 2013). The interview was conducted by the staff of the Ukrainian-Canadian Research and Documentation Centre, Toronto.
2 Vorokhta is an urban-type settlement of the Yaremche City Council in Ivano-Frankivsk Oblast. In 1939 it belonged to the Stanisławów Voivodeship of the Second Polish Republic.

"In your native village of Matiiv[3]?"

"Yes, in Matiiv. In fact, Matiiv remained in the hands of the Polish for another two or three weeks. My husband didn't make it to his duty station because everything was bombed out, so he returned to us. He walked on foot a little, hitched rides a little, and made it to us in Volyn like that. Everything was destroyed already; there was no organized political or military life left. The Poles were at a complete loss.

"Then all of a sudden the 'liberators' arrived ... We heard it on the radio: Molotov announced that Stalin was going to liberate his Western brethren from the Polish yoke. And the Bolshevik army came marching into our area on September 17."

"And what was the result of the Bolshevik arrival?"

"The Poles were completely disorganized already—there was nothing anymore, no Polish rule to speak of—so a committee was formed. Obviously, it was made up of underground fighters, former communists, because the communist party was active in Poland. It wasn't legal, but it had a lot of members, mostly Jews. Those Jews and a few of our village boys, who were already known to be communists, formed this self-government committee. I don't know what it was called. In any case, they somehow had weapons already too, so they became the guards of the town until the military authorities arrived.

"When Soviet rule was installed, it was initially quite benign. When we'd ask the soldiers—and they were Ukrainian—'How are things where you're from?' they'd always respond, 'Just wait and you'll see for yourself.' 'Come on, how are things where you're from?' 'Just wait and you'll see for yourself.' There was nothing more, no real answer.

"Then later when the NKVD arrived, things got worse because they had these different kinds of people that spied on us: some belonged to the Organization of Ukrainian Nationals and some to Petliura's army. People would get pulled out for the occasional untoward word.

"In short, in the beginning still, while there was no NKVD around, we could still manage to have some semblance of a life. But when the NKVD arrived, we stopped sleeping at night. They began to deport people very quickly. First they deported the Poles—the so-called colonists, the ones that the Polish government had settled in our lands. They were mostly from Poznań. The NKVD would take them away and deport them to Siberia at night. And later they took our nationalists too—one here, then one there.

---

3   Present-day Lukiv in the Turrisk District of Volyn Oblast.

"Interestingly, some information would make it through to them, in addition to what our people were reporting to them. There were also people who'd warn others, saying, 'Do you know that you're on the list? It'll be your turn today.' And that would let people avoid deportation. A lot of people went beyond the Buh River; they fled to the General Governorate for the Occupied Polish Region there. But many, many others were arrested and deported. Those were difficult times."

"How long did this last? How long were the Bolsheviks there?"

"The Bolsheviks were in our area from September 17, 1939 to June 1941. And June 22—I think, I don't recall well—that was a big surprise, because those various Soviet officials had resettled their families to our area already. But those families that got their hands on our wealth, they descended on the stores and bought up everything. They were never happy, always saying that they wouldn't be staying there and ... And, in fact, it happened very suddenly, before the outbreak of war, that Hitler struck Ukraine."

"What was the arrival of the Germans like?"

"At first people welcomed them joyfully, because for some reason we Ukrainians thought that the Germans would help us attain an independent Ukraine. That's what people thought at first, so they welcomed them. But that was for only a very short time, because later the Germans showed their true colors, making it clear that an independent Ukraine wasn't in their interests. They just separated us off from Halychyna ... The Ukrainians that were in Halychyna—their lives were easier. But the Germans did much worse things in our region. The further east they were, the more cruelly the Germans behaved. It's worth noting that when the war ended, the POWs passed through our town—heading east, heading home."

"Can you describe this a little more?"

"Yes, of course. The Bolshevik soldiers surrendered en masse, they were taken into captivity en masse, and they returned home on foot. We organized a committee of women and helped them, feeding them and putting them up for the night. They were truly wretched: they had typhus, they had parasites on them, it was horrible. And one time I took a few of them in for the night. I fed them, clothed them: they were wretched and hadn't done anything wrong. And then my child caught typhus and oh, it was very difficult, but, thank the Lord, we saved her. That relief operation was pretty widespread in our region. For example, malnourished children would be brought to our area from eastern Ukraine, and we would feed them."

"When was that? What sort of children were they?"

"Children that had been in an orphanage."

"Where?"

"An orphanage in Kyiv. They were dying of starvation because there was no food to be had in Kyiv. Kyiv had been bombed out, and there was no food to be had, and people there were starving to death. And that charitable service of ours was working everywhere. The wife of Samiylo Pidhirskyi, a former member of the Polish parliament, played a very large role in this, traveling to Kyiv and organizing this whole charitable service and all this humanitarian aid. And she organized a committee there: a teacher named Ms. Yurkevych was the head (she passed away already in America). She brought a group of children to us."

"To Matiiv?"

"Yes."

"How many children were there?"

"There were twenty of them."

"And of what ages?"

"They were all between six and ten years old, those children."

"They were small. And what year was that?"

"That was in—one second, 1941 was the war, so that was 1942. That was 1942.

"And these were orphans?"

"Yes, supposedly. They had no documents that they were orphans. Maybe their relatives had died during the war. Or maybe they were evacuated and the children were abandoned or something. The committee would pick them up, organize them, and try to help them survive somehow. There were

Busia, left, dressed in white. Vorokhta, 1936

these points scattered throughout Volyn. We'd travel to the villages, pick up groceries, and feed those children. And afterward, some time later, they returned to Kyiv with Ms. Yurkevych and another teacher. We revived them a little and found them some better clothes: the children were so pretty when they were heading back."

"So there were children like that in Matiiv and in other towns?"

"There was an initiative like that in other towns as well — to revitalize children from eastern Ukraine.

"What else can I tell you? Maybe this'll be interesting, or maybe you know this already ... When German governance came to our area, at first we were allowed to choose our own town head, our own *wójt*, and our own police. So it all went well because we believed that a Ukrainian state was going to be created. The town council and police were formed from our own people. Their assignment was to maintain order in the town. But when the Germans started being very, very ruthless, and began to snatch young people and send them off to Germany for labor and impose large obligations on the people, then the Organization of Ukrainian Nationalists incited us to resist.

"So the police, who had weapons in hand, were given the order to 'go into the woods' [and join the Ukrainian partisan resistance forces]. But that order reached us a little too late. We already knew that in Rivne and in Kremenets the police had gone into the woods, but in Kovil and in our town of Matiiv, the police were still there. Then one night the Matiiv police also went out into the woods with their weapons. And that's when the Germans were gripped by terror. The Germans sent their soldiers after them, and that whole affair was very, very sad ... You could read volumes of books about it. My husband described it a little as part of the project Litopys UPA (Annals of the Ukrainian Insurgent Army)."

"And what did the anti-Jewish operation in Matiiv entail?"

"Actually, that was done very, very insidiously by the German government. At first all the Jews lived normally; they just had yellow patches on their backs so that it would be visible that it was a Jewish person. They worked and went to work wherever needed."

"But they were living in a ghetto already?"

"No-no, there was no ghetto at all in our town. In our town, the Jews lived in their own homes and had been ordered to choose their own leadership from within the Jewish community. This was called a *Judenrat* in German."

"So they weren't subject to the Ukrainian town authorities?"

"That Judenrat was governed directly by the Germans, by the so-called district commander. One time they told all the Jews to get together. There was this large grove in our town, where there were the former country houses of wealthier landowners, and that's where the German army — the Gestapo — were quartered. Then an order was given for all the Jewish men to gather and for the Jewish women to remain at home. And they segregated them by profession there: butchers off to one side, shoemakers and tailors off to another, then merchants to another side. For some reason they told those whose professions they thought they would still need to sit down, to fold their legs like so and sit down on the ground. And they told the others that they were being sent off for work. They said that the Judenrat knew about this, but God only knows.

In Czech territory, 1945

"They took away the ones for work, and the other Jews that were sitting heard the machine guns firing. They survived, so they heard that, but our people didn't hear it because it was far away. Well, and obviously, everyone then found out that the other ones had been shot. The Germans said that they took them off to work, but no one believed that.

"It was Gestapo agents themselves shooting. And the most important thing that happened — this is horrible to even remember, God almighty, the risks that our people took! — was that the Jewish women, when they learned that all the Jews were being taken, came running to the head of the district, who was my husband. He went and asked our priest to go save those Jews, to say that they were very good citizens. And so, the head of the district and a priest — the priest took a cross — went to the *Gebietskommissar*, the regional commissar.

"We still believed that we could talk to these people, so we started talking to them and pleading: 'These are people, they have

Canadian arrival document

children, don't take them away for work.' Because we believed that they were going to be deported. But there was this one Gestapo officer—his eyes were bloodshot—who said, 'You're a priest, go back to your church where you belong. You're the boss of the district, go back to your office and don't come back here anymore.' Well, that meant that it hadn't helped at all. People were naïve, but that was dangerous, it was dangerous for them as well.

"So that was the Germans' first move. Their second move was very cruel because there was a round-up, and they gathered all of the Jewish people into their synagogue when we had no police left anymore because our police had headed to the woods already. There was a *Schutzmannschaft* battalion, a battalion of auxiliary police, and there were a lot of Poles serving in it, and Germans, and other people non-native to these parts. Well, and they conducted a round-up throughout the town: they surrounded the town and gathered up the Jews in the synagogue.

In Montreal

"That happened at night. Then they led them out of the synagogue and walked them over to the pits where they used to quarry clay—these pits had been dug already—and they shot all of them there. That was a horrible operation. Some managed to save themselves and fled into the woods. Obviously, they couldn't kill everyone: some managed to save themselves. That's what happened. Later the Germans destroyed all of their homes. They destroyed all of the old homes where Jews used to live, but left the new ones. They said that gold was supposedly hidden in the ovens there. Maybe they went looking for it or something? I don't know why they wanted to level everything to the ground completely. As it was, no sign that there had once been people living there was left behind."

"So they essentially wiped out all the Jews in one big operation?"

"Yes, all the Jews in one big operation ..."

"Were there any attempts made by Ukrainians to hide the Jews?"

"Oh! There were very strict orders not to do this, and there were instances ... In the town no, but out in the villages, there were instances of families that hid Jews, and they would get killed together with the Jews."

"Do you know their names?"

"I don't know their names, but I do know for a fact that there were instances of this: several families were executed along with them. Oh, those were horrific times!"

"There were also gallows in Matiiv, no? People were hanged there, correct? Do you know what for?"

"That was for their connections with the Ukrainian Insurgent Army (UPA)."

"Were the Germans doing the hanging?"

"Yes, and when our *Polizei* joined the UPA, the insurgents would attack the town. There was an attack one time on the *Schutz* battalion, and the insurgents took a Schutz battalion unit prisoner with them. Well, and then there was an operation to uncover who had collaborated with them ... The Germans were powerless to fight the UPA openly — because things weren't going their way at the front anymore. All of their forces were concentrated at the front because they were outside Stalingrad at that point. So, they didn't have many troops that could fight the UPA openly. Their fight against the UPA was reduced to them occasionally grabbing someone by night and then hanging them for show, to scare people, to instill fear."

"Were there many such instances in Matiiv? Do you remember any?"

"I don't recall if there were many, but they did happen. There were several instances of people being hanged from the gallows. I don't remember any, because those were horrible times and maybe my husband sheltered me from all that. I didn't even see the gallows for myself because the whole thing was too horrible. People said that upward of seven men were hanged. Those were horrible, horrible times."

"So that happened without any trials, without any sort of legal process?"

"Without anything. There were no trials."

"Was there a prison in Matiiv?"

"There was no prison in Matiiv; there was one in Kovel. The Germans conducted round-ups in the villages and would attack ... Maybe there were some sort of provocations happening, and people would tell Germans to go here or there. For example, the UPA was doing training exercises one day. After those exercises, the boys were all sleeping in the same barn without anyone keeping night watch. A German patrol was driving by on its way to pick up the rest of their contingent and saw them. And so they killed all twelve of those young men right there ... It was all very scary and very horrible."

"And then you left in which year?"

"In 1943, on New Year's Day. An opportunity to leave presented itself right on the first day of 1943; meanwhile, the front was approaching, it was getting closer and closer. We left together with another family. We were heading to Czechoslovakia, and we made it there without a problem. We found a means of transport, left, and survived all those hardships. We succeeded in leaving: we were among the lucky ones. We made it to Brno, but we couldn't find a place to stay, and someone recommended that we go to Pohořelice, this little town not far away. And we stayed there for a while ..."

"How long were you there?"

"Oh, we left in early 1943 when it was still winter, and we stayed there through fall of 1943. Then in early 1944 the locals started giving us a very, very hard time. We couldn't find work in Pohořelice: when we would apply for work, we would get turned away. And that's why the authorities told us that we had to leave for Germany because we would be employable there. We were given transportation and taken off to the Sudetes, where we were able to find jobs, and that's where we were during the next phase of the war.

"The front was approaching. We had no intention of returning to life under the Bolsheviks, so we kept trying to move further and further away, as far away as possible. We obtained a pair of horses and a wagon, and we slowly retreated and retreated. We'd say, 'As long as there's dry land, we'll keep moving, and when we find ourselves before an ocean, we'll go into the ocean—any way not to stay under the Bolsheviks.' And that's how we kept going and going westward. The roads were clogged with German troops that were retreating, and we'd squeeze past them somehow. And we made it to ... I don't remember what it was called, but it was this small locale where we were told that we had reached the end of the war. That was in Austria."

Nataliia Popovych
(Natalka Talanchuk-Hrebinska)

"Oh Mama, Life Is So Hard without You ..."

Excerpt taken from the novel Destiny: The Life of an Extraordinary Woman, *published by the League of Canadian Ukrainian Women (2017).*

My neighbors helped me bury my mother by the fence in our own backyard. We didn't have a coffin. We found a wooden ammunition box, pulled a plank out of its side, and placed my mother inside. The box was a little too narrow and too short, so my mother's feet poked out of the end. We wrapped them with a length of string. That's how we buried my mother — my mother, a woman born into a rich family and the wife of a priest. The memory of my poor mother's legs has haunted me ever since. For me, the dearest place in the whole world became that mound of earth in our backyard.

The front was getting closer. Events developed rapidly, and nothing could stop the German army's offensive. Towns and villages fell one after another. Factories and equipment were evacuated, and archives and anything of value were removed. Anything that couldn't be carted away was set on fire or blown up. By July 1941 the first bombs fell on Dnipropetrovsk.

Deadly chunks of iron rained down onto civilians' heads, destroyed buildings, uprooted trees, ploughed up the earth, and incinerated everything around. The Soviet forces made their dugouts on the left (eastern) bank of the Dnipro River, behind the cemetery that was just up from our street, in dunes overgrown with vines. The Germans were positioned somewhere on the right bank, and we were right in the middle of the line of fire. The shelling from both sides of the Dnipro grew until it became a continuous howl that bit into our already stretched nerves. We were surrounded by chaos, smoke, fear of the enemy, and by death that could happen anytime and anywhere. The city sat face to face with an enemy whose savagery we had read about in the newspapers.

Our neighborhood started preparing for the bombing in advance. In the school yard opposite our house, our neighbors built a bomb shelter with my and my mother's help. It was a primitive bomb shelter with two entrances, and we covered it with layers of leaves, twigs, wooden boards, and earth. We installed benches and a water supply inside. I doubt it would have been much help if a bomb had fallen right onto it. Still, it was at least some sort of protection. As soon as the shelling would start, we would grab a hunk of bread and run into it, hoping to survive.

Mama, Why Did You Go Outside?

It happened on August 30, 1941. The cannon fire started on the left bank, where our troops were. The shelter was filled with people listening intently to what was going on outside. I sat right next to the exit, where there was a little light, and, as always, was reading a book. My mother sat a little further away from me. Suddenly there was a bang, everything shook, and I don't remember anything more.

A shell had hit our shelter, and I was buried by earth; my mother only managed to find me from a shred of my clothing sticking out of the dirt. Something had razed all my hair off; whether it was shrapnel or fire, I don't know, but I was still alive. My mother grabbed me, and we ran, hunched over, across the school yard, shells whistling over us, to another bomb shelter. They didn't let us in because there wasn't any space.

My mother decided to run over to some other neighbors', who had made their own cover in their yard. This family belonged to some religious sect and had little contact with their neighbors, having barred themselves off from everyone with a high fence. There was no way in, and my mother rattled on the closed gates with all her might. The neighbors took pity on us and let us in. Most likely it was my pitiful appearance that influenced their decision: I was covered in soil and my hair had burned off. We spent an anxious night there.

While I slept my mother decided to run over to our house and bring me something to eat and drink. While she was gone, the old fellow sitting with us in the shelter decided to go see what was going on outside and went off to peek through the gate. Unfortunately, at that exact moment a German soldier walked past and just shot the old man dead. Our neighbors ran out just for a second, to drag the poor old man back and put him in their stable—and then the shelling resumed.

Mama, why did you go outside? Why did nobody stop you? You didn't come back for a long time, and I decided to run after you. Our neighbors advised me to take some white cloth. I ran up to the high fence, waving the cloth. I don't know where I got the strength from, but I scaled it. But, Mama, you were already gone.

Death had already taken you: death in the form of a shell that fell by our veranda and destroyed half the roof and the house, blowing out all the windows. There was smoke and fire everywhere I looked. My mother, my dear mama, was dead. She was lying on the veranda, her body torn by shrapnel and blood flowing from her wounds. My mother was half naked, some of her clothes ripped off by the blast and the rest burning up still on her.

The heavens were torn asunder by my cry. Mama ... I was left alone amid the chaos of war, without any material or moral support. I was only sixteen.

Our acquaintance, Ostap Pavlovych, who was deacon of the church where my mother conducted the choir, helped reinstall the windows and patch the roof. He and his wife stayed over at my house for some time before moving back to the Poltava region, where they were from. My neighbors helped me bury my mother by the fence in our own backyard. We didn't have a coffin. We found a wooden ammunition box, pulled a plank out of its side, and placed my mother inside. The box was a little too narrow and too short, so my mother's feet poked out of the end. We wrapped them with a length of string. That's how we buried my mother—my mother, a woman born into a rich family and the wife of a priest. The memory of my poor mother's legs has haunted me ever since. For me, the dearest place in the whole world became that mound of earth in our backyard. I couldn't bear to sit in my empty house, so I would run over to that mound and talk and talk and never get tired of it, and I would pour out my grief and my pain, bent over the cold ground. Mama, how am I supposed to live on? How do I keep living?

"If only we could turn everything back! If only we could turn everything back, back to my childhood, I would have been better behaved, Mama. I wouldn't have climbed trees, or swum in lakes, or gone down to the swamps with the boys; I wouldn't have dirtied my Sunday clothes; I would have prayed more, studied better; I would have eaten that semolina porridge I didn't like. How could I ever have thought you didn't love me? How could I ever have hated you, Mama? I feel such grief that I'll never be able to hug you again and say, 'I love you, Mama.'"

I looked out of the window onto my mother's fresh grave. Now I could look, and nobody could stop me. The one who wanted to protect me from everything bad in the world was lying there, in our yard, while the rain hammered on the window and heavy droplets fell on her grave. My poor mama—she was cold and damp in there. My mother loved the warmth and the sun. My heart was full of the cold and damp. Mama, I wish I could have been able to warm you up, especially your feet. My dear father is gone, and he always warmed up your cold fingers with his breath. You always looked at him with such love in your eyes. Maybe Papa has met you there—there, far away. If only it wasn't like this! Yet the thick raindrops still fall upon your grave.

A knock on the door, sudden and unexpected, rattled my already frightened soul. Who could that be? I was afraid to move, hoping whoever it was would think I wasn't home. But someone kept on knocking. It was a precarious time: people tried to not leave their houses unnecessarily. But someone kept on knocking.

I looked discreetly out the window. A woman was standing outside, wrapped up in a headscarf. She knocked one more time. I opened the door but stood on the threshold, making it clear from my expression that I would not let her inside the house. But she didn't intend on coming inside and started talking straight away. I only knew this woman by sight, and I knew she was Jewish. She had heard about my mother's death and wanted to save her own mother.

"I beg you, I am praying for you, please sell me your mother's passport, we have to leave," the woman said.

Sell her passport? How could I sell my mother's passport? Give away her passport?! My head couldn't reconcile with the thought. But the woman wouldn't listen, throwing herself on her knees, clutching at my legs. While sobbing and pleading, she begged me again and again and again.

How could my heart resist this? It couldn't, of course. I gave her the passport. The dead thus saved the life of the living. Did my mother, Halyna Fedorivna Bolotina, live on in the body and likeness of that Jewish woman? Did she manage to escape from death's clutches? Another unanswered question.

Life under Occupation

The loneliness was slowly killing me. It was easier during the day, but when night came, the terror would swell in every cell of my being. I was a lonely young girl, all alone in her house. I would shutter the windows, lock the doors, and even bolster the doors with heavy furniture. Sometimes the priest's son, Yurii Makar, would come by, but I was wary of even him, even though I had no grounds not to trust him.

The only relation I had left was Auntie Afanasiia, but there hadn't been the slightest bit of news from her since the war had started. She didn't even know about my mother and that I had been left all alone. And how was I supposed to get to her in Kyiv? There was a war raging: Kyiv had probably been occupied by the Germans. After mass bombardment from the air and shelling from the ground, a sudden calm fell over the city. It was a pernicious and troubling calm. What would come next?

Next came the rumble of engines, and the conquerors arrived on our street—specifically, German, Italian, and Hungarian soldiers on big black motorbikes, in full uniform, machine guns slung over their shoulders. They were foreign people, speaking a foreign language, but they acted like they were at home. Terror ... We felt terror before these people. The locals hid behind the four walls of their homes, shuttered behind ten locks on the door and peeking out through the cracks of their shutters to see if anyone was walking up to the house. As if that would save them! The Germans set up headquarters in the junior school. Having them as neighbors brought us nothing but trouble, but I was forced to get used to it and even utilize it to my benefit. The German soldiers had free access to any house at any time. They would come to me to borrow various things: kitchen utensils, firewood, or salt. Every one of their visits would induce great anxiety in me, after which I would run to our household icon and pray before it, thanking God that I had been spared that time, that He had protected me.

I got to know one German, but I now no longer remember his name. He worked as a dispatch rider, transporting various pieces of information and documents by motorcycle. Did he want to fight? Of course not. But one had to carry out the Führer's orders, just like the boys fighting in the Red Army had to carry out Stalin's orders. My acquaintance would come around often, bringing me various magazines, and we would talk about movies and books. Movies starring Charlie Chaplin were being shown in the cinema, and they were extremely popular. Yes, even under occupation people still went to the cinema. I learned German from speaking to the Germans, which later came in very handy. I also learned a little Italian. I had an ability to pick up words and phrases quickly, and I found foreign languages easy to remember. What mattered was that my acquaintance didn't bother making any advances, unlike the others. I didn't know whether I was beautiful or not—nobody had ever told me that I was—but men certainly paid attention to me. Of course, it was no surprise that the German and Italian rank-and-file soldiers, after a long time on the front, wouldn't have minded having some fun with a "Russkie girl."

I have only been slapped in the face once in my life, and that was by a German officer. It was in response to my desperate attempt to fend off his bold advances. Not expecting such a blow, I screamed in terror and ran away as fast as I could. I ran back to my house, slammed the door shut, and pressed my body against it as well. Shaking from fear, I listened to see if the German had run after me. It was quiet, and I didn't hear anything. I stood there like that for some time, until my legs bent of their own accord and I slumped down on the floor. I sat there, swaying and holding my cheek, which had grown puffy from the blow. I barely crawled to my bed, and I fell asleep fully dressed. I was truly terrified as I sat in my house, waiting for the German officer to knock on the door at any point. But nothing happened. I only left the house a long while afterward, still looking around me to see if anyone was there. That German could have forced himself upon me at gunpoint or just shot me, but, thankfully, that didn't happen. God protected me.

Day passed after day, each with its own worries and problems: how to live — well, maybe not live, rather survive — from one day to the next. Fall came, rain fell, and damp seeped into the house, leaving big yellow stains on the walls. In order to keep warm, I only lived in one room of the house, burning everything I could. I found a few wooden boards in the shed outside, and my neighbors helped me saw them down into smaller pieces of kindling. I dug up all the hard coal that still remained in the cellar. There were no fences or gates left anymore: either they had been stolen, or they had been taken down by their owners for firewood.

The loneliness oppressed me the most. I was alone, completely and utterly alone. Nobody was there to care about me. Everyone was living their own lives, which were filled mainly with terror about the occupiers, constant hunger, and the cold. There was no electricity: everyone used kerosene lamps, turning the flames down as low as possible.

Food and necessities could only be found at the outdoor markets. Everything was sold in glass jars. I mostly bought corn because it was the cheapest. To save on fuel, I would soak it for two or three days before boiling it and seasoning it with burnt oil — the oil that was burned by our retreating troops before the Germans arrived. Why hadn't they not distributed the oil to the people? Nobody thought about the local population getting left behind enemy lines, and we were left to fend for ourselves.

Simple domestic chores became a big problem for me. The water pump on our street stopped working, and I had to go to Shoseina Street to draw water. When the fighting returned to Dnipropetrovsk, the aerial bombardment and artillery fire practically never ceased.

I was already experienced at war. I already knew that when a plane was flying right above your head, you didn't need to worry. Bombs don't fall straight down but fly along a certain trajectory. You should worry when a plane was flying at some distance away from you. Perhaps it has already dropped a bomb. How many times did a plane suddenly appear while I was hauling a bucket of water back home! I would throw the bucket aside and dive behind a wall, nettles stinging my body all over. I would cover my ears with my palms to muffle the vehement whirring of the engines. I would pray fervently that death would pass me by.

One day I had boiled water to bathe and was pouring it into a big tub, peering from time to time through the crack in the shutters (during the war we tightly sealed the windows to create a blackout) to see whether planes were flying overhead. I was in the middle of washing myself when I heard the roar of aircraft. Naked and covered in soap, I threw myself under my bed. I don't know how long I lay there on the cold floor.

Washing laundry took away my strength. Unused to hard work and not fully grown for my years, I could barely lift the sodden and heaven linen, I could barely scrub it with my hands, and I could barely wring it out. "Mama, life is so hard without you," my soul cried while my hands carried out the work. I found life so hard then.

After the arrival of our invaders, life in the city slowly improved. It was good that the bombing was over. The churches that were still standing were reopened, and people could find some solace there. I couldn't understand the occupying powers. On the one hand, they murdered people by the thousands, throwing them into concentration camps, but when they arrived in the city, they allowed spiritual and cultural life to continue. I too went to church, but I didn't receive the peace that typically came with church and faith.

My father was the source of my discord. I would step over the church threshold, and thoughts about him, about my poor papa, would fly into my head. What had he done to them that was so bad? He had merely taught people to love God and one another. I prayed fervently, beseeching that somewhere out there, in Siberia, God would protect my father.

Local Ukrainian committees were set up—, under German supervision, of course—that tried to establish at least some sort of civil society in the city. I was fortunate to get a job in the Amur-Lower Dnipro City Council, where I carried out various assignments and issued bread tokens. I don't know where they found the ingredients, but for a while, employees were given a bowl of hot soup with a piece of bread. I got a pittance for my salary, but it was money nonetheless.

It took a lot of effort to get to work. The tall snowdrifts slowed me down; sometimes I had to wade through them up to my waist. With great effort, I would pull my body out of the snow and wade on, bending over from the force of the wind that snaked into any gaps in my clothes and penetrated my bones. My lovely boots would quickly let in moisture, and my feet were frostbitten more than once. It was a long walk.

Spring of 1942 brought hope of my mother's reburial. The coffin cost three hundred rubles. I took my father's suit and shoes and went to the outdoor market. At first, I was ashamed: we had never sold anything of ours at the outdoor market. During the war, the market became an important facet of life. Here, you could buy something, barter, or get hold of information. Luckily, I managed to sell my father's things. I was floating from joy: my mother's feet would no longer be cold in the ground. The exit was quite crowded, and a woman brought to my attention that my bag was open. I frantically rummaged around in my bag looking for the money, and when I couldn't find it, I threw all the bag's contents onto the ground. I couldn't believe it: my money had gone missing. I walked back to my house, weeping: I couldn't see anything in front of me but my mother's cold feet.

A few days later I found some more of my papa's clothes and sold them. It was enough to buy a coffin. My kind next-door neighbors helped me dig my mother up, lay her in the coffin and dig a grave in the cemetery. They also made a wooden cross with a sign, which I painted green. We then reburied my mother in the same cemetery where people who had died of starvation were once buried.

I don't remember whether this cemetery had a name, but it was on Manuilivka Street, and you had to walk down Shoseina Street to a hill at the end of the village, which was quite far on foot. Considering that there was a war happening, my mother's funeral was quite well attended. I suspect that there were also people there who were curious about the reburial itself, which was a rare event — perhaps the first to happen in our area.

My neighbors organized a wake and a traditional *tryzna*, or funeral meal, in accordance with the old Slavic customs. Every part of Ukraine has its own traditions for commemorating the dead. We made rice with raisins and placed it in a large bowl, and everyone present ate a spoonful of it. The priest performed the funeral service without taking any money. Maybe it was because he had a good heart, or because I was an orphan, or maybe because I was the daughter of a priest. My mother was buried properly, in accordance with our faith and our Christian traditions, and it felt like the weight of a mountain had been lifted off my shoulders.

She remained there in the cemetery. Oh, destiny, you couldn't even let me stay close to my mother, let me go to her grave and plant flowers, or leave her a *paska* cake on Easter Sunday! People would come to their relatives' graves on these holidays to leave paskas and decorated eggs, and sit around reminiscing about their dearly departed. That was what we did in the Dnipropetrovsk region. Oh, destiny, you didn't even let me fulfill the final duty of children toward their parents—to look after their graves!

Did my mother's grave survive intact after all the terrible bombing that razed my city to the ground? People said that after the war Dnipropetrovsk was left in complete ruins. If her grave did survive, is someone now looking after it? I want to believe someone is, I truly want to. I believe in good, and this helps me. I pray for my mother's soul and gaze in my mind at that mound of fresh earth, which has been imprinted in my memory forever. And where is my father's grave? Who knows. I pray for him too.

Oles Kulchynskyi

As She Watched the News Years Later, My Grandma Used to Say, "I'm Stupid for Not Having Grabbed a Revolver after the War!"

I want to share the story of my maternal grandmother, Mariia Ivanivna Bezvershenko, née Kolomiiets (1916 – 2003).

My grandmother was born in the small town of Yerky in the Cherkasy region. She's from the same town as Viacheslav Chornovil, incidentally. They were even neighbors.

After the Holodomor she was left an orphan. Having witnessed the horrors of the war from its first day to its last, she hated both Hitler and Stalin. Yet throughout the remainder of her life, she remained strong willed, energetic, joyous, and full of optimism.

As a child, on occasion I would ask her the inane question, "Grandma, did Grandpa Sashko kill people while he was at war?" "I don't know, sweetie, maybe he did," she would reply. Up until her death, every May 9 Grandma would solemnly get ready for the parade: she would put on a white headkerchief, don her best suit, and pin on all of her tarnished medals. She was even buried with them on.

Like many frontline veterans, she didn't like to talk about the war much, though she did leave behind a few stories about it.

The Military Commissar

As a professional pharmacist, Mariia was called up on the very first day of the war to make and dispense medicines. She was attached to one of the battalions. As she crossed the threshold of the field enlistment office after being called up, she was informed that she had a few hours to gather her things, taking only the necessities, and that she would be heading to the front.

The woman's first reaction was tears and requests to be dismissed from duty. The unmoved and tired military commissar responded to this with all of a few words: "You have a choice: Either you go to war and have a chance at surviving, or I'll shoot you on the spot." Of course, my grandma chose the front.

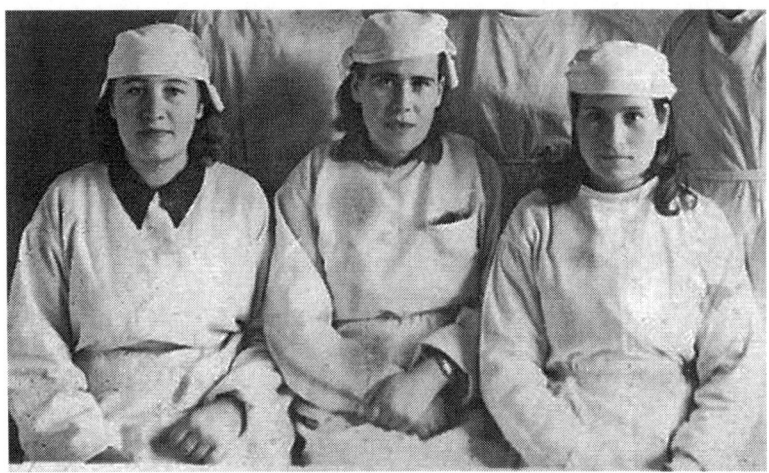

My grandmother (right) with her fellow pharmacists. May 1945

My grandma also described on more than one occasion how, while en route to their first duty station, the conscripts met evacuated compatriots from throughout Cherkasy Oblast, including people from their own villages. As she recounted it, their lamentation was so great it could rival that of hundreds of our central-Ukrainian funerals held at once.

The Reason

Perhaps the most frightening thing that Grandma lived through over the course of the war was the so-called "Kharkiv cauldron" of 1942: Soviet forces were attempting to liberate the capital of the Sloboda region, but due to the command's ineptness ended up encircled, and at least 200,000 lives were lost.

My grandma, by some miracle, managed to survive. Just imagine: she saw with her own eyes and later recounted how one multistory urban building after another collapsed under a torrent of German bombs, how thousands upon thousands of soldiers died ...

Many years after these events, she ran into a friend she had met in battle — a first aid nurse that also made it out of the Kharkiv cauldron alive. As Grandma described it, she was immediately made wary by something unusual in the woman's behavior and her disjointed speech, which was interspersed with incongruous recollections of those events.

She later learned that after that battle the nurse had gone mad.

Watermelon Jam

After Kharkiv, the Caucasus awaited my grandma, in particular the city of Grozny in Chechnya. Grandma Mariia has only the most positive memories of Chechens, Georgians, and other Caucasian peoples.

Despite all the myths promulgated during both Soviet and modern times, Grandma always characterized Chechens aptly and succinctly: "They're good people." She had witnessed the deportation of this people—the old and the young, from elderly men to women with small children—and could never bring up the subject without shedding tears.

As everywhere else, she made a friend in Grozny—a Chechen woman, who invited the "Ukrainian woman in uniform" over to savor some jam made from watermelons, which my grandma had never tried before.

The amiable Chechen family and the woman from the front were just finishing a lunch of Ukrainian *varenyky* prepared in honor of the guest, and the lady of the house was already placing a few jars of freshly cooked, reddish-colored preserves on the table for dessert, when suddenly they heard yet again the sound of bombs, explosions, and German aircraft.

The people in that house survived, but as soon as my grandma raised her head after the bombing, she encountered a macabre scene: the entire room was spattered with reddish-pink clots.

She never did taste the much-anticipated preserves. Fortunately, however, these clots were just jam, not clots of blood!

The General and the Hair Dye

Even though my grandma knew how to shoot and ride a horse and pull a wounded soldier out of battle, she was very highly valued as a pharmacist and was utilized first and foremost in this capacity at the front.

Working in wartime conditions, she often had to prepare medications herself—liquid mixture after liquid mixture, pills, ointments—using powders, herbs, and oils with medicinal properties as her basic materials.

One time while at the front, my grandmother was charged with a peculiar task—to restore the hair color of one of the generals. Completely exhausted and stressed, the general had turned horribly gray, aside from which his hair had become brittle and started falling out. My grandmother made an infusion based on recipes known only to her, which had to be rubbed into the scalp for natural hair color renewal.

This wasn't a modern, artificial dye, but a natural, herb-based "revitalizer." She first tried it out on her own early grays. As the story goes, something similar could later be spotted in Soviet pharmacies now and then in the 1950s and 1960s. The infusion helped. The general was "rejuvenated," and my grandmother was celebrated with honors.

As the bizarre laws of fate would have it, she herself, however, later contracted a disease, after which she always wore a headkerchief. While spending the night during one of the battles right out in the freezing cold and snow, the young woman, as a result of a weakened immune system, contracted lupus. The illness would also leave its mark on the strength of her hair.

Afterword

My grandmother and I talked quite a bit in her later years. It sometimes felt as though she were trying to use these endless stories to teach me something in the height of her old age. Yet other times it seemed as though she had been horrified by war forever. It's not even worth getting into the effect the two Holodomors had on her …

Yet now and then, from among the horrors buried within her subconscious, something seemingly incomprehensible to us weaklings would burst out into the open—something arising from the power of her spirit, or some insight gleaned from the challenges she had lived through: "I'm stupid for not having grabbed a revolver after the war when they were offering me one!" she was capable of blurting out as she watched the evening news. Or, "If there's another war, I'll be the first one taken off to the front. I've been there already and know how it all works. You just wait and see!"

Stepan Semeniuk

Seventy-Nine Days in a Death Cell

Insurgent fighter Stepan Semeniuk spent seventy-nine days in a Rivne prison in a cell for prisoners sentenced to execution. In February 1945 Soviet authorities commuted the twenty-five-year-old insurgent's death sentence to hard labor. This is an excerpt from the Volyn resistance fighter's memoirs of these events. His dry and factual description cannot leave anyone unmoved by this story, even today.

On the night of February 14, 1945, my death sentence was commuted to twenty years of forced labor.

I passed through all the "best" prisons and camps in Russia and travelled over thirty thousand kilometers in prisoner trains, ships, and prison vans, and time and again I would find myself outside of Ukraine. I lost everything: my friends, my love, my family, and my health.

Three of my brothers were felled by enemy bullets, and my father died of starvation when he was exiled beyond the Urals. When for the first time in thirty years I saw my mother, who had twice escaped from exile in Siberia, she said to me almost reproachfully, "My son, you are wasting your energy in foreign lands."

My time in these foreign lands began for me on the 13th and 14th of February 1945, or rather on the night between them, with my release from a so-called "death cell." But could I ever forget that cursed place? No, never. All that hardship has translated into an array of wounds that do not heal, and they are always with me.

In Lieu of a Diary

Your heart grows heavy when you see people for the last time. Perhaps one of these condemned men might be able to pass on a letter to the outside or get the chance to see a family member, or—God willing—he might return home a free man, and though you will not, you don't hold it against him.

You only have one thing left—to die in silence. Your death will be unmarked, but you will die a Ukrainian, as a Ukrainian resistance fighter. That is no small thing. Yet it still weighs so heavily on your heart and soul!

Rivne Prison No.1: I find myself once again underground. The Chekists (NKVD agents) have told me to take off my shoes, and I throw off my wooden clogs and my footwraps.

"Pick up those rags," says my jailer.

"Why would a man sentenced to death need them?"

"Shut up, you fool, you'll be building cities for the Motherland yet," the Chekist, a senior officer in this purgatory, says in Russian as he shoves me into the cell and locks the door.

Several dozen eyes stare out at me from the darkness. Dante himself could not have conceived of more pitiful creatures than those lying prostrate in front of me, and I have become one of them.

"What, are you scared? You'll be just the same as us in a few days," someone says.

Some people slowly push up off the floor and sit leaning against the wall because they are no longer able to sit without the wall for support. The cell is basked in a permanent twilight.

"My friend, this is Cell No. 14. The whole underground of the prison is for people sentenced to death. It's like a waiting room for heaven, for the other side. But they won't shoot you right away; you must wait your turn and become a shadow of a human, like us. Well in any case, tell us what it's like outside. How is our side doing? You were there not long ago. You're probably closer to the outside and got arrested later than us," someone says, barely audibly. That is how my life as a condemned man began. Hnat (I no longer remember his last name, unfortunately), who was from somewhere in the Mykhailivka District in Chernihiv Oblast and had been a platoon commander in the Ukrainian Insurgent Army (UPA), pulls me toward him.

My first reaction is one of horror. The announcement of my death sentence doesn't induce fear in me. Every revolutionary is always ready for death and prepares himself for it. But one cannot prepare oneself for a death cell in a Russkie prison because it's impossible to imagine what they're like.

Looking at the other condemned, you might think that you're in an anatomical research lab and that you're surrounded by human skeletons wrapped in skin, or living mummies.

The day in the cell would begin with the wakeup call. The Chekist warden would bang on the door, open the tray slot and bark, "Get up!" He would do an inspection through the tray slot: we'd be ordered to sit against the walls or kneel, and they'd count us. After that they'd give us some hot water, not for washing ourselves, but for our breakfast. During the day — but not every day — they would give us 100 – 150 grams of black bread each, or sometimes instead of bread we would get flour boiled in water. For lunch we would have soup, generally a concoction made from potatoes or some other vegetables.

We were given the soup in tin canteens—which they insisted on calling bowls—but without spoons. They would give us one canteen for the two of us. We sat opposite one another and slurped the soup in turns; first I would slurp it and hand it to the other prisoner, then he would do the same and hand it back to me, and so on until the "bowl" was empty.

Sometimes we were given hot water again in the evening. To deceive our empty stomachs, some of us would drink more of this hot water, convincing ourselves that the water would fill the space bread should be occupying. A diet like that quickly brings your body to the point of exhaustion, to the point at which you can only survive. You not only lose your physical strength, but your mental strength as well.

In such conditions, how is it possible to deny that purgatory exists?

In the corner next to the door stood a two-hundred-liter slop pail that functioned as the prisoners' toilet. The prisoners had to feel along the wall to get to it, leaving finger- and palm prints on the wall. If a prisoner wanted to squat over the pail, several other people had to help him since he couldn't do it by himself. The guards would take the slop pail out of the cell, which was then carried out of the corridor by "domestic offenders," who would return it to the cell once it had been emptied. During this process we would be told to keep away from the door and sit down.

The cell itself was five meters long and just over two meters wide. High on the wall was a small window, like in a cellar, covered with a grate and boarded up. The outside wall was more than a meter thick. At the turn of 1944 – 45, there were forty-two prisoners occupying this "living area" in Cell No. 14 of Rivne Prison No. 1. We slept head to toe, my outstretched feet reaching the chin of a comrade lying next to me, and his reaching mine. We could only sleep on our sides as otherwise there wasn't enough space. We'd all lay down together and only turn over to our other side at the same time. If someone turned over without the others, he could lose his spot because the mass of human bodies would squeeze into the gap. Everyone slept on the bare floor.

Once a week a female doctor would peer through the tray slot and ask, "Is anybody sick?" Sometimes someone would complain of a headache, and the doctor would hand them some powder wrapped in paper, which then had to be returned to the guard. What were they afraid of? The little sticks they used to fasten pieces of bread into paper also had to be handed back. Whenever the guards weren't near, the doctor would sometimes say something comforting in Ukrainian. We all got scabies because of the dirt and the excreta overflowing from the slop bucket, and this itching disease gave us no rest. Scabies was treated with an ointment made from gunpowder that viciously scoured the sores off our skin, but the scabies would disappear and the pubic lice with them.

Isolation, a lack of movement and air, and hopelessness dull the human mind. That's why some of us fashioned chess pieces out of chunks of bread, then dried them. The Chekists would take them away at the next inspection—they were "against the rules"—and once again we would make chess pieces out of chunks of bread. Alexander Herzen once wrote that an intelligent person is quicker to adjust to prison conditions than simpler folk, but that can't be said about a Bolshevik prison. Perhaps that's how things used to be, seeing as Herzen used to get books, letters, and even food sent to him from the outside and paid for with his own money.

The guards would check the strength of the window bars, the ceilings, the floor, and the walls almost every day. Then the officer would scream in Russian through the peephole, "Lie on your front! Arms by your sides! Legs in the air! Turn your head to the door!" We would lie on our stomachs, arms stretching down to our legs and our legs bent up in the air. After that a few Russkies would run into the cell with big wooden hammers and bash them against the window grilles, the walls, the ceiling, and the floor. Those hammers would often hammer at our bones too. There was a similar process when someone was being called for execution, only then they did not enter the cell. It was only when we were lying on the ground "as per the rules" that they would open the tray slot, which some NKVD agent captain would then stick his snout into. He would look at us in silence for a long time, then leave. These were terrifying moments because that night someone would be taken to be executed, and each man prepared his soul for death, though our bodies had been prepared long beforehand.

In all my seventy-nine days in that death cell, I never saw someone go to their death exhibiting fear, pity, or crying—and there were children in our midst. Everyone exiting the cell for execution wished for those left behind to be released. The OUN members always bid us farewell with the exclamation, "Glory to Ukraine!"

Sometimes the Chekists in the corridors would talk loudly among themselves about a hanging or shooting, possibly with the goal of tormenting us mentally. And since it would be quiet in the cell because talking loudly wasn't allowed, we could hear all those conversations.

During my time in the death cell, we were taken only once to the bathhouse, which was in the other wing of the prison. The Chekists stood as a solid human wall along the corridor and in the prison yard, telling us to run as they beat us with sticks and shouted in Russian, "Run, little wolves!" To be fair, we probably didn't look like people: we were unshaven, ragged, barefoot, and dirty. Although it wasn't possible to clean ourselves properly, not having any soap, enough water, or a change of underclothes, our bodies still felt somewhat lighter after a rinse.

In the bathhouse, someone in the next stall over asked me my name through a hole in the door. It was M. Lebid talking, whose lot had already been "pardoned"—how lucky! I expressed my happiness that he was no longer a condemned man, and he shared his joy at my being still alive.

"They'll probably pardon you too, that's why they took you to the bathhouse," he tried to comfort me.

The whole of the underground floor of the prison was inhabited by prisoners awaiting execution. Before 1945 there were practically no cases of commuting "the highest measure of punishment" (execution) to imprisonment. Only recently Lavrentii Beria himself visited the prison and inspected the executions. According to a study by Professor Patsuly, on January 1, 1945 there were 372 persons sentenced to capital punishment in Rivne Prison No. 1, in Prison No. 4 there were 2, in Dubno prison there were 349, and in Ostroh there were 44 in all. There was a total of 767 persons sentenced to the "highest measure of punishment" in Rivne Oblast, including women and young people below the age of eighteen. How many were there across all of Ukraine? And who will present Moscow with the amount?

After I had spent a few days in the cell, a young man with a big beard (we all had beards and mustaches) shifted over to me and asked where I was from. I answered him, and he smiled, saying that he knew the place, and we didn't return to the subject. It was only then that I recognized him. He was a youth leader from Ostrozhets District, from the village of Kniahynina, I believe. While still on the outside he had caught tuberculosis of the knee and had been treated by the unforgettable Dr Gross, but in here his knee, left untreated, had grown like a melon, and he couldn't bend his legs. He joined the liberation movement in 1942, and all his activities, like those of his comrades, were directed against the Germans. The Russkies executed him in 1944. All glory and honor are yours, young heroes!

Among the other prisoners in our cell were two brothers from Chortoryisk, a village in Polesia on the Styr River. One of them was not yet sixteen, and the other was seventeen. They had been in the death cell for half a year by then and were so starved that they couldn't even talk or get up. One of them was executed. On his way to his execution, the brothers, still children, courageously said

Stepan Semeniuk with his fellow exiles (seated, far right)

goodbye to one another, like grown men. What threat did these children pose to the Empire? What barbaric right did Moscow have to shoot children?

It was customary in the prison for the convicts to write or etch their names onto the walls. Looking at these historical inscriptions marked there over the decades, you could make a list of people's names in various languages. You could even read the names under the fading plaster, especially those marked in paint. Though our invaders were exchanged for different ones, the prisons remained full. Someone learned from these wall inscriptions that one of the Radziwiłł princes had been in this prison in autumn of 1939 until Stalin handed him over to Hitler. The prince then lived in Warsaw, making use of all his estates in the General Governorate for the Occupied Polish Region. He was taken in by Hermann Göring, with whom he had to be detained to solve the matter of the Polish Catholic clergy. Well, everybody should enjoy freedom; that is one's natural right, Radziwiłł princes included. Then again, the Radziwiłłs were, according to the proclamations of communist ideology, "exploiters of the masses," "the vilest enemies and enslavers of the working people of Lithuanian, Belarus, and Ukraine," and so on, which was not very far from the truth.

So what was it that happened here? Did the prince become a member of the proletariat, or did other interests play out? Could these young boys have had a more guilty class position than Radziwiłł? They were his former subjects, also sentenced to death: seasonal workers, hirelings, and simple Polesian peasants from his estates in Polesian Volyn. Anyone with a working brain could likely figure out what was going on here.

Man is a strange creature. He may be sitting in a cell, awaiting execution, but he will still think and dream. He'll dream about what Ukraine should become and what it will look like as a free state. We dreamt in our sleep too—especially about delicious lunches and dinners. I often dreamt about my mother, although I didn't know where my family was as they had been deported on May 15, 1941. I also dreamt of my Kvitka, my love, who came to me in my dreams as an angel and gave me strength in the prison and in the camps.

"We must feel that we are Ukrainians: not *Halychany*, or Bukovinians, but Ukrainians without official borders"—Ivan Franko. This sentiment of Franko's united all of us Ukrainians, regardless of whether we were from the east or from the west of the country. Regardless of whether the political borders of foreign states had divided us for centuries, we were one.

The "Westerners" knew perfectly well about the awful events that had transpired in the USSR, about the repressions and the famines. Certain social movements had occurred almost simultaneously in the USSR and in the Polish lands, such as Ukrainianization, or the struggles to use our native language, for an autocephalous Church, or for the preservation of our identity. The difference lay in the fact that in the USSR authorities intervened in these protests and put them to a brutal end, whereas in Poland people could claim such rights themselves in the framework of civil and political organizations.

In December 1944 someone tossed a Ukrainian-language newspaper through our cell window (here's some news for the Ukrainians, they said), which contained news of the death and funeral of Metropolitan Sheptytskyi, known as the "Prince of the Church."

The photograph in the newspaper showed an "honorary" division of Red Army soldiers taking part in the Metropolitan's funeral. The deception and hypocrisy of it all! The people of Lviv knew perfectly well that this "honorary" division of Chekists was not there to pay homage to the Metropolitan; they were there to prevent any protests and keep up appearances for the outside world since there were many western Allies in Lviv at the time. As I looked through that old newspaper, I remembered how Stalin had told Metropolitan Sheptytskyi via Kost Levytskyi that he— namely, Stalin—would not let Sheptytskyi become a martyr. And

Stalin kept his word, ordering that Sheptytskyi be buried with full honors. But after the death of its metropolitan, what would happen next to the Greek Catholic Church?

Mid-way through February, just before the 14th, we were awoken at night by people running up and down the corridor. Everybody knew what that meant: someone was to be called to their death. But they called people from several cells at once, brought them all out into the corridor, and then told them to sit on the floor.

I was called out too. There were several other prisoners in the corridor that had been sentenced to execution previously. They were surprisingly gentle with us.

Then a commander came over and started calling people over to a table one by one. He told each of them that the Supreme Soviet of the USSR had commuted their death sentence to twenty years of hard labor. There had never been a case like this, where so many people were "pardoned" at once — both those who would and those who wouldn't call this a "pardon" later.

Next we were thrown into different cells, which weren't as crowded as our death cell, with only eighteen people in each. In the morning the prison warden visited us with a retinue of the entire prison staff. He asked us how we felt, then promised us that as soon as we had regained our strength, he would send us off to the camps. The Chekist who had first led me into the death cell had told us the truth: the Motherland needed free labor to "build a new city for the country."

They started taking us out for ten-minute walks, though not every day because they wouldn't have been able to fit all the prisoners in the yards if they took everyone out every day. On our walks we could sometimes catch some news from the next yard over. This mattered a great deal to us since we had been so isolated.

However, there was a sense of tragedy to these walks as well: these "exercise rings" were situated on the part of the prison yard where prisoners, shot by the retreating Chekists in June 1941 and by the Germans in 1942, had been buried.

How many of our brothers lay beneath these "exercise rings"? Would their descendants ensure their names weren't forgotten? Would the world ever learn of the criminals who had shot thousands of prisoners, and would those criminals ever be punished? Such were the thoughts that ran through our minds as we walked over our graves.

Who were these "brave knights" that were the first to enter the fight for their people's freedom and for the nation of Ukraine? Below are some of those with whom fate brought me together in those heroic and turbulent years.

Serhii Kachynskyi, a.k.a. Ostap, was first commander of an UPA division and son of a poor farmer from the village of Piddubtsi, near Lutsk. His family's property consisted of only a one-bedroom house and a thatched-roof barn, without even a separate kitchen or small threshing barn. His brother Stepan was a tailor and musician, who died in a hospital for the terminally ill in Belgium. His parents and his sister Zina were deported in 1940.

Mykola Mostovych, a member of the OUN leadership, was the son of an Orthodox priest from the village of Malyn in the Dubno region. His parents were deported to Siberia in 1940.

Liuba Hnatiuk, a.k.a. Bila ("Fair One"), Rusalka ("Mermaid"), and Kvitka ("Flower"), was the daughter of a peasant from the village of Harazdzha, not far from Lutsk. She served as a women's officer for the Kovel Okrug of the OUN and for Volyn Oblast. She was also head of the Ukrainian Red Cross within the Turiv "Military Okrug" (a combination of UPA military units) and the UPA's Zavykhost military field hospital. Her family were deported in 1941.

Anatolii Koziar, a.k.a. Hai ("Grove") and Volodymyr, was the son of landless peasants from the village of Piddubtsi. He was the regional leader of the Volyn OUN.

Mykola Yakymchuk-Kovtoniuk, a.k.a. Hrisha, from the village of Piddubtsi, was the son of poor farmers, an administrative official of the OUN for the Lutsk region, and first commander of Turiv Military Okrug, also known as "OLEH."

Kuzma Muzychuk, a.k.a. Karkolom ("Neckbreaker"), was the son of a shepherd from the village of Harazdzha and a clerk in the regional OUN Security Service.

Yaroslav Harasymenko, a.k.a. Ya. Mova (literally "I Am the Language"), was from a family of Ukrainian intelligentsia from Lutsk. He was an editor, linguist, and poet.

Yurko Myskovets was the son of a road worker from Lutsk and an emigrant from the east of the country.

Yaroslava Skab, a.k.a. Ivha, was the daughter of a rural school teacher from Tomashiv (Tomaszow) and an administrative official of the Ukrainian Red Cross.

Olena Mostovych, or Verba ("Willow"), was the daughter of an Orthodox priest from the village of Malyn in Mlyniv District (now Rivne Oblast). She served as a women's officer in the OUN network PZUZ, and as an organizer and first head of the UPA's branch of the Ukrainian Red Cross.

Vasylyna Demchynska, a.k.a. Tsyhanka ("Gypsy"), was a poor peasant woman from Piddubtsi and head of the UPA's military hospitals in the Kolky region.

Serhii Manko, a.k.a. Yashchur ("Blight"), from the village of Sadiv, was the son of a Poltava native, and the administrative officer of the OUN for the Kovel region.

Yukhym Vakh was an immigrant from the Kholm region (Chełm Land).

There were also hundreds of thousands of others. These are the fallen "bourgeois nationalists" and "children of kulaks," as they were known in Russian terminology. Stories like theirs could be found across all of Ukraine.

Yevhen Klimakin

"My Grandfather Was in the SS."
"And Mine Was Killed in Auschwitz."

A Love Story[1]

A conversation with Uwe and Gabi von Seltmann, descendants of SS member Lothar von Seltmann and concentration camp prisoner Michał Pazdanowski, about the need to know one's own history and the ability to forgive.

It was 2006 in Kraków. Gabriela, a Polish woman, was spending a merry evening with friends in the Singer Café. Jokes, dry wine, and conversations about mutual acquaintances and travels flowed. The group decided to take a photograph.

A man sitting alone at a neighboring table offered to help. Was he a Pole? No. A Ukrainian? Also no. He spoke with some kind of strange accent. It turned out that Uwe was German. He joined the group, and they started talking.

Gabi and Uwe simply couldn't get their fill of conversation. An hour passed, then a second. The other friends were starting to take their leave already, but Gabi and Uwe just kept talking and talking – till daybreak.

"Why are you in Kraków?"

"I'm drawn to this place. The thing is, my grandfather was in the SS."

"Why'd you say that?! My grandfather was killed in the Auschwitz concentration camp, in Oświęcim," Gabi cried in almost a yell.

An hour later the descendants of the executioner and the victim were walking down Szeroka Street in silence. And a year later Gabi and Uwe were married.

Today the couple travels all around the world advocating the need to know one's own history and the ability to forgive. They explain how the past influences the present and the future.

Tens of thousands of people have already attended Gabi's and Uwe's presentations, and books about their story and the lives of their ancestors have become bestsellers.

---

1   Reprinted with permission from the website Culture.pl.

Gabi and Uwe von Seltmann. Photo: Yurii Druh

Yevhen Klimakin: I, like many others have, will ask you to share your story.

Gabi von Seltmann: You know, as I was on my way to this interview, I was thinking about the fact that we tell our story and the story of our ancestors with completely different emotions now.

Y. K.: What do you mean?

Uwe von Seltmann: We do it more calmly.

G. S.: Yes, we learned the entire truth in order to forget about them — so that the truth may allow us to live peacefully, without glancing back all the time.

U. S.: No one had even told us the story of who our ancestors were, how they lived, whom they helped, or what crimes they committed. We had to travel the world, searching through archives and collecting information one bit at a time.

Y. K.: What was your life like before all of these discoveries?

G. S.: There's a saying in Poland about "sweeping things under the rug" — that is, hiding whatever's uncomfortable or unpleasant to see. For a long time we lived, pretending that everything was normal, that there was nothing there "beneath our feet," and then we ended up having to "sweep out from under the rug" everything that our predecessors had hidden there.

Feeling Guilt for One's Grandfather's Crimes

U. S.: For a long time I lived with a feeling of guilt for my grandfather's crimes. In 1999 I traveled from Germany to Kraków as a journalist to write an article about Kraków's Kazimierz District, where over sixty thousand Jews lived prior to the war. When I was visiting the Remah Synagogue, I noticed a man in a dark suit, who was reciting a prayer for the deceased. I inquired if I could ask him a few questions.

He agreed, after which he was the one to bombard me with questions.

"Why did you ask to speak to me?"

"I'm writing an article about Jewish Kraków. I studied Judaism."

"Why not Islam? A feeling of guilt? What year was your father born?"

"1943."

"And your grandfather?"

"I don't recall for sure, but I think 1917."

"A-a-ah." My conversation partner paused for a while, then deduced, "Your grandfather was a Nazi."

"Yes, he was in the SS," I replied. "I don't know any more than that."

"Everything's clear now. You live with a feeling a guilt for the wrongs your grandfather committed," he concluded.

How I hated my grandfather Lothar von Seltmann at that moment! I had been tormented by guilt from age twenty because of him.

I realized that thanks to someone who was only supposed to offer a few words for a piece I was writing but instead managed to turn my life upside down.

Y. K.: After that, from what I understand, a protracted search began. Uwe, describe what you managed to ascertain.

U. S.: I had always wanted to know who my grandfather was, what he did for a living. When I was a little boy, I found my father's passport. "Kraków" was listed in the Place of Birth section. That really surprised me. I asked him, "Kraków — where is that?" "In Poland. My parents were there. Son, don't ask me about anything more because I myself know diddly-squat about it," my father replied.

He really didn't know anything. When my father was two, my grandfather passed away. Two years later my father's mother, my grandmother, died. My father and his brothers and sisters were sent to orphanages and various foster families. He didn't know why he ended up in a small town not far from Dortmund.

Y. K.: Your father had a lot of brothers and sisters?

U. S.: Five of them. His older brother Helmut was born in Vienna in 1938, and the youngest was born in 1945. My dad was the second-to-last child. He, his brothers, and his sisters didn't realize that their father had been a criminal. I ended up being the one to reveal this terrible truth to my family. I began to investigate it when I was thirty-five. Even now, eighteen years later, I sometimes stumble on bits of information about Lothar von Seltmann.

Y. K. What exactly have you learned about your grandfather?

U. S. The most horrible discovery for me was that in 1943 he personally killed people in the Warsaw Ghetto. I collected information about him piecemeal.

I found out, for instance, that during the war he spent time in Lublin, Lviv, Chernivtsi, and Odesa. Even before I had learned about this, without realizing it myself, I had traveled in my grandfather's footsteps. I had been drawn to these places.

Why Young People Became Captivated by Nazism

Y. K. Was your grandfather a zealot?

U. S. At age thirteen he became a member of the Hitlerjugend. When he was sixteen he was arrested as a young Nazi for criminal activity. At the time my grandfather was blowing up trains and preparing all kinds of incendiary actions with other like-minded individuals.

In 1934 he fled from Austria to Germany and enrolled in an elite Nazi school. There he met his future wife, my grandmother, Wilhelmine Fritsch.

In 1938 Austria joyously welcomed Adolf Hitler, while the local Jews were being forced to clean sidewalks with toothbrushes. After these types of events, my grandmother and my Nazi grandfather came to Vienna without any apprehension. At age twenty-two my grandfather began working for fascist organizations and became acquainted with Odilo Globocnik.

Y. K. The originator of the idea of extermination camps?

U. S. Yes, this man was the Reichsführer-SS's delegate for the establishment of an SS structure and extermination camps on the territory of occupied Poland. Globocnik expressed an interest in working with my grandfather, and he and my grandmother moved to occupied Lublin.

Y. K. From your book *Gabi and Uwe*, I also learned that your grandfather had dealings with Heinrich Himmler.

U. S. Yes, that's true. With time my grandfather made a career for himself in Nazi circles and had dealings with the most influential Nazis.

Y. K. Uwe, why did the idea of Nazism enthrall such a young person? You've surely asked yourself this question, no?

U. S. My grandfather's parents were very conservative people—monarchists. And Nazism struck young people as very contemporary, even fashionable. It became an alternative to the monarchy. When I look at what's going on in the world today, I always remember that dramatic story from the last century. Today people who don't want to hate are also called conservative and old-fashioned. We're all witnesses to nationalism spreading its wings. On the eve of World War II, there was a similar situation.

The "Work" That Interfered with Enjoying Spring

Y. K. While he was in the occupied territories, your grandfather sent letters to his parents. What did he write about?

U. S. Not a single word about the war, and not a single word about the fact that Germans had turned the lives of millions of people into a nightmare. He wrote only that he was very busy and that he had a lot of work. When my father was born, my grandfather was staying in the Warsaw Ghetto. In letters to his own mother, he was seemingly proud of the fact that he had had a son in Kraków. He regretted not being able to be with his family because of an important operation in Warsaw.

He also described that a beautiful spring had begun and that nature had awakened, but that because of work he couldn't fully enjoy all of this. It's appalling, but at that exact time he was personally killing Jews in the Warsaw Ghetto. This "work" kept him from taking pleasure in the spring and being with his newborn son, my father.

Y. K. What did your grandfather do before the Warsaw Ghetto?

U. S. He worked in propaganda, including publishing a propaganda magazine. He was also responsible for the search for people with German roots. The Third Reich believed that it needed to support its own. And that's what their work entailed: imprisoning or killing Poles and Jews, and rescuing ethnic Germans and bringing them to Germany.

Y. K. What are your thoughts on the responsibility of those who have worked or are working now in propaganda?

U. S. It's a serious crime. Propaganda is the foundation on which all kinds of horrible things can be built. Without propaganda Hitler wouldn't have been able to actualize that whole horror. Without a doubt, propagandists are criminals that should be held accountable for their crimes.

George Orwell once wrote that truth is the first to be killed. When I read these days about journalists that are imprisoned or killed for their professional activities, I understand that Orwell wasn't mistaken.

Y. K. Where did you look for information about your grandfather?

U. S. In archives in Poland, Germany, and the United States. For instance, in the United States, there are entire collections of documents pertaining to the Warsaw Ghetto Uprising. I collected information from wherever it happened to be. I managed to recreate my grandfather's life.

For example, I learned that in February 1945 my grandfather curtailed his own life. Not long before his death, he had met his wife's sister, showed her a pistol, and told her that in the event of a Red Army victory, he knew what to do.

I'd like to think that he regretted the crimes he committed, but that likely wasn't the case.

When in 1944 the SS killed half a million Hungarian Jews, Lothar von Seltmann was very happy. He wrote then, "Finally, Europe's last Jews are being killed." The irony of it is that Jewish blood flowed through my grandfather's veins too.

Y. K. Tell us more about that.

G. S. In 2012 we were invited to Hungary to give a book reading. We couldn't remember at what time the event was starting, but decided to not trouble the organizers and check online ourselves.

Uwe typed two words into the Google search bar, "Seltmann" and "Budapest," and we were shocked when we saw results with information about a Seltmann, who was a Jew and Hungarian rabbi.

It turns out that a part of Uwe's family hails from Hungary. Some of them converted to Christianity and left. Those who remained were killed during the war.

It's unclear to us whether Lothar von Seltmann knew about his Jewish lineage.

A Fated Meeting

Y. K. Uwe described his grandfather's story in the book *If the Perpetrators Will Not Speak, Their Grandchildren Will*, which became a bestseller in Germany. Not long after the book came out, your fated meeting took place. Tell us about how you met.

U. S. I sometimes lead tours from Germany to Ukraine, where I show the visitors Lviv, Chernivtsi, and other cities. In 2006, on our way back from one such excursion, the group and I stopped in Kraków for the night. In the evening I went to the Singer Café.

G. S. I was there with friends that same evening. We were drinking dry wine and joking around. Then we wanted to take a picture, and Uwe, who was sitting at the next table, offered to help. We immediately realized from his accent that he wasn't Polish. Uwe joined us at our table, and we started talking. I found him very interesting. Later he admitted that his grandfather had served in the SS. That was a shock!

Y. K. Gabi, how did you feel when you learned about this?

G. S. I felt like I had been hit on the head with a ton of bricks. In response to his "My grandfather was in the SS," I blurted out, "And mine was killed in the Auschwitz concentration camp, in Oświęcim." There! My words, my trauma, my story are greater than yours!

It was hard to control my emotions.

However, later I understood that there was a person next to me that was trying to somehow remedy this horrible past, that wanted to figure it all out. I had never before met a person that could speak so sincerely about such things.

Y. K. Gabi, what do you remember the most about that evening?

G. S. I remember everything. I'll never forget the anger that consumed me then. Toward morning Uwe and I were walking near the old Jewish cemetery, and I was thinking, "Why is all of this happening to us?" I had met a good and educated person. What did it matter to anyone what our ancestors had done? He and his grandfather were two separate people.

I was aware of this but could in no way control the anger that had appeared in my heart. Two weeks later Uwe came to Kraków again. I liked him. I thought to myself, "He's an interesting man. He's definitely either married or gay."

Lucky for both of us, I turned out to be wrong. Our relationship progressed rapidly, and a year later we were married.

Meeting Uwe was an important signal for me: thanks to my husband, I realized that the time had come for me to get to know my own story too.

Y. K. Your grandfather's story?

G. S. Yes. My mother didn't allow us children to go on school field trips to the Auschwitz-Birkenau concentration camp. It seemed to her that by doing so, she was protecting herself and us from that horrible truth, from that tragedy. You don't know about it, don't see it, and don't think about it, so you sleep more peacefully. I realized that that was the wrong approach.

Y. K. How did your family react?

G. S. Unenthusiastically.

A Taboo Subject

Y. K. Uwe, and how did your family—your father and his brothers and sisters—react to your desire to know the truth?

U. S. My father's older brother Helmut—the only one who remembers anything—was categorically against it. He wouldn't tell me anything. The others with time understood that it was important.

After my book was published in Polish, a Polish woman reached out to us. She wrote, "I recognized the apartment I grew up in in one of the photographs in your book. Your grandfather's family lived there before us. If you want to come see it, write to me. The apartment still belongs to us."

From that began my relatives' "pilgrimages" to Kraków.

Y. K. Gabi, your grandfather lived in Kraków as well?

G. S. He was an impoverished member of the *szlachta*, the Polish nobility. He was educated at the Jagiellonian University, then studied in Switzerland.

After that he moved to Verkhovyna, located on what was then the eastern border of Poland (present-day Ivano-Frankivsk Oblast, Ukraine). In 1935 he began construction of a school there and became its director. Interestingly, that building is still standing. Even photographs of it from the time have been preserved. Today the district hospital is located on the premises of the former school.

When I arrived there I met Ms. Vasylyna, who told me about my grandfather and about the fact that he valued Hutsul culture and traditions a lot. I was very concerned about what kind of person he had been. Let's be honest: in those days, some Poles behaved horribly there.

Y. K. What was your grandfather like?

G. S. While we were researching my grandfather's story, we found records of others informing on him in the archives.

Y. K. Who wrote the denunciations?

G. S. Other Poles. They were complaining that he wasn't Polonizing the local residents. I'll confess that I sighed with relief when I read those denunciations. Uwe once said that I was lucky with my grandfather: he was a good man.

Y. K. What was your family doing when war broke out?

G. S. In 1939 my grandfather and grandmother gathered up their belongings and decided to return home with their two children. My mother hadn't been born yet. On the way, their daughter, my aunt, began to cry a lot and was asking her parents to go back. My grandparents thought about it, then turned their wagon around. They arrived, and not long after horrible events began in Verkhovyna.

Y. K. What kind of events?

G. S. There were Soviet troops there until 1941. According to local residents, the Soviets killed all the influential Ukrainians almost immediately.

Then the Germans came. My grandfather was arrested and deported in 1941. At the time they were arresting Poles that were directors, supervisors, priests, etc. Most often it was locals informing on them to the Germans.

At first my grandfather was transported to Kolomyia, then to Stanislaviv (present-day Ivano-Frankivsk), and then on to Lviv.

He ended up in the Majdanek concentration camp outside Lublin and eventually in Oświęçim, in Auschwitz-Birkenau, where he died.

At about that same time, all the Jews in Verkhovyna itself were killed. They just led them out into the woods and executed them.

Y. K. And what happened to your grandmother?

G. S. That's when the period of Ukrainian Insurgent Army (UPA) activity began. They tried killing my grandmother a few times. Fortunately, a certain Ukrainian teacher would warn her about the impending danger. In 1943 she managed to escape with her children. No one from my family has been back there since.

I was the first one to go back.

Thus, it was only after seventy years that a Polish descendant of Isabella and Mikhał Pazdanowski set foot again in Verkhovyna.

Ukraine was a taboo subject in our family. Verkhovyna was some sort of cursed place for us.

However, I was constantly asking myself: If it was a cursed place, then why did my grandparents live there? Why did they return there? That must mean that not everything about it was that bad. That's how I mustered up the courage to visit there.

The First Encounter with the Past

Y. K. But you didn't know anyone there, did you?

G. S. We first met Anna, who spoke Polish, and then went with her from house to house, showing a photograph of my grandparents and asking people if they knew anything about the Pazdakowskis.

At first people were curious if we were planning on trying to reclaim property. We said that we weren't. Some man even came and promised to help us reclaim our family home, but I said that I didn't need anything, that I just wanted to learn more about my grandparents and about that time.

Then some people called and told us that Ms. Vasylyna lived next to the school and might remember something. She was eighty-five at the time.

Y. K. You went to go see her ...

G. S. We showed her the photograph, and she immediately said, "This is Michał, and that's Isabella." She recognized them instantly. I'll never forget that day!

That's how I met an old woman in the Ukrainian mountains, who knew more about my history and my ancestors than I did. I was so anxious! My heads were trembling from trepidation; we all cried like children.

Ms. Vasylyna kept repeating over and over, "Where have you been for so long? Why didn't you come earlier?"

During the war my grandmother was living in Verkhovyna hand to mouth. One day Vasylyna came to visit her and saw that Isabella, who had been left on her own with three children, only had a few beets at home. Vasylyna told her grandmother about this, and the old woman began to give her food, which the girl would secretly bring to our house. Vasylyna essentially saved our family from death by starvation. Every day at dawn she'd bring my grandmother food, then quickly run away so that no one would see her. Vasylyna's father was in the UPA and, naturally, knew nothing about this. Do you understand how complex and ambiguous history can be? Can you imagine what that meeting meant to me?

Y. K. Is Ms. Vasylyna still alive?

G. S. She died in 2015. She waited for four years to see my mother again.

Y. K. And did she get to?

G. S. Yes. When all those horrors were happening in Verkhovyna, my mother was a small child. She doesn't remember anything, but she inherited some sort of genetic fear, this type of frustration.

My mother is a shining example of a person who spent many a decade carrying the burden of a previous generation's tragedy and experiences. She doesn't remember her grandfather being arrested or people from the UPA coming: she didn't actually see anything that happened, but she spent her whole life living with a feeling of dread.

I tell people about her, and they respond that there's no need to pick at the scabs of the past, that it's better to forget everything and not broach painful subjects. That isn't true! The past has an active effect on us and our present lives.

You should've seen how scared my mother was of going to Verkhovyna!

Y. K. But it did happen, correct?

G. S. I convinced her to. We visited the house in which our family had lived during the last century. A teacher named Ms. Maria lives there now. She welcomed us very warmly, prepared a meal, invited us to sit...

Ms. Maria suggested that my mother spend the night. I'll be honest, my mother didn't want to, but I insisted. I understood that she needed to overcome her fear, to realize the absurdity of her phobias — that she should spend some time in the house in which she had spent the first years of her life.

My mother couldn't fall asleep for a long time. Then Ms. Maria went out into the garden and brought back all kinds of herbs from there and brewed some tea, after which my mother fell asleep. And she woke up a different person!

Our entire family sensed that my mother had changed. The end of a horrible story that had always made its presence felt finally arrived in her life.

Y. K. And how did you feel when you first traveled to Verkhovyna?

G. S. I was scared too. Uwe took me there almost by force. What was I scared of? Of people with machine guns or axes? It was absurd! You see, it was an irrational, panicky fear. You comprehend that nothing bad is going to happen, yet you can't help yourself. It's sewn somewhere into your subconscious. Locations activate your memory.

Y. K. What do you mean?

G. S. When I was spending the night in Verkhovyna for the first time, I woke up at three a.m. in a panic. I kept feeling like someone was coming, that there were conversations happening somewhere in the distance, that the gate was opening. I later learned that my grandfather had been arrested at three o'clock in the morning.

The location where this had taken place was activating the resources of my subconscious. I conquered this fear, and I felt better. I was also scared of going to Oświeçim.

Only at age thirty-nine, thanks in large part to my German husband, did I find the courage to go where my grandfather had been killed.

There I realized that the Auschwitz concentration camp is an educator. Auschwitz shows us the truth about us humans.

Memory as Salvation

Y. K. What are your thoughts right now about the terrible events of the last century?

G. S. Every nation has some kind of sins on its conscience. The Poles have their own, the Germans their own, and the Ukrainians or Russians their own.

Every nation also has its own traumas. Those who think that forgetting or silence heal are deeply mistaken.

U. S. The residents of villages in northern Japan discovered for themselves in 2011 just how important memory is. In many spots along the shore, there were large stones into which rules of conduct during a tsunami had been carved several centuries ago. Unfortunately, the stones of the ancestors were neglected and their advice forgotten. The price for this was paid during the 2011 tsunami by the thousands of people who didn't know how to behave during the catastrophe. Only in one small village, Aneyoshi, did no one die. Everyone in the village knew what was written on the stones. The children were even taught about it in school. Owing to this knowledge all of the village's residents managed to flee to the mountains in time.

Y. K. Memory saved them.

U. S. The Japanese professor Fumihiko Imamura, who studies natural disasters, notes that the memory of a terrible event or catastrophe fades by the fourth generation.

The fourth generation after World War II is currently sitting behind school desks in educational institutions around the world.

I want to ask the people who talk about the need to forget everything the following: are we raising cannon fodder for the next war?

Peace and freedom aren't obtained once and for all. In order to preserve harmony, we need to converse, listen to one another, and remember the price that humanity pays for the inability and unwillingness to understand their fellow men.

Y. K. How else does the past influence the present?

G. S. Take, as an example, the fact that the women in my family don't have children. My grandmother, as she was fleeing Verkhovyna, underwent a horrible shock and deep fear for her children. My mother did nothing with this phobia she had inherited for most of her life. As a result there's no generation of grandchildren to continue the family line.

My grandmother had three children, who gave birth to fourteen grandchildren. None of us have continued the family line. Incidentally, this situation is rather typical for these kinds of families. How do you explain that? Whether or not we want to, we're reaping the past's fruits.

Y. K. Without realizing it ourselves sometimes ...

G. S. Yes. For instance, the descendants of victims often suffer from depression and suicidal tendencies. They themselves don't realize what's happening to them. That's a fact.

If you're struggling and not at peace, and if you know one of your ancestors had a complex biography, it's imperative to learn more about your parents and grandparents and their lives. Your problems and the problems of your loved ones may be buried in the past. Someone in the family should, for once and for all, break the chain by which subconscious fear, depression, and phobias are passed on.

Likewise, the descendants of executioners often change their places of residence. Prior to meeting me, Uwe lived in thirteen different cities. The descendants of wrongdoers subconsciously flee and are constantly hiding from something.

What's important is that both the descendants of executioners and the descendants of victims need to do this sort of work on themselves.

It's no secret that the victim is also often aggressive. I don't tire of repeating that we need to take an interest in our past, at the very least out of a healthy self-interest.

Each of us has only one life. It's worth living it with joy.

Executioners and victims, in my opinion, only exist in the first generation. In the second and third generations, everyone's a victim.

That needs to be remembered.

U. S. I'd like to say one other important thing. My grandfather's story is shut and done for me. All the i's have been dotted. I live without a feeling of guilt, yet I've developed a feeling of responsibility.

When I look at the world and what's going on in it right now, I'm aware that we're living in a very explosive time and milieu. Proponents of democracy have one final chance to stop something very bad from happening. The current situation in the world resembles those on the eves of the First and Second World Wars.

People who are free, candid, and tolerant must stop nationalism. Nationalism always leads to conflicts and wars. Let's not forget that.

Volodymyr Parkhomenko

Surviving Fire and Water: My Father, Who Escaped Bombing and Drowning in the Dnipro

Until recently I had the habit of visiting the Liutizh Memorial every May 9, on Victory Day, to pay tribute to my father and his fallen compatriots from the 340th Sumy-Kyiv Division. This year I will probably choose another day to do this.

When the war between the Germans and the Soviet Union broke out, my parents, both born in 1924, had just finished their second-to-last grade of high school.

My mother, Liudmyla Kolodiazhna, was an orphan and lived with her guardian, appointed by the local collective farm, in the village of Hlynsk in Sumy Oblast.

My father, Hryhorii Parkhomenko, was born in the same village but lived in Alchevsk, which is where my grandfather, Tymofii Parkhomenko, moved the family in 1925. My grandfather worked at the local metallurgy factory as a welder and later headed the factory's so-called "residential section."

Although Alchevsk was occupied by the Germans later than other parts of Ukraine — on July 12, 1942 — schools appear to have been closed during the 1941 – 42 academic year, seeing as my father did not complete his grade level that year. Instead, he worked on the collective farms with his classmates and dug trenches. One time they were caught in an air raid, during which the parents of his classmate Vasyl Protsenko died.

Meanwhile, in the summer of 1941 my father's brother, Mykhailo, was serving in the Soviet military on the Soviet-occupied Finnish peninsula of Hanko. For several months the Soviet forces beat back the enemy, until they were evacuated sometime in November via the Gulf of Finland back to Leningrad, then already under siege by the Germans and the Finns.

During the crossing several transport ships were sunk by the Germans, and thousands of fighters perished in the freezing waters of the Baltic. In Leningrad fate brought Mykhailo together in the same squadron with his cousin, Semen Parkhomenko.

Mykhailo Parkhomenko (far left) on the Hanko peninsula during the Second World War

In September 1942 Semen was blown up by a shell right before his cousin's eyes. Mykhailo himself died at the beginning of January 1943 during an attempt to break through the Leningrad blockade. He was buried in those faraway lands.

My mother's brother, Arkadii Omelianovych Kolodiazhnyi, born in 1922, had just graduated from his second year of the Naval Academy in Leningrad when the war broke out. As a side note, he once told us about the school's political commissar, Miroshnychenko, and how, in confidential conversations with the Ukrainian cadets, he would express his belief that Ukraine would soon gain its independence (granted by the Germans) and would need its own naval officers.

Soon the naval cadets were sent to defend Tallinn, where, my uncle said, he was the commander of an artillery support unit. In late autumn the decision was made to evacuate the school to Baku, Azerbaijan, where the cadets could finish their training for service in the navy.

Since Leningrad was already surrounded, the cadets were taken onto Lake Ladoga outside the city and loaded onto a rotting old barge riddled with holes. In the middle of the lake, the overloaded vessel was hit by a small wave; it broke up and sank, and most of the cadets on it drowned. My uncle was one of the few to survive.

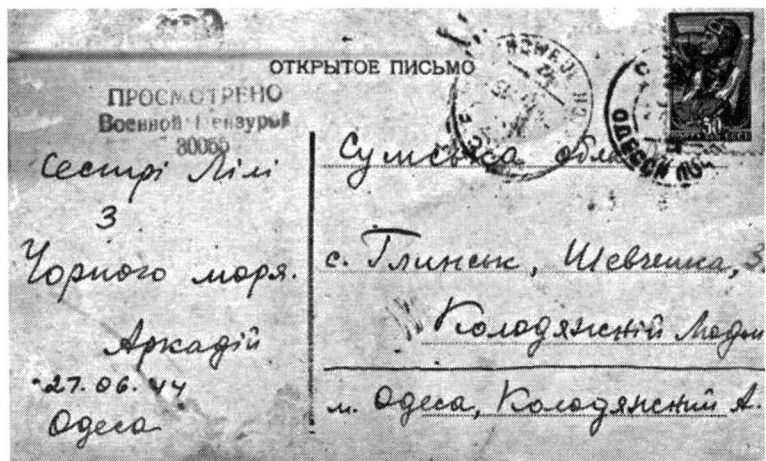

News of Lieutenant Arkadii Kolodiazhnyi from liberated Odesa reaches his sister.

After finishing his year in Baku, he fought first in the Black Sea in 1944 and later with the Danube Flotilla. He survived, was awarded several Orders of Glory, and graduated from the Naval Academy. Through all this he was a devoted national-communist, who believed that Ukraine should be independent yet remain communist.

Given A.O. Kolodiaznyi's title of Captain 1st rank, as well as his hydrographic research, a few years ago UNESCO named an underwater mountain in the Atlantic Ocean after him: Mount Kolodiazhnyi. Arkadii Omelianovych didn't live long enough to witness this honor himself.

When her hometown was occupied in September 1941, my mother started work as a laborer on the occupied version of a collective farm, otherwise known as a "community yard." After a short time, even though you could tell "from a mile off" that she still had a couple of years of high school left to finish, the girl was appointed as an accountant. Every time there was a recruitment drive to take people to Germany for hard labor, she would hide in the next village at her aunt's, whose son was in the police force, which ensured they'd be left alone.

In occupied Alchevsk, my grandfather was out of work because the occupied metallurgical factory had stopped operating. He wasn't drafted into the Red Army because of his age. My father's sister, Nastia, also lost her job. The Soviet military hospital where she had been working beforehand and where she had been lightly wounded during an air raid was evacuated when the Red Army retreated, but she stayed behind with her parents. Life for them was miserable in Alchevsk, and they had to exchange their meager belongings for food.

Meanwhile, the forces occupying Donbas started rounding people up for hard labor in Germany. My grandfather was taken away and put into a line of people being marched to the train station. Instead of taking a bag with him, my grandfather quickly grabbed an old bucket, in which he threw a piece of bread and something else for the road. Deciding to have a rest next to the road, he set the bucket upside down and sat on it. He was older and had a beard, and so he looked like an old man. The guards didn't pay any attention to some old grandpa sitting there by himself because there were plenty of people standing along the roadside as it was, so they left him alone. The line moved on, and my grandfather went home.

My eighteen-year-old father evaded being sent to Germany in whatever way he could. One time he was caught up in a round-up at the local market, where he had been selling drinking water from a bucket by the mug. The crowd was surrounded by Germans, who quickly separated young from old and then marshalled everyone into groups, loaded them into cars, and took them in batches to the station.

One or two Germans accompanied each group. When there was only one group of people left with only one pair of Germans supervising them, my father daringly made a run for it. The Germans shouted, "*Halt! Halt!*" but didn't chase after him (otherwise the rest would have run off as well) or shoot him (as the market was teeming with people).

A letter from Liudmyla Kolodiazhna to her brother on the front

On another occasion my father was hauled off to an assembly point near the station. It was an area fenced off by barbed wire, which was illuminated at night by a searchlight from a watchtower. The night before they were due to be loaded into wagons, my father and some other young men ran away, hastily throwing their coats over the barbed wire and climbing over while the searchlight was shining the other way.

In the end, with nothing to eat in Alchevsk, the family decided to move back to their home village of Hlynsk, where they still had a house occupied by some lodgers. In early spring my Aunt Nastia was sent there to try and resolve the issue of getting a patch of land to grow on. Nastia got to Hlynsk and wrote a statement to the head of the local council, but she was denied the land as a "daughter of a communist," though my grandfather had never been a communist.

"Aren't *you* a communist?!" my aunt, then still a young girl, couldn't help asking.

The council head was outraged and went for her, but he didn't chase after her.

Finally, the family moved to Hlynsk. Some relatives gave them some land and they ploughed up a patch. All of them started working in the "community yard" mentioned above—something they had no way of getting out of.

One time my father had to harness a horse. Because he had grown up in a city, he did it clumsily, which meant he received a whipping from the community yard monitor appointed by the

Surviving military railway servicemen after the war. My father, Hryhorii Parkhomenko, is circled

Home at last! My maternal uncle, the sailor Arkadii Kolodiazhnyi, with his family and neighbors, 1946

occupiers. The boy, always a hothead, went after the man who'd wronged him, but some well-meaning people pulled them apart. The yard monitor didn't pursue the matter because the sound of the approaching gunfire could be heard coming from the East.

By September 1943 the Red Army had advanced onto the left bank of the Sula River. The locals held up the towns for them, and our boys showed some of the units where the best places were to ford the river. The Germans were swiftly driven back to the Dnipro.

In the village, which was the district center, there was a field recruiting station. Within one or two days, all the men who were even slightly capable of service had been conscripted, and a day later they were already marching to the front, most of them as part of the 340th Sumy Division. My father was exempted from service: he had only about five percent vision in his right eye. However, he joined the army voluntarily. His only reply to his mother's lament was: "What else can I do? Don't you think Mishka [his brother Mykhailo] would've liked to have survived as well?"

The recruits were taken to Kyiv straightaway, but in their own clothes: why waste military uniforms on men on a suicide mission? People solemnly referred to them as *chornosvytnyky*, the "black jackets." They were also low on arms, though my father, being a hard worker, was given a rifle to himself. He joined a group destined for the Liutizh Bridgehead on the Dnipro River. Countless of their men drowned in the Dnipro, forced under by the heavy shelling of their improvised watercraft.

The raft that my father was crossing on was blown apart by a shell. My father couldn't swim: where could he have learned to in Alchevsk amid the dry steppe? And how could you swim and save yourself in the cold November waters, while fully clothed and carrying a rifle? But my father was lucky: he was pulled onto a boat by soldiers more fortunate than he.

In September 1967, twenty-four years later, I was a freshman at the Kyiv Polytechnic Institute and was doing agricultural work in the village of Moshchun, near Pushcha-Vodytsia outside Kyiv. When my landlady learned where I was from, she burst into tears. "Oh, my dear son! So many of you poor boys from Sumy were slaughtered there, on the fields beyond the Dnipro! Their bodies were piled up in droves ..."

My father mentioned that only twelve men from his company survived after the crossing and the fighting. He complained bitterly that most of them lost their lives because of their ignorance of even the most basic rules of battle. No one paid attention to battle rules; they just ran at machine gun fire like cattle. Till the end of his life, my father was convinced that in this way Stalin wanted to exterminate the Ukrainian youth that had briefly experienced life without communism.

The remainder of the units that had defended Kyiv were withdrawn and reorganized. That's how my father ended up all the way in Penza, Russia. He recounted terrible things about his time there, such as soldiers going without food and many of them dying of starvation. Later I found evidence showing that this had happened as well in other places where troops were temporarily deployed far into Russia.

It was only on December 18, 1943, more than two months after his conscription and after already taking part in fighting, that my father was sworn into the army. His fallen brothers, it turns out, weren't even awarded this honor, and so the Motherland was never indebted to them in the slightest.

The military medical commission examining the surviving liberators of Kyiv finally rejected my father from the infantry on account of his vision and deployed him with the military railway service. From that point on in the war, he took part in restoring the railway and railway bridges in Western Ukraine, Poland, and Manchuria — sometimes under bombardment.

After the Soviet authorities were restored to power in Hlynsk, the high school there resumed teaching. As such, my mother was finally able to finish her final grade, and as a first-class student she was accepted into the Kyiv Medical Institute without needing to take entrance exams. The institute's teaching and residence buildings were scattered all around the large city, and public transport was non-functional, so the students had to do a lot of walking. On the weekends the students, together with other city residents, helped dismantle the ruins on Khreshchatyk, Kyiv's main boulevard. Even back then people realized that the buildings' destruction was not the work of the Germans, but of the Bolsheviks, but they could only talk about it in whispers and with those they trusted.

Meanwhile, the war had come to an end, but as an orphan my mother had no money with which to support herself in the capital. Everything, especially food, was terribly expensive. Therefore, she dropped out of school, returned to her native Hlynsk, and accepted a job in the district state administration office.

In 1947 my father returned to the village from the armed forces, where he and my mother met and were married.

I was moved to take notes of these extraordinary events and record the lives of my parents and my closest relatives, who lived through the darkest and most desperate times of the war.

P.S.: Until recently I had the habit of visiting the Liutizh Memorial every May 9 to pay tribute to my father and his fallen compatriots from the 340th Sumy-Kyiv Division. This year I will probably choose another day to do this. I don't want to provide comfort to the puppets of the Kremlin, who use Victory Day for their own gains, by laying flowers beneath the bloodstained flags of an inhumane regime that hated its own citizens and slaughtered them by the million.

Boris Artemov

The Two Lives and One Victory of Yukhym Eisenberg

This is the story of how Yukhym Eisenberg, a Jew from Dnipropetrovsk born in 1924, died in the summer of 1942, and Viktor Borisovich Artemov, a Russian from Mozdok born in 1921, survived in his place.

I'll open with a facetious observation: everyone knows that Ukraine's Jews didn't starve in the famine in the early 1930s, but waited out the Great War in Tashkent. Because there was nice weather, *plov*, and fruit there. And, most importantly, people there weren't going to shoot them. And since everyone knows this, there's no point in debating it—all the more because my story corroborates it.

In 1933, my father's small family—just he and his mother—were living in the village of Veseli Terny in the Kryvyi Rih region, which meant they witnessed the results of Stalin's collectivization with their own eyes.

My father's mother, Kateryna Yukhymivna Briliant, was the village midwife, and my father, Yukhym Eisenberg, attended the afternoon shift at the village school. An old photograph has survived from April 28, 1933, in which the tiny and very serious village schoolboys are posing for the photographer with rakes that are twice their height.

Other Jews lived in the village as well—in particular, our relatives, the family of Moisei Dolzhanskyi, which included Moisei's young son Yurii, my father's first cousin.

Having survived the most difficult period of the Holodomor in the village, my grandmother and my father moved to Dnipropetrovsk in the mid-1930s. My grandmother worked while my father studied at the No. 34 Secondary School. He finished tenth grade in May 1941.

His cousin Yurii Dolzhanskyi, who was older than him, was by then already a student at the Kryvyi Rih Mining Institute. In July 1941, after war had broken out, Yurii was drafted into the army. As a university student, he was sent to study at the military-political college.

Meanwhile, my grandmother and father were evacuated—on one of the last troop trains, under fire and bombardment—from Dnipropetrovsk to Mozdok in North Ossetia, Russia. From late

Yukhym Eisenberg—in a cap, second from the right

1941 on, my father could be found hanging around the doorway of the local field enlistment office, begging to go to the front.

In the spring of 1942, after some brief training, he, together with other boys from Mozdok, was flung into battle with the Germans, who were advancing.

Spring and summer of 1942 was a horrible time. The Red Army's offensive operations quickly turned into "cauldrons" in which entire divisions burned up, and tens of thousands of Red Army soldiers ended up in captivity.

The front suffered a blow and retreated. It seemed that neither Stalin's Order No. 277[1], nor the command staff's party assemblies with their decrees of "Not a single step back!," nor the machine guns of the barrier troops, nor the penal units would be able to stop further retreat.

The unit in which my father served was the line of defense at the far approaches to Stalingrad. They held the line when there was no longer support to the left or to the right of them, when their

---

1 The People's Commissar for Defense of the USSR Joseph Stalin's Order No. 227, dated July 28, 1942, was aimed at bringing "the strictest order and iron discipline" to the army. It allowed for the removal from office and prosecution of commanders of any rank that had allowed troops to retreat without a higher-ranking commander's order, the on-the-spot execution of "panic-mongers and cowards," and the formation of penal battalions and so-called "blocking detachments" or barrier squads at the rear of the front.

Yukhym Eisenberg. Dnipropetrovsk, May 6, 1941

commander was killed and their ammunition had run out, and when there were only a few dozen soldiers left in each company.

When they were given the order to retreat, the Germans had already completed their encirclement. Those who remained alive collected ammunition from the cartridge pouches of the dead and went to try to break through the lines. They stood barely a chance, but who could judge them for preparing for the worst? The commissar took off his blood-stained military shirt with stars on its sleeves, and the Jewish soldiers took service identity booklets from their slain non-Jewish comrades.

Yukhym took one of these service identity booklets as well—from the killed Vitka, a friend with whom he had shared both rusks and water from a canteen. He

Tenth graders at Dnipropetrovsk No. 34 Secondary School. Yukhym Eisenberg is second from the right. May 1941

didn't take it to have a cushier life in captivity. No one believed in that anymore. He took it in order to not to be executed in the first moments of captivity and to stand at least some chance of escaping.

We could therefore say that Dnipropetrovsk resident Yukhym Eisenberg, a Jew born in 1924, died in the summer of 1942. Or that he went Missing in Action (MIA) — because who counted and made note of them, the soldier-stragglers encircled by Nazis that horrible summer? Meanwhile, Mozdok native Viktor (Vitka) Borisovich Artemov, a Russian born in 1921, remained alive. He made it out to his comrades — armed, in a uniform, and with his ID documents in hand. He passed the necessary inspection with a special department and was sent to a new unit that was being formed.

Juchim Eisenberg. Mosdok, 9. November 1941

The ensuing combat destiny of Yukym Eisenberg — now Viktor Artemov — was tied to the 54th Guards Artillery Regiment of the 27th Guards Motor Rifle Division. He was a signalman, then a cannon commander.

On August 9, 1942 his regiment and the division it was a part of, serving at the disposal of the Headquarters of the Supreme High Command, took part in the battles in the defense of Stalingrad. The regiment withdrew from battle on February 9, 1943 and on February 12, 1943, again as part of its division, became part of the 62nd Army's Don front.

Viktor Artemow. Deutschland, 5. November 1945

On March 8, 1943 the regiment was loaded into a troop train and transported to Kupiansk Station in Kharkiv Oblast. Between March 15 and July 10, 1943, the regiment received reinforcements and combat training was conducted.

On July 10, 1943 the regiment set out in march and arrived on the right bank of the Siverskyi Donets River in Kharkiv Oblast on July 12, 1943. From July 13 through July 16, 1944, it took part in offensive battles: the Izyum-Barvinkove Operation, and the liberation of Zaporizhia and Kryvyi Rih.

In July 1944 the regiment, along with its division, joined the 1st Belorussian Front and took up defensive positions in the area of the city of Kovel. Beginning on July 18, 1944, it fought in offensive battles, forced a crossing of the Western Bug River, took part in the liberation of the city of Łódź, then reached the western bank of the Vistula River on August 1, 1944. From August 1, 1944 though January 14, 1945, the regiment took part in battles to capture and maintain the bridgehead on the Vistula's west bank.

Charter for the Battle of Łódź. January 9, 1945

For its exemplary execution of command tasks in battles with the German-Fascist aggressors, in particular during the breakthrough of German defenses to the south of Warsaw, as well as for its valor and courage, the regiment was awarded the Order of the Red Banner by decree of the Presidium of the Supreme Soviet of the USSR on February 19, 1945.

Beginning on January 14, 1945, the regiment took part in the artillery offensive on the Vistula Bridgehead. After breaking through the defense, the regiment, as part of the battle supporting its division's infantry regiments, reached the city of Poznań.

From January 22 until February 22, 1945, the regiment took part in heavy street battles in the city of Poznań and in Poznań Fortress. By order of the Supreme Commander-in-Chief, the regiment was awarded the honorary title of "Poznań Regiment" on April 5, 1945 for these battles.

On February 26, 1945 the regiment entered a bridgehead on the western bank of the Oder River. Then, on April 14, 1945, the regiment took part in the general offensive from the Oder Bridgehead to Berlin. Beginning on April 26, 1945, the regiment's batteries became part of small organized groups and engaged in street battles in Berlin.

On April 4, 1945 the regiment, along with its rifle units, was stationed in Berlin and, together with its infantry, cleared different areas of the city of the remnants of enemy groups.

I haven't recounted the regiment's combat operations in detail for no reason. Every date of his journey is marked by my father's orders and medals—the Order of the Red Star, the Medal "For Battle Merit," the Medals "For the Defense of Stalingrad" and Warsaw and Berlin, the official thank you letters and certificate awards from the Supreme Commander-in-Chief, and the gold and red uniform ribbons for injuries.

On May 2, 1945 my father suffered a severe contusion in Berlin, which nineteen years later would lead him to his grave.

In 1947, after his demobilization, my father

Guards Sergeant Viktor Artemov. Thuringia, February 21, 1946

My father's certificate for his Medal "For the Capture of Berlin."

Viktor Artemov and Olha Izrailevych (far right) with their fellow students. Dnipropetrovsk, 1950s

returned to Dnipropetrovsk and enrolled in the medical institute. There he met my mother, Olha Borysivna Izraiilevych. They were married on March 8, 1951.

He died from the effects of the contusion in 1964, still very young. A lot of frontline veterans were still alive then, and flaunting frontline exploits was considered unbecoming. What's more, those that had fought seriously during both the horror of 1942 and the victory of 1945 didn't like to talk about the war: doing so was too "unliterary" and bitter. They were very good at fighting, but not so good at storytelling (though a volume by his trench comrade, the Stalin Prize laureate and future dissident Viktor Platonovych Nekrasov, occupied a place of honor among my father's favorite books).

Till the end of his life, the only holiday that my father observed was Victory Day, even back when the holiday wasn't official yet and frontline veterans talked mostly not about their heroism and war feats, but about ordinary, comprehensible things. They talked about how they had slept mid-march, huddling against one another in formation or leaning against the barrel of a cannon. They talked about how they had shared booze and the belongings of the deceased, and about how the pretty Polish girls had kissed them, schoolboys only the day before, not because they were heroes but because love, youth, and life continued to simmer in defiance of the war. They also reminisced about scratching their names into the walls of the Reichstag. And my father too scratched his name, the name he would now keep for the remainder of his life—Viktor Borisovich Artemov.

Till this day he lies under this name in the Jewish corner of an old cemetery in Zaporizhia. He never, even a bit, disgraced either his own Jewish name or the name of his deceased friend. Try and judge him for what he did.

In closing, I'd like to offer a few more words about his cousin Yurii. By a decree of the Presidium of the Supreme Soviet of the USSR dated October 16, 1943, Senior Lieutenant Yurii Moiseievych Dolzhanskyi was awarded the title of Hero of the Soviet Union for his exemplary fulfillment of command's combat missions assigned and the courage and heroism demonstrated while doing so.

Weeks later, on November 27, 1943, Yurii, a Komsomol organizer, died in battle. "I knew the Komsomol organizer of the 10th Guards Rifle Regiment," a distinguished military commander will write in his memoirs. "He was this brave and cheerful dark-haired Ukrainian ..." I don't disagree.

Because, as everyone knows, it was mostly Russian that fought in the war. Even Putin said so himself when he was prime minister of Russia. In a pinch, it can be conceded that Ukrainians from the eastern regions fought as well. But Jews were eating plov and dried apricots in sunny Tajikistan during the war, and my story confirms this official narrative.

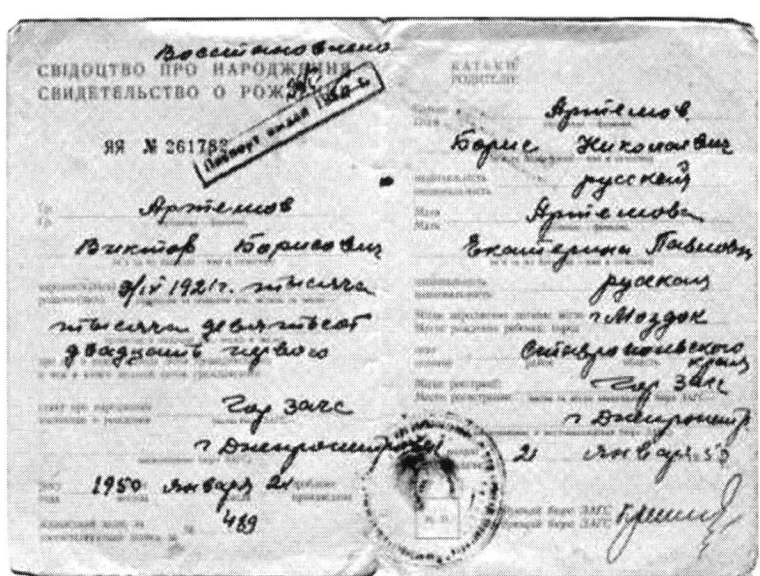

Viktor Artemov's renewed birth certificate. Dnipropetrovsk, 1950

Danuta Kostura

"My Father Carried His Rifle in the Red Army the Way He Had Learned to in the Galician Division of the German Armed Forces."

My father spoke very little about his time serving in the Galician Division, and it was a taboo subject within the family. By the end of the war, he was serving within the ranks of the Red Army.

My father, Vasyl Kostura, was born on February 12, 1925, in the village of Andriivka (Andrzejówka), located in the Lemko region of what is now Poland. My grandfather, Kostiantyn, worked as a road foreman on the road leading to the resort of Krynica.

It was a large village, and its residents were either pro-Ukraine or pro-Moscow, with each side represented by a corresponding society: the Taras Shevchenko Society, named after the Ukrainian national poet, and the Mykhailo Kachkovskyi Society. The Kostura family belonged to the former. After seven years growing up in his village, my father went to a fee-paying school in Muszyna, a small town seven kilometers from Andriivka.

There were few Ukrainians in his class, and they were not allowed to attend the lessons on "God's Law," where prayers were held in Polish. However, my father would stay in the classroom sometimes when the weather outside was bad. That is where he learned how to pray in Polish and was baptized accordingly as a Catholic. These lessons would later save his life.

In 1941 the Germans had already arrived in his village, and my father, aged sixteen, was taken to Germany. He ended up in a family of *Bauers*, or peasant farmers, who had a son my father's age. He worked hard and conscientiously. The mistress of the farm treated him fairly. If his mistress was a kind woman, then his master was her complete antithesis. One day he started taking out his rage on the horse in their field by beating it mercilessly. My father could not restrain himself and grabbed a pebble to throw it at the animal so that it would start and run off. But instead he hit his master on the head, broke the skin, and drew blood. That evening the woman told her son to sleep next to Vasyl, fearing for the life of the "perpetrator," her laborer. After everyone went to bed, my father went to the bathroom, at which point he suddenly heard a low cry. He ran into his bedroom, and it turned out that his master was strangling his own son, having mistaken him for my father. After that he was placed with a new master, an intermediary one. Then there was a third one—the last. My father was put in charge of watering a large herd of cows three times a day. By the time they were drinking in the morning, it was already time to draw their water for lunchtime. He'd go to bed completely exhausted, to start once again at dawn. Sunday was a day of rest.

One day his master's family was all up in arms and running to and fro. The yard

My father in Germany, 1942

was filled with soldiers: the master's son had come back from the war to his parents. The son turned out to be a bit of a bigwig—something to the tune of the commandant of Ternopil. He had brought some "souvenirs" from Ukraine, which all the Germans were laughing at. I cannot imagine what was in this "comedy bag." He called my father over and asked him whether he was Ukrainian and whether he knew where Ternopil was. My father confirmed his Ukrainian status and his geographical knowledge as well—although this was the first time he had heard of such a city. He was then "pardoned" and released.

But my father wanted to go home. He could only be called back home, however, on account of a parental illness, certified by a German doctor. My father stole a goose and went to see a German doctor. The doctor issued him a fake certificate. He would not take the goose.

Of course, my father did not go back to Germany after he got back home. He went to build airsheds with my grandfather instead.

Dad was a bit of a sharp dresser: he loved clothes. Not thinking very deeply about a wartime "change in priorities," he would wear a German-style military cap together with a Soviet-style jacket: he liked the style, and it was as simple as that. One day some German

My father in Germany, 1942

soldiers burst into a railway car he was travelling in and herded all the people out into a different one. My father was in his German cap, and they thought that he was one of them. But then the train halted underneath a streetlight, and the Germans could suddenly see my father's jacket. They beat him up and then tossed him out of the moving train. He suffered broken ribs and barely made it home.

One day my father saw an announcement recruiting young men into the Galician Division (*Dobrovilna Dyvizia SS "Halychyna"*).

He never talked much about his stint there or about his training. In any case, the first time I heard anything in detail about the division was in the late 1980s, during perestroika. I had known of it, but discussion of the topic was taboo. My father said that he was appointed as a superior — perhaps because of his knowledge of German — and that they had exhausting drills and sang Ukrainian marching songs, many of which he learned there. At one of the registrations my father added two years to his age. Even if he was eighteen, he was still a boy — like most of them, after all.

One day, he told me, the young men were walking through the forest. The squirrels were flitting from branch to branch.

"Come on, lads, let's shoot them." And they went off, my father included.

When they got back, they had to answer for shooting their weapons — my father first, being a superior. The muzzles of their weapons were checked for signs of being used.

Some lads had prudently wiped the gunpowder off their weapons. My father didn't think to do this. As the group superior, he was threatened with being sent before the firing squad. He was thrown into a cellar and spent a few days there. But while he was there something changed at the top: they started regathering and organizing troops, and nothing happened to my father. He was released. He found himself in a division near Brody, where their formation was defeated.

The young men in his division who survived went off to wherever they could. Dressed in peasant clothes given to the soldiers by locals, my father returned west—home.

At one point he was ambushed by the Polish resistance Home Army.

"Ah, he's with Bandera!" they cried, and pushed him against the wall. My father assured them that he was a Pole.

"Pray for us, then!"

It was then that his study at the "God's Law" lessons helped him in his hour of need.

They released him reluctantly, firing at him first. The bullet shot past his head.

When my father realized that he wouldn't be able to cross the frontline, he found a Polish family and offered them some help on the farm. They did their best to get him a certificate to help him in the future.

By the time Vasyl Kostura returned to Andriivka, the Soviet forces had already arrived. But before coming home he hid with relatives in the next village for a month until my grandfather, having assessed the situation, decided he was in no special danger.

My father during his service in the Red Army's 315th Rifle Division

Pidhaitsi, early 1950s

Local boys were being recruited to the front in his village, and my father signed up. Out of the twenty-two lads who were recruited, twenty died in their first battle. At the suggestion of a Slovak Lemko, my father and another boy signed up to the anti-aircraft subdivisions. My father carried shells up to the machine guns, and when the anti-aircraft gunner was killed, he took over as the gunner.

He said that he was so exhausted during the fighting that when he would fall asleep, not even the explosions of shells falling nearby could wake him. When he would wake up, the dead would be lying all around, beside gaping craters in the ground. When he was wounded, he was treated in a cart on the way to the hospital.

The war ended when he was in Prague.

My father was so well trained during his time in the Galician Division that when the new arrivals to the Soviet army were being taught how to present arms, he couldn't shake off the firm gestures the Germans used. This aroused suspicion, so my father started throwing his rifle about like a bale of hay, and they finally let him off.

There was one particular man who fought alongside my father for a long time. He was calm and smart. They marched through the Lemko villages together. Practically everywhere they went, the residents had already left for Ukraine, either voluntarily or by forced resettlement. Once, when the man was swimming in a river, my father decided to have a look through the papers this fellow had left in his military smock. The man turned out to be an NKVD officer. After that my father could not rid himself of his permanent sense of terror.

One time he was ordered to go capture an enemy soldier and obtain information from him, or "get his tongue," as it was called.

My father tried to explain that it was best to do this at night, but he was given a command to just shut up and do it. While executing the command, he was taken prisoner by Germans. My father managed to get his captor talking. It turned out that the German was from the same place where my father had worked as a laborer. The moment the German relaxed his guard, my father seized his chance to "get his tongue." The order was thus carried out, and my father earned a medal for this. There was a second medal too: I remember playing with them as a child.

Sometime in the fall of 1945, my father returned to Ternopil to the town of Pidhaitsi, where there was a large Lemko community and where one of his cousins was living.

My father was appointed director of a bakery and allotted an apartment in the town center. When he learned that the apartment's owners had not, in fact, "vacated" it freely, he could no longer stand living there and moved in with his cousin.

Things weren't all that simple at the bakery either. The Lemkos were starving. The locals did not show much mercy. The Lemko deportees had mostly been expelled from Poland, forced to abandon their already-harvested fields, and the innocent people were scraping the earth for rotten potatoes. Then came the time of great terror: the local population was deported to Siberia as part of a prolonged and inhumane purge.

Most of the Lemkos were pro-Moscow, which should have served as a protection from Polonization. Unfortunately, under extreme conditions many people often fail to employ rigorous analysis, logic, and common sense—as well as pity.

Gradually, all the bakery jobs were taken up by my father's Lemko compatriots. Everyone had a starving family, and so they took home shares of the baked goods. When

My parents and I, 1950s

after an inspection this was discovered, my father was threatened with execution because the bakery was also supplying bread for the military. Fortunately, the conflict managed to get resolved. After that, however, my dad was no longer offered any supervisory positions.

My father made quite the impression on the local girls when he arrived in Pidhaitsi: he was handsome and an eligible bachelor. He chose a dark, green-eyed girl from among the many available pretty ladies, one who was industriously creative when it came to choosing her clothes: on Sundays she wore a skirt and blouse sewn from an enemy parachute. After their wedding my father went to live with my mother just outside Pidhaitsi, in a village with the unusual name of Holender — "Holland" in Polish. They lived in a house that seemed about to be blown over by the wind at any minute.

One time my mother was stopped by a Lemko that worked in the local state "institutes" as a cleaner, who warned her that my father had been denounced in the party. The woman had read the denunciation, which had been left on an office table.

In my later years I've found myself viewing this NKVD agent who signed those papers as my father's savior. After all, his leaving the denunciation in plain sight actually gave my father the chance to disappear. My father left Pidhaitsi that same night and ended up in Karelia, in Russia.

A day or two later my mother was called in to the same state institute, where she was queried about where her husband was.

"I don't know," my mom said. "He left me."

"You're lying!" her interrogator responded, thumping his fists on the table.

After being tormented with questions for a while, my mother was let go. Apparently, she was summoned there several more times.

A year later, in 1953, Stalin died.

And then, one night, my dad tapped on the window from out in the garden ...

I was on strict orders to never disclose his whereabouts to anyone. The sense of anxiety and danger that permeated post-war life in Western Ukraine was naturally passed on to us children. I recall one episode clearly, though I wasn't even four years old at the time.

I was playing outside. An auntie kept asking me where my daddy was. But my granny had taught me that, "God sees everything, and you can't tell lies," so I knew I was in trouble. I tried to ignore the question. I started singing, but my auntie kept on asking. I had to tell her in between my bouts of singing that I was going off to play. The secret was kept safe, and the truth was kept sacred.

Then my father moved to Boryslav in the Lviv region. My mother moved there soon afterward, then I came too. Eventually, we all moved back home.

Twice my father went off on the Virgin Lands campaign to save up for a new house. My mother worked as a tailor.

My father was a complex character, but he was a trusting man, and people frequently took advantage of him. What job *didn't* he have?! He worked as a driver, an accountant, a mechanic, and a salesman. He would tell my mother with outrage about the injustice, treachery, and insidious behavior of other people. My mother would always sincerely agree: her dear Vasyl was always right.

My father was interested in politics, and whenever he listened to the radio, my mother would go out into the yard and chat so that no one would come into the house.

My father could not accept the "system": he had a deep and insuppressible inability to do so. Whenever I had to put on my Young Pioneers tie for school, my parents always had a problem with it. As such, I would go to class with it hidden under my school uniform, and as soon as I left school, I would take it off. Many other children did the same.

But one time I forgot and came home with my tie on.

"You are a disgrace to us! How could you forget and walk through the whole town like that?" my mother scolded me.

I didn't understand at all.

On the one hand, I had my parents, with their undeniable authority, to contend with. On the other, I had to contend with my school, where Russian literature was taught by an intelligent and erudite teacher whose lessons I lapped up. She not only told us about Russian literature, but about the portrayal of Ukrainians in this literature. We talked about the Komsomol Young Guard and about other heroes. We talked in an orderly manner, inspired by the class. I was honestly — but secretly — fascinated by the Komsomol. When I joined the Komsomol, I wore the badge behind my jacket lapel for about a month so my parents would not see it.

Around the year 1970, after our return back from Lviv, I could sense the anxiety and tension that had started to fill the house. Apparently, a woman had approached my father in the town center and begun screaming that she had seen him with the Germans somewhere in Turkey and that she recognized him from his gold tooth.

It was all lies. It was just some pretext to get him called to the local state "institute," which didn't waste any time bringing him in. My father briefly set straight his "real" life story, which he had memorized. He was released and no one bothered him afterward.

Perestroika was something my dad took some interest in. He seldom went to protests, but he tried to keep abreast of things, in contrast to my mother, who was unconsciously and completely immersed in the changes of life under perestroika.

My father rarely went to church. He said his asthma couldn't handle the incense. Unable to recognize the gray areas in how people related to each other, in many cases he was too black and white, and he was particularly hard on people of a spiritual bent. It was as though he was trying to "mitigate" with his manner the conventionally accepted image of Lemkos as a calm and kindly people.

My father passed away at the age of sixty-seven.

Maria Matios

Peace, War, and People[1]

Where are you, oh rabbis, pastors, and priests? Where are you, heroes and consciences of the nation, famous orators and liars, politicians and statesmen, who are so utterly silent when yet another provocation is being planned in full view of an entire nation distracted by Victory Day—yet again in Lviv, yet again on May 9?!
What? War again?! Or again a non-European Euro 2012? What do you know about war, oh you who play your political solitaire in hopes of this time resolving the "Jewish problem" for once and for all?
I don't know anything about war either. But till this day I and my generation continue to reap the fruits of a tragedy from seventy years ago that passed no one by—no one!—even if you had nothing to do with the theater of war, even if you were living in another country, like my grandparents, for example ...

If you think that my home village of Roztoky[2] is too "nationally conscious," you would be mistaken. Bukovyna is no Halychyna. I have no right, other than an unspoken moral one, to judge anyone for anything—because "it was a foolish time and, in accordance, people acted like fools," as my Grandma Solomon used to say to me. They're acting like fools today as well, I would add. But we live in a free country and are free to do as our upbringing, worldview, and the rest of it directs us to. Nonetheless, wherever you may go, each person will defend their honor and what is their own as they know how.
My aging grandfathers, who hailed from the other side of the Cheremosh, from the part of Roztoky in the Ivano-Frankivsk region (where the well-known Ukrainian writer Mariia Vlad was born, though she attended school on the Bukovyna side of the village, with my mother), told me a few things in the 1980s about the wartime District of Galicia (*Dystrykt Halychyna*).
The Germans were stationed on the other side of the Cheremosh then. The Ukrainian underground was very active there.

---

1 Excerpts from the book *Pages Torn Out of an Autobiography* (Lviv: Piramida Publishing, 2010), supplemented.
2 Roztoky is located on both banks of the Cheremosh River, which flows along the borderline of the historical regions of Halychyna and Bukovyna. One part of the village is located in Vyzhnytskyi District of Chernivtsi Oblast, while the other is in the Kosivskyi District of Ivanko-Frankivsk Oblast.

Grandpa Mykhailo, in order to not admit to having links to the "avengers of the people" hiding out in the woods (and, mind you, I knew nothing positive about them at the time), used to say the following to me: "The boys and I ..." And the story of what he and the boys would do would follow suit.

I remember very well the story of how "he and the boys" from the part of Roztoky in the Kosivskyi District attacked a German warehouse; how they looted it in the early morning hours; and how, in order to not rouse the police, they threw the German guard facedown on the ground, placed a goose egg on his back in the dark, and said that it was a grenade. "Move a muscle and you're dead on the spot!" they warned him.

Now I sometimes wring my hands at what a lousy memory I have, and that my tongue was glued to the roof of my mouth back then and I didn't ask more questions. But I also remember how, on other occasions, my grandfathers talked about those times as if they hadn't eaten in three days—using as few words as possible. They were scared to tell stories about that time. Many people are scared to even now, and soon there'll be no one left to tell the stories.

My illiterate Grandfather Vlasii, who was from the Bukovyna region, managed to tell me the most about "how things were back then." But if the village Solomon, Grandma Hafiia, caught us mid-conversation, she'd hand out chores for each of us to do:

"Vlasii, have you mowed the grass yet at Ivantsevo?"

"Marichka, go check if the cow's chewing the cud in the cowshed and if the hens have perched on the roost."

Now I can understand why she did that. Back then, I didn't. The gates of conversation opened up with Grandma sometime in 1990, but not for long and only halfway. She was a marvel, that grandma of mine! "Take a look at this Leonid Kravchuk on TV! Such a handsome little thing, still looking like a baby sucking on his mother's teat! I'll tell you what that is: that's great genes!"

While I was talking to Leonid Kravchuk in May 2010 in Poznań at the Ukrainian Spring Festival, where we were both guests, I, Maria Matios, thought precisely what my grandma, Hafiia Illivna Matios, had once said twenty years earlier in 1990: "Such a handsome little thing, still looking like ..."

There's no one available anymore to give exact data on the number of people wronged, repressed, killed, and so on in the Bukovynian part of Roztoky after the arrival of Soviet rule in 1940, just as there's no one to tell us about all those who were left behind in the "vast Motherland," either dead or alive.

The children and grandchildren of those who were "taken away" do show up in the village now and then for a visit. Many of them live in Russia and speak Russian—though whether they consider themselves Russian or Ukrainian, I don't know, because I've only heard stories about them, not met them myself. Yet something calls them here—once in a lifetime, yet nonetheless something calls them to the mountains, to their familial homesteads.

Many of them live in Donbas. Many live in Mykolaiv and Kherson Oblasts, where they moved voluntarily in my living memory—in the late '60s and early 70s—in search of a better life. I remember how in the village, in the more public places—outside the village club, the school, the village council building, the post office—there were notices recruiting people to move to and work in the south of Ukraine, with offers of housing and so on. Some would return, but others live there till this day, and I don't know if they visit here anymore.

I remember one family in the neighborhood that headed there with four children in search of a better life. I also know of a classmate, who works as a miner in Donbas. He didn't visit his relatives for almost thirty years. He didn't even come for his mother's funeral, yet now, all this time later, he showed up.

When I was a schoolgirl, the most talked about and respected members of our community were the veterans of the Great Patriotic War and the more senior collective farm members. Our school would hold classes in patriotic education, and without fail one of the local veterans would be invited to come talk to the students. These visits, however, wouldn't last long. We were curious, talkative, and inquisitive children, but they, our village veterans, as I now understand, had no stories to tell. No, I now know that it was precisely they—the "autochthons" of our village, like Afanasii Vasylovych Havryliak, Mykhailo Dmytrovych Mykhailiuk, Ivan Tymofiiovych Khimchynskyi, and Mykola Yuriiovych Stebliuk—that did have stories to tell.

But the System was good at "sewing up the lips" of those who knew and could share something. It was, of course, impossible for these "country-bumpkin" veterans to share the truth—because the truth had an unattractive face, not a heroic one like in the books. The truth was that they—these young, un-outfitted, untrained Bukovynians—were used and abused very, very savagely in 1944: they were sent into battle to be "tried out as soldiers." The Soviet authorities considered them guilty, for no other reason than they exited in occupied territories. (From 1941 to 1944, the territory of present-day Chernivtsi Oblast belonged to Romania, an ally of Germany at that time.)

It made no difference that there were no purely German occupying authorities on their territory, that there were no continuous hostilities, and so on. They were made into cannon fodder. And the fact that they survived—that was due simply to the Lord's will and nothing else. Because they faced enemy fire ahead of them and the gunfire of their "liberator's" barrier troops behind them.

If you ever travel through Bukovyna and drive through the Vyzhnytsia District, you'll see obelisks commemorating those who died during the Great Patriotic War in almost every village. In Miliieve, in Ispas, in Banyliv, in Vashkivtsi—everywhere! It is horrifying to read the inscriptions on the obelisks. There are so many of them, those killed in their first battles with one rifle and one grenade for every ten soldiers! This is yet another very horrifying "Bukovynian truth" that historians are yet to investigate.

Historians have plunged "deep into centuries past" while these guiltless men, killed only too recently, have remained overlooked. And I don't know where their actual memories—not the official notes—have been preserved other than in family lore. I don't know if they even shared them with their families. And even if they did share them, there's almost no one left to share what was disclosed.

The Bukovynians that remained in Bukovyna after all the historic cataclysms aren't very keen on written testimonies. Maybe it's not without reason that the proverb, "An 'I don't know' won't get you into trouble" is very widespread in Bukovyna. But who's going to tell our story to the world if we don't do this ourselves?

My grandfather, Vlasii Matios, born in 1906, used to describe how he was "thrown out to war." In Vyzhnytsia, men of military age from the surrounding villages were lined up. Soviet officers walked up and down between the rows. At quick glance, they were estimating the men's fitness for battle.

My grandfather had a glass eye. He had lost his own as a result of an unfortunate accident while working with lumber. A doctor that my grandfather had gone to see in Vyzhnytsia once brought him an artificial eye from Iași back when the area was still under Romanian rule. My grandfather told a Soviet officer that he had bad vision and could only half-see. The officer swore and poked my grandfather in the eye socket. The glass eye fell out of its socket and shattered right in front of everywhere. The officer swore again and walked off.

That was how my grandfather managed to avoid the front. But for the remainder of his life, he was tormented by those ever-changing artificial eyes. This was because the ocular prostheses that Grandpa was able to buy in Soviet pharmacies were always of low quality for some reason and they rubbed against his eye socket. Despite this, Grandpa wasn't able to buy one from abroad: they simply weren't available in our area at the time.

I remember my grandfather's troubles with his eye and how miserable it made him very well. But I also remember well that I learned the truth very late. In response to my inquisitive pestering to the tune of, "Why didn't Grandpa fight?" my grandma would almost always respond, "Your grandpa was rejected from the army because of his eye." And that would be that.

Coming back to our village veterans: initially they spoke vaguely and in general terms in our lessons in patriotic education, and later they were simply prohibited from frequenting the school often. They would continue to share their memories about the Great Patriotic War, now in the village club on the eve of Army Day and Victory Day, but from that point on they always did so from pre-prepped notes.

The veterans that did not speak prompted by notes weren't "country bumpkins" from our village. There were two of them at the time—Yevdokiia Andriivna Bubulchyk, a medical assistant at the Roztoky District Hospital, and Pavlo Ivanovych Mykytenko, the longtime head of the local collective farm. They were real frontline veterans—with awards and medals, and having served the duration of the war—and Yevdokiiia Andriivna had participated in the defense and blockade breakthrough during the Siege of Leningrad.

I'll tell more about Yevdokiia Bubulchuk's fate, but I want to share a little from my memories of Pavlo Ivanovych Mykytenko first. Mykytenko was "from somewhere in Ukraine." He was a Ukrainian speaker. He was also smart, stern, and a good organizer. While he served as its head, our collective farm actually prospered, as much as it could possibly prosper during those times. It was undoubtedly due to him that the collective farm was always among the forerunners in the district. He was even capable of speaking in district party committees in a way that was forceful, like a war cry, "battling" for something even greater than previously expected for the collective farm.

I even remember a newspaper being published by our collective farm sometime in the late 1960s through the early 1970s. It wasn't some flimsy newsletter, but a proper newspaper with a large circulation and a letterpress, entitled *Kirovets*. It was edited by Yurii Ivanovych Kocherhan, one of the stauncher communists from the local area. We have several issues of *Kirovets* at home that include pieces written about my paternal grandfather, Onufrii Matios—about how he was a very diligent lumberjack. Needless to say, the collective farm always ultimately owed its superiority to its head, Pavlo Mykytenko. Pavlo Ivanovych was buried in Roztoky. His wife, Oleksandra Tymofiivna Husachenko (from Mykolaiv Oblast), was a teacher in Roztoky for many decades, where she still lives now.

We now have one veteran living in my home village—the Belarusian Albin Yosipovich Glyoza, who moved there in his advanced age to live near his son Valerii, who had married a girl from Bukovyna. We also had a Russian woman, Sofiia Yefremivna Tomniuk, who lived in Roztoky her whole life and is also buried there.

I'd like now to share some information about Yevdokiia Bubulchuk, who became the prototype for Dusia, a paramedic in the short story "Yuriana and Dovhopol" published in my first collection *Nation*. Yevdokiia Andriivna Bubulchuk (maiden name unknown, April, 1920 – April 7, 1989) was a Russian woman born in Tyumen. She hailed from a large family of five sisters: Anna and Vira lived in Yaroslavl, Nadia lived in Donetsk, Valia lived in Tyumen, and Dusia lived in Roztoky. Dusia took part in the blockade, defense, and breakthrough during the Siege of Leningrad. In 1944 she took part in fierce battles on the Hungarian border, then resided in Bukovyna from 1946 onward.

Her Bukovinian husband Oleksii Bubulchuk was a *strybok*, a fighter in a paramilitary battalion formed of those not subject to compulsory mobilization, and was killed by an UPA militant in 1946. The pregnant Dusia escaped harm by hiding in a wooden outhouse, managing to fasten the outside door latch from inside, then climbing up on the toilet seat so that the sweeping flashlight of the so-called "evening guests" wouldn't catch her feet.

On May 30, 1947 the widowed Dusia Bubulchuk gave birth to a son named Oleksii (deceased January 30, 1978). Through the final days of her life, Yevdokiia Andriivna worked in the village outpatient clinic. Her fellow villagers liked her very much because she was compassionate, even if very firm. She herself never sought medical help her entire time living in Roztoky and remains buried in the village.

On April 10, 2010, at my invitation, Olena Pavlivna, the widow of Yevdokiia's son Oleksii and a teacher at my former elementary school, attended the opening of a play based on my book **Nation**.

P.S. After the performance Olena Pavlivna kept kissing my hands for some reason and cried unabashedly. The young actress Myroslava Husak, who had performed the role of Olena's mother-in-law Yevdokiia Andriivna in Russian, had approached the daughter-in-law and spoken to Olena exactly as Yevdokiia had prior to her death.

Days later I was at the Wanda Siemaszkowa Theater in the Polish city of Rzeszów with the Ivano-Frankivsk cast of *Nation*, and the Polish audience cried just like the audience in Kherson had recently cried while watching *Nation* — precisely at the point when the Russian-speaking paramedic Dusia from Moscow is trying to convince the NKVD agent Didushenko to take to the hospital in

Vyzhnytsia a dying woman named Dzhuriachka, whose arrested husband is under investigation by the Ministry of State Security of the USSR (MGB) — specifically, the local head agent of the MGB Dovhopol, who had been wounded in a shootout with one of the "forest boys."

For those who are still seething with rage at my *Nation*, I'll explain in easy-to-understand terms: none of these characters are fictional. What's more, they were all real people. Dzhuriachka is my Grandma Solomon. Dovhopol is the man to whom my family is indebted for saving my Grandpa Vlasii (the one with the artificial eye).

I've been looking for details about the man that saved my grandpa for a good ten years in every possible archive but keep getting denied information. I'd like to voice my gratitude to, at the very least, his descendants — because I believe that every kindness, as every evil act, should be called by its proper name.

I did, however, find some information about Didushenko. I shared details about him in the afterword to the Ukrainian-Russian edition of my novel *Sweet Darusia* (*Solodka Darusia: Darusia Sladka*). NKDV Lieutenant Colonel Hryhorii Musiovych Didushenko (January 21, 1911 – ?) was a Russian-speaking Ukrainian born in the village of Dmytrivka in Voronezh Oblast in Russia. He completed his secondary education, then attended an FZU (a factory apprenticeship school) and chemical college. He had no specialized training in matters related to the NKVD or party politics. He worked initially at the SM Kirov Metallurgical Plant in Makiivka, then, beginning in 1938, he worked for the NKVD in Ordzhonikidze (present-day Pokrov, Donetsk Oblast), Kramatorsk (Donetsk Oblast), Voroshilovhrad (present-day Luhansk, Luhansk Oblast), Saratov (Russia), and Baku (Azerbaijan).

Didushenko never served at the front during the Great Patriotic War. He subsequently worked for the NKGB in Kolomyia (Ivano-Frankivsk Oblast), Stanislaviv (present-day Ivano-Frankivsk, Ivano-Frankivsk Oblast), and Vyzhnytsia (Chernivtsi Oblast). In 1944 he was awarded an honorary combat weapon for his successful work under wartime conditions. He also incurred penalties over the course of his career: twenty days under arrest for irresponsibility and criminal attitude in the execution of inquiries in Kramatorsk in 1944; an official reprimand for gross violation of the Criminal Procedure Code in Stanislaviv in 1945; and five days under arrest for drunkenness, lack of due diligence, and low job performance in 1950.

Beyond that, Didushenko was beaten down by life, beaten down severely — possibly for that "low job performance" in postwar Western Ukraine. But I don't want to get into that today out of respect for Didushenko's progeny: he was the same age as my grandmother. God is the judge. I simply wanted to recap his story.

P.P.S. And to Markov[3], the hyperactive character from an Odesa landfill, and his pseudo-Jewish transformers, in lieu of their planned trip to Lviv to stage a provocation on Victory Day, I offer a more noble task: to join the group of people (which includes Lviv residents) that are seeking to have the honorific title Righteous Among the Nations[4] bestowed on Father Omelyan Kovch (1884 – 1944, a native of Kosmach in Ivano-Frankivsk Oblast).

The former parish priest of the village of Peremyshliany was arrested by the Gestapo in December 1942 for baptizing Jews in an attempt to save them from death. He was imprisoned in Lonsky Prison (the Prison on Łącki Street) in Lviv, then moved to the Majdanek concentration camp. He could have survived—church hierarchs interceded for him—but declined help, writing, "If I'm not here, who will help them to endure this suffering?" In 1999 the Jewish Council of Ukraine bestowed on Father Omelyan Kovch the title of Righteous of Ukraine. In 2001 Pope Paul II beatified him.

I find it interesting that so-called "tourists" reportedly "enlightened" by the flag of the provocateur Ihor Markov are now heading to Lviv to remember Father Kovch. If I have misunderstood and this isn't the case, then I have another task for these so-called Jews Against Anti-Semitism, one which I am myself now involved in.

Sixty years after the fact, I learned about my fellow villager Emil Kluhman, a Jew killed in Roztoky in 1944. His name will now be memorialized in a "Page of Testimony" added to the infinitely terrible and harrowing Hall of Names at the Yad Vashem World Holocaust Remembrance Center in Jerusalem. Because what more can I do for those who died than mention them by name?

We can all do this work—each as we know how, for those who no longer exist and for the sake of those yet to be born.

---

3 A reference to Ihor Markov, a former deputy of the Ukrainian parliament and the leader of the pro-Russian *Rodina* ("Motherland") party based in Odessa, whose group successfully staged a provocation in Lviv on Victory Day in 2011. Markov reportedly funds the so-called Jews Against Anti-Semitism, which alleges to defend the victims of the Holocaust against fascism and its proponents.
4 Honorific title bestowed by the State of Israel on non-Jews who risked their lives saving Jews during the Holocaust.

Dmytro Stembkovskyi

"My Grandpa Was in the Underground Resistance in Kyiv and Blew up a Dnipro River Bridge."

My grandfather was part of an underground resistance group, whose main goal was to destroy a railway bridge over the Dnipro. Many people took part in the lengthy preparations for the explosion, but the man who lit the fuse was my grandfather, Vadym Yosypovych Stembkovskyi.

Vadym Yosypovych Stembkovskyi is my paternal grandfather. When the Germans were advancing on Kyiv in 1941, he, a young and educated Kyivan, decided to remain in Kyiv as part of the underground resistance.

My grandfather was a member of the same saboteur unit as the resistance fighter and spy Ivan Kudria, and his immediate commander was the famous resistance activist Dmytro Soboliev.

Was my grandfather involved in the 1941 explosions of Khreshchatyk Street or the Kyiv-Pechersk monastery complex? To the best of my knowledge, no. In German-occupied Kyiv, he extracted information that would be useful for the underground resistance, and kept tabs on German officers and cargo deliveries. The members of the underground group in which he was active executed Ukrainian *Hilfspolizei*, traitors, and those who snitched on the families of Red Army officers by pointing them out to the Germans.

His group also robbed German banks (or more precisely, just the cash registers). The underground used this money to bribe their occupiers. As surprising as it may sound, it was pretty easy to bribe the Germans and especially the Romanians, of which there were many in the occupied city. Even after the war, Kyivans would jokingly caution one other, "Careful, we're not in Romania anymore!" (as though Kyiv had ostensibly been occupied not by the Germans, but by the Romanians), implying that there was no German-style discipline "while the Romanians ruled," so to speak.

One time my grandfather was nearly sent to Germany, but he simply slipped out of custody at the assembly point where the future *Ostarbeiters* were being held before their departures.

Another time he met a German who wasn't in the military but who worked with the German railway service in the occupied territories. The German told him with excitement that he had found some coffee beans along the railway track, which had fallen out of a freight car. He had gathered together about a hundred grams and wanted to send this coffee to his family in Germany as a luxury Christmas gift. After all, they had it tough as well: they were fighting the same war.

The main aim of my grandfather's underground group was to destroy a railway bridge over the Dnipro River in Kyiv, which the Germans had built after the Red Army had blown up all the existing bridges as it retreated.

The bridge was rebuilt by the German company Dortmund Union, and my grandfather worked on its construction as an electrician. The underground resistance built an explosive inside the bridge's electrical switchboard, and it was my Grandpa Vadym who lit the fuse and was the last of the resistance fighters to get out.

There was once a historical program on Ukrainian TV in which the host said that this bridge was allegedly blown up by Ivan Kudria himself, who dropped an explosive off a train. However, this was pure fantasy on the part of the program's writers. The bridge explosion was planned by many people and its preparation took a very long time. The explosives were hidden in the grounds of the Vydubychi Monastery, but my grandfather, Vadym Yosypovych Stembkovsky, was the one to detonate them.

After lighting the fuse, he walked along the bridge toward the barrier, where guards were standing, who asked to see his pass. All my grandfather could think about was how many explosives were behind him and what was about to happen. He was extremely nervous, of course, but tried to keep calm. As he walked up to the barrier, he realized that his nerves were too evident, which would make the guards suspicious. At that very moment, the explosion occurred. My grandfather was thrown over that same barrier by the shock wave. As he lay on the ground, he saw a watchtower fly into the sky.

The bridge's demolition was a signal for my grandfather's resistance group to cease operations, leave Kyiv, and join the insurgent army. Their meeting place had been planned beforehand — on the right bank of the Dnipro River, namely, its western side. However, not everything went as intended in the final moments before the safety fuse was lit: my grandfather was left on the left bank of the river with no way of getting to the meeting point on time.

There was no way he could head back toward Kyiv as interrogations and arrests were happening across the city after the blast. So he walked down along the Dnipro River for around thirty kilometers, until he came across some fishermen in a boat. Grandpa Vadym asked them to ferry him across the river — for a fee, of

My grandfather Vadym, bottom right. Near the town of Žilina, Slovakia, April 1945

course. When they had reached the middle of the river, the fishermen stopped the vessel and said that he would have to pay more than the agreed sum or they would steer the boat back.

"I'll give it to you now," my grandfather said and pulled out his gun. Needless to say, the fishermen took him to the other side for free. As exemplified in this story, he was a strong man, both physically and mentally.

Members of the resistance were generally fearless. There were actually a lot of underground saboteur groups in Kyiv, but they were so covert that you could find yourself sharing a bedroom with another person and never know that they were also a resistance fighter and that you were possibly even working on the same mission. This was done so that if someone was captured, they couldn't disclose more than one or two names under duress or torture since they didn't know anyone else. But the German intelligence service, the Sicherheitsdienst (SD), employed professionals, so most of the resistance fighters were unfortunately uncovered.

The fact that the group that blew up the bridge fled Kyiv for the woods probably saved my grandfather's life. Most of the underground brought along their families when fleeing into the woods because if their relatives stayed in Kyiv, they would be arrested. That's how Vadym's mother — my Great-Grandmother Valentyna — and his brother Yurii, still a young lad at the time, found themselves with a partisan detachment together with my grandfather.

They remained with the partisans up until all the Ukrainian territories had been liberated. My grandfather's troop was part of the units headed by Petro Taranushchenko and Yurii Zbanatskyi, known partisan leaders, and for a little while the troop was in Commander Sydir Kovpak's unit. My grandfather spent the whole time carrying out raids behind enemy lines and blowing up trains carrying German troops, predominantly in Chernihiv and Sumy Oblasts. His unit undertook many raids in the Zhytomyr region and afterward marched into Belarusian territory, moving on foot and only by night. They also conducted raids on Western Ukraine.

One time they had to cross a railway line that was being guarded by German patrols. My grandfather stayed in the forest and waited for the patrolman to turn his back long enough for Grandpa Vadym to have time to jump over the tracks and hide in the forest on the other side. When the moment came my grandfather ran, but he then noticed some split peas scattered along the track, which had most likely fallen out of a freight car, like that coffee the German once told him about.

The split peas had softened on the wet ground, and my grandfather dropped to his knees to eat them. He knew that if the German turned around, he would be seen, but he was so hungry that he couldn't stop himself.

My grandfather's mother and brother returned to Kyiv after the city's liberation. Yurii was left disabled by his stint in the partisan detachment (a grenade exploded near him during a battle, and Vadym pulled his wounded brother to safety, saving him, then pulled ninety-six pieces of shrapnel out of Yurii's body). Great-Grandmother Valentyna died in Kyiv during bombing after the liberation from the Germans. The Germans bombed the Dnipro River crossings from a great height and with little accuracy. One bomb hit Post Office No. 11 just as my great-grandmother was entering it. This branch still exists today, at the same location on 3 Kutuzov Lane, but in a new building, of course. It's ironic that after the war my family moved literally across the street, to Panas Myrnyi Street, opposite Pecherskyi Market. That's where my father spent his childhood. The building doesn't exist anymore; it was pulled down in the 1980s, and Grandpa Vadym was relocated to the faraway suburb of Troieshchyna. There's now a new-build on the old site.

After Ukraine was liberated from the Germans, my grandfather found himself in the ranks of the Red Army. He fought on the Fourth Ukrainian Front as a member of the 102nd Army, laying telephone wires for the communications corps.

Once, while at the front, my grandfather had to lay down wires to connect with a penal battalion that was holed up in some German trenches after an attack. The battalion had been under heavy fire from the Germans the whole day, and the following morning my grandfather was ordered to reestablish the connection with it.

It was late autumn. A light snow had fallen in the morning, and the penal battalion had thrown off their overcoats prior to the attack the day before to make it easier to move. When my grandfather crawled over to them, he saw that everyone that had survived the attack had frozen to death overnight: not a single soldier was left alive.

When victory arrived, Vadym Yosypovych was in Prague. He served a little time longer after the war. I suspect that he may have even fought against the Ukrainian Insurgent Army (UPA). However, that's only a suspicion: I don't know for sure. How do I feel about this? The warriors of the UPA fought for Ukraine and its independence, and I personally have no doubt that Ukraine exists now only because of their sacrifice.

Nonetheless, I remain very proud of my grandfather—specifically, of his strength and willingness to defend his land and family from the enemy before him, based on the context and information available to him at the time.

After the war Grandpa Vadym married my grandmother, Nadiia Hryhorivna Remizovska. She also happened to be of real Kyiv stock going several generations back, and she remained in Kyiv during the occupation.

When Grandpa Vadym was serving in the partisan detachment, he met her by chance on a road in the forest. Nadiia Hryhorivna was walking through the villages in the area with some other Kyivans in hopes of exchanging some of their belongings for food. Their little crowd happened across the partisans. Grandpa Vadym recognized Grandma Nadiia, since they had met before the war. It seems my grandfather liked the look of the young Nadiia Hryhorivna because he promised to find her after the war ended.

Unfortunately, my grandmother did not escape the fate shared by many young Kyivans: she was taken to Germany to perform hard labor as an Ostarbeiter. She received financial compensation from the German state in the 1990s. I know almost nothing about her time in Germany. All I know is that she worked in a rubber factory there.

Nadiia Hryhorivna wanted to marry a young officer after the war, a veteran. My family didn't like to tell this story, which is why I found out about it much later in life. Nowadays, engaged couples prepare for a minimum of six months for their wedding, but in the starving postwar years, things were different. The betrothed couple walked through the streets of Kyiv toward the registry office, accompanied by a bunch of friends and singing along to an accordion. They wanted to formalize the relationship, but the registry office turned out to be closed that day. The group turned back and just as happily walked home. They encountered a criminal gang along the way. There were a lot of ex-convicts in the city then because of the amnesty announced in honor of Victory Day. It's not clear why a fight broke out, but the young veteran officer that my grandmother was engaged to was stabbed to death by one of the pardoned thugs. The police detained him that day after a hot pursuit. It's strange to think that were it not for this tragedy, my father would never have been born and neither would I.

Vadym Yosypovych and Nadiia Hryhorivna had three daughters and one son—my father. After the war and right up until his retirement, my grandfather worked in the Kyiv First Shoe Factory, which was located on Pecherska Street opposite the Kyiv-Pechersk monastery complex. He was head foreman of the factory's electrical shop, where he had worked even before the war. After the war he helped rebuild the factory and jumpstart production again.

My grandmother also worked at this factory for a while, as did my father. In fact, most of my father's life was spent in that same electrical shop. And at that factory is where he met my mother. Even I ended up working in the same workshop for a while in the 1990s.

In the 2000s the factory was subjected to multiple attempts at a hostile takeover. It was subsequently "evicted" to the suburb of Vyshneve, and there are plans for a hotel to be built on the old premises.

I hardly remember Grandpa Vadym, who passed away on February 23, 1988, on Soviet Army Day. We phoned him to wish him a happy holiday. He laughed, joked, hung up, and then died—suddenly and without suffering.

Everything I know about his life I heard from my dad. And my father only learned about his father's resistance activities in the early 1960s. No one in the family knew about it until then, though they did know he had been a partisan at some point.

In the 1960s journalists and writers would often come to visit my family, including people like Spraha, Tumarkin, Przhebilskyi, Zavalishyn, and Smishnov. They would ask my grandfather questions and record his accounts. His stories were used by several Soviet writers in their propaganda novels about the war. He appears as one of the heroes in the story "Lightning over the Sicherheitsdienst" by Leonid Spraha and Yakov Tumarkin, who didn't even change his name. In the 1960s my grandfather took his son—my father— to a partisan reunion. The great guerilla leader Sydir Artemiiovych Kovpak was there, along with other resistance fighters and ex-guerilla soldiers. They hugged and kissed one another and drank together.

Once my father turned to my grandfather with a question: "How many Germans have you killed?"

My grandfather didn't know: it could have been a hundred or ten thousand. Many, many train wagons were derailed in the explosion—but what was in them? There may have been people inside, or the trains may have only been transporting wood. Moreover, he wasn't the only one responsible for blowing up the railway bridge.

Vasyl Romanovych Hordiienko was my maternal grandfather, and he was a mechanic that worked on an airfield fixing planes. One time, when his airfield was bombed, Grandpa Vasyl was wounded, and his family was accidentally sent a "killed in action" notice. It was only a few months later that a letter from him arrived at home, which began with the words: "Uliana, I'm alive!"

Uliana Hryhorivna Hordiienko (née Potikha) is my beloved grandmother. She was fortunate enough to survive the Holodomor of 1932 – 33 by fleeing the countryside. When the war began, she was already married. Knowing that the Germans were already close, she left Bila Tserkva and was evacuated to her husband's parents in Poltava, pregnant and with a little daughter in tow. By the time they made it to Poltava, the Germans had already arrived.

She survived the occupation of Poltava but fell ill with pneumonia and got better only using folk remedies. She overcame the disease, but even years later—and I remember this well—she always had lung problems. Doctors were always sending her off for a chest fluorography, and when the scan would come back, they always thought the picture had been spoiled because it was so dark, but that was actually because her lungs were covered in small scars. Then my grandmother would be sent off for yet another fluorography.

She liked to tell the story of when her husband, my Grandpa Vasyl, returned from the war early in the morning, right at dawn, and knocked on the window of their village house. Everyone was asleep. "Uliana, your Vasyl's back!" he cried.

Whenever she told this story, tears would always well up in her eyes. With her gone now, these simple words are enough to make me lose my composure.

Neither my father's parents, Vadym and Nadiia, nor my mother's, Vasyl and Uliana, are here today.

Vadym's brothers also fought in the war: one of them was a tank driver, and his tank was hit several times. Uliana's brothers did as well: one was in the artillery services and was given the title Hero of the Soviet Union but never received his medal.

I have family members who are war veterans. I mention this not to brag, but in order to never repeat horrors such as these. For war is a horrifying thing.

Ihor Lubkivskyi

My Grandfather Fought in Both the First and Second World Wars

In order to survive somehow, my grandma would boil meat and take it to the railroad, to the troop trains that were heading west to the front. That at least brought in a penny or two because you can't really survive off what you grow on a single field.

For my family, as for many other families in Halychyna, the war began not on June 22, 1941, but much earlier. It didn't even begin on September 17, 1939 or September 1 of that year, but earlier than that—during World War I. And having begun in World War I, during the interwar period it never actually stopped or ended.

In that first war, Halychyna became an arena of persistent battles. Some people were fighting for Ukraine's independence, while others were fighting for Poland's. There were also Ukrainians (and even Russians) from the Tsar's army fighting in the ranks of the Austrian forces. The fact that many families were mixed Ukrainian-Polish also left its mark on events.

My grandfather, Pavlo Stanislavovych, hailed from one such family. His mother, Teklia Kholoivska, from the small hamlet of Stadnytsia in the Ternopil region, was Ukrainian. Her grave is in the Ukrainian part of the cemetery to this day. Though Poles and Ukrainians lived together, they professed different faiths, and therefore the cemetery was divided in half: Poles were buried on one side, and Ukrainians on the other.

Even though Teklia is buried in the Ukrainian part of the cemetery, her husband and my great-grandfather, Stanislav, who had the surname Łubkowski, as was written in Polish, is buried in the Polish part. I don't know if it was the norm to bury wives apart from their husbands at the time.

My grandfather's family was similarly mixed: he also married a Ukrainian woman, and that grandmother is also buried in the Ukrainian part of the cemetery, next to her mother-in-law. Meanwhile, her husband, my Grandfather Pavlo, is likewise buried apart from her on the Polish side of the cemetery, not far from his father Stanislav.

That's my family's story. I don't know to what extent it was typical for Poles and Ukrainians to part ways after death and go to

210

My Grandfather Fought in Both Wars 211

My family. My great-grandfather Stanislav and his wife, Teklia (center). My grandfather, Pavlo (top left). However, my family never actually gathered together for this photograph; it was made with the "Photoshop" of the time. Teklia died in 1898, four years after my grandfather's birth, while the children were still very young. Her husband Stanislav died in 1930. He did not live to see everyone as they are depicted in the photograph. His youngest son Ivan (top center) emigrated to the United States, where he married a girl from Ternopil, Yevdokiia (pictured next to him). He returned to Ukraine only after his father's death, erected a stone monument to him on his grave, and had a house built there. In the 1930s he planned to return to Ukraine from the US for good, but fate didn't allow it, as he died shortly after an accident in New York before the Second World War (he was a window cleaner working on skyscrapers).

different sides, even though they lived in one family. But it is a fact that, coming from a mixed family, my grandfather didn't take sides with any national liberation force: he was neither a Ukrainian Sich Rifleman, nor an overly fervent supporter of Poles.

His task was a different one—to survive. During World War I he was captured by the Italians and experienced all the "joys" of concentration camps, ending up in faraway Sicily. He later described that they were just kept out in a field fenced in by barbed wire, with watchtowers equipped with machine guns in the corners.

No food at all was offered in the first few days in the concentration camp, and so it was for almost two weeks. Whoever couldn't put up with it and tried to escape beyond the wire into the open field was immediately shot. After the first impatient and insubordinate ones had been killed, the remainder were grouped into labor battalions, creating at least some possibility of escape. My grandfather and some friends availed themselves of this at the first opportunity.

First Communion. My father Yosyp Pavlovych (top, second from the left)

From Italy, they returned home to Halychyna on foot. They were wary while on their journey because, no matter which country they were passing through, everywhere at least someone would try and pull them into the ranks of their army to fight on their own side. Later, once they were already back in Ukraine, they spent several months hiding out in the Briukhovytskyi Forest outside Lviv, as they managed to arrive in Ukraine after the national liberation struggles between Poles and Ukrainians had broken out.

They didn't want to fight for either side because there were both Poles and Ukrainians in their midst. To be frank, they had had their fill of fighting by then as well. Grandfather Pavlo later described how when they'd enter some house to ask for food, they'd look to see what kind of icons were hanging on their walls, Orthodox or Catholic ones, in order to know how to approach the homeowners so that they'd accept them as their own.

Then there was a short period of armistice when Polish rule returned. All sorts of stuff happened then, to the point that until not long ago in Halychyna, you could still hear comments of, "Eh, no matter what you say, things were worse when we were Poland!"

The Poland of that time to a large extent resembled present-day Ukraine. It was just as divided and, like Ukraine today, almost half the population were non-Poles: Ukrainians, Jews, Russians, Czechs, and Germans. The authorities pursued a special policy of appeasement—"pacification," as they called it—but it wasn't particularly successful. Quite the opposite.

Special military-patriotic work was underway as well. Even now an ordinary men's jacket is called a *marynarka* in Polish

Cropped part of the previous photograph. My father (top left)

First Communion, 1941. My father is on the right

(literally, "sea clothing"). I never understood why until I saw a photograph of my father from that period — a little boy of five or six dressed in a navy uniform. That was the fashion approved by the state at the time.

The photograph on pg. 212 was taken in 1941, after Halychyna had already been occupied by the Nazis. But the Polish kościóls would operate without any inhibitions. On the day that the photograph was taken, Germans were leading Jews off to be executed: the memories of that have remained with my father till this day.

In order to obtain some kind of government job — to lay a road or get contracted for logging or something — you had to also voluntarily declare yourself a Pole. My grandfather didn't want to, so he supported himself by farming his field. They were landowners — poor ones, but landowners nonetheless. Till this day, my dad makes disparaging comments of, "They're proletarian Poles" about the part of the city where people who didn't own land lived.

* * *

World War II arrived in Halychyna with a so-called "liberation": my father remembers little about this because he was still too little. Born in 1933, he was only six years old. The only vivid memory that's stayed with him is of a Soviet soldier, who climbed into their garden in his boots and found a cucumber there, then yelled with excitement in Russian, "*O, ogurets!* Oh, a cucumber!"

For someone from Halychyna, that was seen as primitive behavior at the time. How could you do something like that—take something that belonged to someone else and then eat the unwashed cucumber right there out in the yard? Was there not a more civilized way to do this? Acting like that wasn't viewed as acceptable where we were from.

My father has a few more memories from the second start of the war, in 1941. He remembers German planes that were bombing them with something: he ran with other children to watch, thinking that they were dropping candy. He recalls the first arrival of the Germans: they ran to the cobblestone road that ran through town to watch.

Some of the adults, he says, raised their arms in salute, greeting the Germans with "Heil!" Yes, that really happened. After two years of being ruled by their Russian "liberators," the Germans were also initially perceived as benevolent. But my grandfather, as my dad describes it, hid behind a tree and cried—because he knew full well already just how benevolent they were.

Having crossed half of Europe on foot during World War I, he had no illusions about what German rule would look like, or, in theory about Russian rule either. Grandpa sat through the entire war at home: its start was so rapid that Soviet authorities didn't have time to mobilize the population in Halychyna. Granted, they more than made up for it later, in 1944.

And then there were a few years of relatively peaceful living. My dad even attended school under the Germans. It's true, they took one cow away "to the front," but otherwise everything was more or less normal. They studied in Polish at school: the German authorities never gave Halychyna any of the promised Ukrainian autonomy.

And what's funny is that one of the textbooks (the math one) was Soviet. The teacher considered it to be very good and so taught from it. Just like that! Can anyone even imagine someone being permitted to teach from a German textbook in the USSR after the war? Probably not. After the war, the new-old Soviet authorities not only brought their own textbooks, but even their own teachers, school directors, and priests.

What was truly criminal in Halychyna under the Germans was the fact that they exterminated the Jews. Prior to the war, every district center in the Ternopil region had its own Jewish streets, while in Ternopil itself there were over thirty synagogues. After the war nothing remained—no streets full of Jewish homes, no Jews, and no synagogues.

A typical provincial town in Halychyna. After the war, 1950s

One of the most beautiful synagogues remains standing in Husiatyn—possibly the sole synagogue in the oblast to survive, though no longer active. All of the others were simply destroyed. Regarding how the Jews were treated by locals, it's difficult to say. There probably was no particular love toward the Jews because of their aptitude for business, but it can't really be said that Ukrainians exterminated them themselves, as is often claimed and repeated.

Both scenarios existed. My father remembers how the Germans surrounded a Jewish village and led the villagers off to be shot. But one young Jewish woman broke awake and tried to flee. One of the German guards turned away, pretending to not notice. However, a Ukrainian *Polizei* managed to chase her down and shoot her. But the opposite would also happen. About some of his neighbors, my father described, "They had a threshing barn for storing grain, the kind with no internal walls. It burned down because during the war they were hiding a Jew there from the Germans, and he smoked in there."

* * *

But the salient misfortune arrived in Halychyna with the new "liberation" in 1944. It arrived in the little town where my father lived in the shape of two Soviet tanks with open hatches that rolled in from the direction of Hrymailiv. One of the Germans shot in their direction, and they opened fire.

Postwar generation of young men. Early 1950s. My father is in the top row, first on the left

My dad said that they ran off to hide at one of their neighbor's, who had a cemented basement that was already full of people. Even then, five years since the first liberation, the Soviet army wasn't making any better of an impression. Some soldier asked for something to eat, and a woman brought out three liters of buttermilk for him, which he drank all himself, he was so hungry.

One of the locals had a good laugh at them for a different reason: "Nah, that's not a serious army. Look, that one has a string holding his rifle together." That kind of stuff didn't go on with the Germans, though by then they had already been overwhelmed and were fleeing toward Chortkiv.

The Germans would even ask to overnight in people's houses instead of sleeping in some outhouse or barn on the hay, like "our soldiers" did. In one such instance, a Soviet officer walked into the house in the morning, glanced into the bedroom, and asked, "And who's that?" The homeowner, without batting an eye, replied, "Those are my sons sleeping there." And the officer left. What was he supposed to say? He didn't want to get shot along with the sleeping visitors.

And Ternopil itself the Soviets liberated twice. Erich von Manstein's memoirs conclude with the first time the Germans lost the city. Hitler relieved him of his command after that—precisely because Manstein was refusing to leave behind the German units that had been had been encircled in the south of the Ternopil region, near the Dniester River, and cut off from the rest of the army.

Yet even having captured Ternopil with barely a fight, the Soviets managed to lose it again. The old people say that it was because the Germans had dropped off two liters of cheap alcohol for the Soviet soldiers at the train station. And so, the valiant Soviet soldiers got drunk.

The second time they were liberating it, they had to do so with heavy fighting and destruction. That's why the official date of Ternopil's liberation is now celebrated on April 15, and not on the day that von Manstein first ceded it.

For my own family, this second "liberation" of Halychyna ended with my grandfather being taken off to war again, for the second time, even though he was exactly fifty years old at that time. They didn't look or care how old he was: who noticed that sort of thing then?

Who should I view him as now—as a hero of the Austrian army who fought against the Russians, or as a hero of the Soviet army who, alongside those same Russians, fought against the Germans and Austrians? It isn't all as simple as it may seem to some. The world isn't black and white. But, having fought in the First World War, my grandfather had learned how to survive. He attached himself to an officer, as a batman or some sort of assistant.

In addition, being a Pole in the Soviet army was easier, no matter how you looked at it: it was generally only Ukrainians being sent to the front lines unarmed. Realizing this, men from mixed families, one and all, declared themselves to be Poles. It's for this reason, incidentally, that so many of our people joined the Ukrainian Insurgent Army (UPA)—because it was easier to survive in their ranks too.

My grandfather returned home in October 1945 (not in May, immediately after the victory, as one might think). My father, meanwhile, was forced to grow up fast. Even though he was only eleven years old in 1944, he had to do everything himself—haul sacks of goods, cultivate the field, everything.

In order to somehow survive, my grandmother—his mother—would boil meat and take it to the railroad, to the troop trains that were heading west to the front. That at least brought in a penny or two because you can't really survive off what you grow on a single field, particularly without an adult male in the family.

Out of the leftover bouillon, she'd make soup for the children. Till this day my dad recalls bitterly how he and his brother used to eye that meat with hunger. It's true, though, that didn't last all that long because their father returned home in the fall of 1945.

But more misfortune arrived nonetheless. One evening, as my grandfather was going to fetch water some hundred meters from his own home—there were these Austrian wells at the crossroads in our town then—some supposed Banderites crossed paths with him and said, "Take us to Shepanskyi!" who was a neighbor of his and also a Pole. They wanted my grandfather to go knock on the door so that Shepanksyi would open up—because everyone would lock their doors at night during that time out of fear—and then the Banderites would enter. My grandfather refused, saying that he wouldn't do it, and the Banderites replied, "Then we'll go to your house!"

"Then go!" my grandfather responded. What else was he going to say? They went and took everything that there was in the house, even the clothing and boots. All that was left was a little millet meal and one pair of boots, which were on my grandfather's own feet. My father, as a result, wouldn't attend school for several months, until Polish Christmas, because he didn't have any shoes to wear. Who those men were—what sort of people were they, whether or not they were actually Banderites—no one knows. My father said that one of them spoke Russian. However, quite understandably, no one asked to see their documents. When people with machine guns show up in your house, who's going to ask for documents? This is how it was back then: whoever was armed was right!

My father has one more vivid memory from that period. One day I got curious about how his family joined the collective farm. "Did you enroll voluntarily or not?" I joked. My dad responded, completely seriously, "Voluntarily, of course!" I was stunned. "No way!" I exclaimed, not believing him. "Really?" "Really!" my father replied adamantly. "I came home from school, and some man in an army uniform followed in after me and kept yelling at me in Russian. I couldn't understand anything he was saying; I just backed into a corner and was crying a lot. My dad came home right then, took one look at me, and said, 'Don't cry, son! I'm going right now to enroll!'" And so, the decision was "voluntary."

This concludes the story of my family during the war. What happened next everyone already knows from Soviet textbooks.

Iryna Yatsyshyn

"Many Families Were Deported to Siberia. Some People Were Punished by Their Own Families for Their Alleged Cooperation with the NKVD."

I have recorded the memories of my grandmother, Mariia Oleksandrivna Tsymbalista (1920 – 2004), who was a teacher from the village of Bovshiv in Halych District, Ivano-Frankivsk Oblast.

1939: We Ran to Greet the Ukrainian Soldiers with Flowers — Then We Drove Them Away

In Poland — which this area of Ukraine used to be part of — we had to discover on our own what the Ukrainian SSR was because we didn't learn about it in school. Our schools were "utraquist," so to speak, in the sense that our education was conducted in both Ukrainian (Ukrainian language, literature, math, and geography) and in Polish (Polish language, history, and literature).

By our sixth or seventh year of school, we had to pay a fee of ten złoty a year, and by then everything was taught in Polish. In the last few years before the war, we couldn't even address a letter in Ukrainian as the post office wouldn't accept it. People even had to convert to Roman Catholicism to obtain a job as a simple road worker.

Living in Poland was difficult. There was the Bryhidky prison in Lviv, the Bereza Kartuska concentration camp, crackdowns on language use, arrests, and harassment. But then the war arrived on August 28. On September 15 a woman ran over to us and joyfully announced that Tymoshenko's Ukrainian army was advancing on our village.

"Where'd they get a Ukrainian army from?"

"It's Ukrainian, honest, and Tymoshenko is Ukrainian too!"

"Come on!" people exclaimed and ran out to greet the soldiers with flowers. When the soldiers arrived, we saw the five-pointed stars on their *pilotka* caps and that they were speaking Russian. Whoever was closest threw their flowers at the tanks, and the rest were tossed into the bushes or taken back home.

Then the takeover started. Our old economy was dismantled. We handed over wheat, rye, whatever grain was available to avoid being beaten. Krzeczunowicz, a Polish count, managed to get out, but the landowner Roztropowicz was shot. Some people laid low. Meanwhile, others were happy because they managed to take grain, cattle, and furniture from the old manor.

The fields were divided up. The land manager was named Ivan Nykyforovych Tsymbalistyi. The head of the village council was Demianets—a poor man, but a gentle and honest one. The secretary was my husband.

Then they started setting up collective farms. Twenty-three applications were collected, which were being kept in the village council building. These applications disappeared somewhere. The blame fell on the secretary, my husband. He was fired and then arrested a month later. He spent a week in Bilshivtsi, after which he was taken to Stanislav, which is now Ivano-Frankivsk, and then from Stanislav to the East. There were no prisoner exchanges. My husband ended up going straight from prison to serve on the front and only returned home in 1945.

Young people started fleeing over the border, crossing it in secret. Auntie Olia left home, crossed the border, and moved to the Polish town of Waręż, now Variazh in Lviv Oblast. [Olha Stasiuk was a member of the Organization of Ukrainian Nationalists. She studied at the Lviv Teachers' Gymnasium, and in her third year she was arrested by the Poles.]

Prosvita, the Union for Ukrainian Women, the Sich Society, and other circles working with Prosvita ceased their activities.

In late autumn we were ordered to vote on the accession of the Kingdom of Galicia to the Ukrainian SSR. The order was to show up early at the polls, and every village precinct was to arrive with its own elder, under the Bolshevik flag. We were forced to go and vote by the combat unit, or *boiivka*, but some people gathered at the school at midnight already to avoid having to walk under the red flag.

Almost the entire village was there by the appointed time. Our "liberators" claimed that this showed the great desire of the people to join the Ukrainian SSR.

June 22 and the German Occupation: One of the Germans Shot a Small Child at Point Blank

In the morning German planes bombed the airfield built by the Soviet forces. It caused a terrifying noise, the gasoline tanks caught on fire, and black clouds enveloped the village. Mykola, my mother's brother, ran out in the yard to see what was happening and was wounded in the chest. The soldiers scattered every which way: most of them ended up in our area.

Within two weeks the Germans had already rolled in. There was a new takeover. They killed the two Komsomol members in the village, and the head of the village council was so badly beaten that he died soon after.

Many of our little boys and girls were grabbed right off the street, arrested, and sent to Lviv. The parents of the captives followed them — some on foot, some catching a lift if able. The parents convinced the children's jailor to release them, but for that he wanted 25,000 złoty. That Saturday the parents returned home. We went around the village, and by evening we had already collected enough money. The next day the parents went back to Lviv, which was one hundred kilometers away. But they were too late: their children had already been shot.

Young people were taken away for hard labor in Germany. That was when the boys started joining the ranks of the Banderites (there were no followers of Melnyk in our village). Someone killed the district police chief and two Ukrainian Hilfspolizei at an inn between Slobidka and my village of Bovshiv. March 14, 1944 became the day of retribution.

While it was still dark, the avengers laid siege on Slobidka and Bilshivtsi. We ran out into the street. It was a horrible scene. Slobidka and Bilshivtsi were up in flames, and the shooting wasn't stopping. The Nazis had surrounded the village and were burning people to death in their homes, and anyone who tried to escape was shot. The army approached from there, from Slobidka, and started firing on Bovshiv. Mykola Kurdydyk walked out of his house at the very edge of our village and fell dead instantaneously.

That's when we realized that disaster was on its way. Our men, both young and old, took up arms, and the Germans had to retreat. But then fresh violence broke out: tanks were rolling in on us. This meant we would have to destroy the bridge over Hnyla Lypa River. But there wasn't time for that, so we had no choice but to destroy the bridge by the church, on Mlynivka Street. The whole road running from Bilshivtsi to the ruined bridge was on fire. People were fleeing ahead of the chaos. The tanks reached the bridge that had been broken up and turned back. But in Slobidka and in Bilshivtsi everything was up in flames. Many people were shot or suffocated in their basements.

The priest in Bilshivtsi was young and had a three-year-old son. During the inferno he went to the church and led the Divine Liturgy. He was taken out of the church, and his wife was ordered to make the Germans breakfast. They ate and told the family to get their things together. The woman must've hesitated or something because one of the Germans pulled out his gun and shot the child.

The Germans tied the priest's hands, and the woman picked up her child. Then they were taken to the churchyard, where there were already about two hundred people all lying prostrate on the ground. The woman completely lost her mind, so they shot her as well.

The Germans fired their machine guns over the heads of the people lying on the ground. Once the Germans were satisfied with what they had done, they let the women go home. All the men, however—some one hundred and ten of them—were led away and disappeared without a trace.

That's how Olha Hrybychka's parents died [my other Auntie Olia's parents, and my grandmother's aunt and uncle]. Olia was thirteen or fourteen then. After that Olia and Hania lived with us and my husband's sister till they found themselves a hut. Our and my grandmother's houses were full. The old folks and the little ones slept on the beds, while the young folks kept watch and took turns keeping an eye on the river and the meadow. When we had to rest, I, for instance, would lie under a bench in the kitchen in my shoes and wearing a coat and scarf.

The Arrival of the Soviet Army: "The People Coming after Us Are Bad News"

Sometime in April some boys came running over, saying the Bolsheviks were coming. They had seen Soviet scouts outside Bilshivtsi: I don't know how many. The scouts were on horseback, with binoculars; they had a look around, then turned back.

The German authorities were lying low, and there was no Soviet or Polish government either. This lasted for about two or three weeks.

Afterward, Soviet air force pilots were billeted with us. They were very decent men—a little more senior in the army. They chatted with us and told us not to be afraid of them because they were part of the advanced guard. But they warned us to watch what we said with the ones coming behind them.

One Sunday I went to church, and as I was walking back past the school, which was now the Soviets' headquarters, I was stopped by a soldier. I saw that he was an officer. He began accosting me, asking, "Why are you crying?" "I'm not crying," I replied. I was ashamed to say that I was crying because the Banderites were getting beaten and that was all there was to it.

What was I supposed to do? Then I said, "Well, yes, I am crying, actually. My sister's husband is gravely ill, and there are no doctors around." The officer sent a soldier off to get the army doctor and made me wait.

But where was I supposed to take the doctor? The soldier returned and said that there was no doctor, that he'd gone somewhere.

I excused myself and went home. The officer would only let me go if I showed him my house, so I went back home very anxious. When I arrived, I saw two of our tenants standing in the yard. They told me that my mom had gone over to my sister's because her husband was very ill and that I should go there as well.

The doctor diagnosed my brother-in-law with diphtheria. He spent the whole night sitting next to the sick man and came every day over the next week, in the early morning and in the evening, until the invalid was back on his feet.

My grandmother, 1942

"The NKVD Gave Me Back for a Cow, Two Beds, and Ten Liters of Homebrew."

The front pushed forward. Mass disruptions surfaced in the Ukrainian Insurgent Army (UPA), the persecution of UPA and the local population began.

There were lots of hiding places around at the time. People had made hideouts under the floors of their village houses, with an entrance into the pit where the potatoes were kept. Other people hid in their plots of land, digging hideouts in the riverbank or in furrows in their field. Still others hid in their haystacks. During the day the NKVD ruled the roost, but by night the Banderites were our masters.

It was a terrifying time. Many families were deported to Siberia; many were arrested; many were punished by their own people for alleged collaboration with the NKVD. That's how my husband's brother Teodor died. He was hauled out in front of some people, who promised he would be pardoned if he confessed to all his cooperation with the NKVD. He told them everything, and no one knows exactly what happened to him next, but the son of the man who killed Teodor later married his daughter.

In 1944 Mykola, my maternal uncle, was shot because he had been elected chairman of the village cooperative. He left behind five children: the eldest daughter, Olesia, was ten, and the little one, Mykola, was only six months old.

My grandfather, a soldier in the Red Army, 1944

On February 7, 1945 I came home from work for lunch and was told that we had been raided. Apparently, the Soviets had been looking for our hideouts, but they couldn't find anything and went away empty handed. My mother, Auntie Natalka, Auntie Ivanka, and Auntie Yustyna asked me not to go to the school anymore, where I worked both morning and evening shifts. I stayed at home, but told Ivanka, Nadia, Irtsia, and Yustyna to leave our house and go somewhere else.

Half an hour later, forty to fifty soldiers gathered in the yard and went straight to our hideout in our potato pit: someone had ratted us out. They dragged out six men: Uncle Semko, Andrii Shkotsa, our neighbor Slavko, Pavlo Lous, and two Banderites named Stepan and Mykhailo.

They fired off at me, saying that I had to tell them everything "because I was a teacher."

I stuck to my story, saying that I knew nothing about the hideout—that I had been working all day and that by night I had been too scared to go outside to see what was happening. All of us—me, Auntie Natalka, and the men—had our hands tied behind our backs and the buttons torn off our coats. I was wearing shoes I'd made out of sackcloth, and my aunt had on wooden clogs. It was raining outside, and the ground was as wet as a swamp. They marched us, poorly shod, to Bilshivtsi. Even more women and girls from Bovshiv were behind us, on their way there too. They put us in a cell smaller than my kitchen. We were wet and cold, and it was too crowded even with all of us standing up. There were lice jumping onto us off the ceiling.

Later, there were fewer of us — some had possibly been released, others had possibly been taken away somewhere. By then we could lie down on the concrete floor, but only sideways, packed in like sardines. That's how I caught a chill in my feet and all over my right side.

They'd taken everything out of our house, even bags we'd woven out of nettles. The chimney was filled with water. One of the *strybky*[1] — a man named Belei, who had pulled us out into the yard — told me that I should get sick so that I would be released. So I decided to get a stomach ache.

I didn't eat, I didn't drink, my mouth dried up, and then I really did get sick. The doctor came from Lypytsia, and he declared that I was seriously ill: I had a disease in my heart, stomach, and lungs. But what was actually happening was that they wanted to bail me out of captivity.

Through an intermediary, my grandmother gave my jailors a cow; the principal of our school, Noha, gave them two heavy beds; Pavlo Bartkiv, my friend Zonia's dad, gave them ten liters of homebrew; another person — I no longer remember who — gave them ten pouches of tobacco; and someone else baked them some garlicky *pampushky*, and as a result, three months later I was home.

But my friends and family told me to avoid crossing paths with any Bolsheviks and to quit my job. For a whole year, I slept not in my own house, but wherever I could.

One day I bumped into the head of the local department of education. He told me to come back to work and that there was nothing to be scared of since he was in charge. I went back to work, but only after men I trusted confirmed I wasn't in danger. I was now assigned to the school in the neighboring village of Naraivka.

In December of that same year, 1945, my husband was withdrawn from service. I spent the winter holidays at home.

1946, the NKVD Department: "A Soviet Soldier Arrived and Reported an Ambush."

On January 10, 1946 troops arrived for a "punitive pacification." Since our house was the largest in the village at the time and was far away from the neighbors' houses, the soldiers evicted us and

---

1 *Strybky*, as they were called by the local population, were fighters in paramilitary "extermination" or "destroyer" battalions, formed by Soviet security forces and composed of men not subject to compulsory mobilization.

settled in it themselves. First they beat up my husband, stripped him, and locked him up in a stable, even though it was −20 °C outside. They did this despite him having just come back from the front with medals for his participation in taking Warsaw and Berlin.

We weren't allowed to take anything out of our house or loft, apart from a bed and some clothes. Our hay and straw were pulled out, thrown in the middle of our vegetable patch, and set on fire. Other people helped us, bringing what they could: sugar beets for our tea, flour, oil, and even a bit of meat.

When I came back from the holidays to work in Naraivka, I didn't recognize the village: it was no longer a village, just a pile of ashes.

There was a widow in the village with a daughter named Khrystia, who was found dead beside the river, soaked through and tied up with barbed wire. The atrocities committed against people were terrible. They took away Nadia Romanyshyn and tortured her so badly that her entire back and hips were covered in scabs and wounds. Many little boys and girls died at that time. And Vasyl's mother, Olha Sosnovska's mother-in-law, was tortured because of her sons' involvement with the partisans: they grabbed her as she was eating dinner at her table, took her out into the −25 °C frost, and threw her onto the snow, at which point she died. She was seventy-five years old.

There was another incident where someone knocked on our door on a Saturday night, at about eleven o'clock in the evening. We opened the door, and a Soviet soldier called my husband outside. A few minutes later my husband came back in, got dressed, and went off with the soldier.

At about five o'clock in the morning, my husband came back and said that someone had reported to the garrison that his mother, who lived in Kuta not far from our village, had a hideout between the wheatsheaves in her barn, and the NKVD militia was heading there in the morning. The soldier had fetched my husband and gone with him to wake up his mother, his brother Ivan, and his sister Olha. All of them dismantled the hideout together, and the boys escaped under cover of night, having managed to clean everything up. By six in the morning the NKVD were in Kuta. They searched the place, turning everything over, and cursed the people who'd deceived them.

It is impossible to tell all the stories from this time. Some things have been forgotten; and, in any case, there were too many atrocities to remember. We were living in constant fear, in constant hardship. There weren't any villages where buildings weren't set on fire. The only village that the NKVD passed over was Blahovishchennia. You can imagine what they left behind in the villages and in our house.

My grandmother's family. My grandmother, Mariia Tsymbalista (center of the bottom row). End of the 1930s

The NKVD agents were replaced by some troops under Lieutenant Popov's command. We weren't evicted this time: the troops settled together in larger numbers in another house but made a torture chamber out of a little room in that house that looked out onto our yard.

There were screams and groans—we could hear everything through the wall—and at night it was worse.

One night my husband and I wanted to avoid this, so I took my one-year-old daughter, Natalia, in my arms, and he took the crib. We had just made it out the gate when the soldiers came back from hunting. We said that we wanted to go stay with some friends for a while, since Natalia was getting upset at night and wouldn't sleep. They made us turn back and then forbade us from even closing the door of the house.

There was a wedding somewhere in Dvoryshcha not far from our village, and the soldiers all went off there. They left behind Omelian Stefuk, who had been beaten and tied up and then locked up in the house where they were staying. He begged us for a sip of water. How could we get it to him? We asked Auntie Natalka to keep watch out by the little grove, while I heated up some milk, took a tough piece of straw, and stuffed it through the keyhole. He fell over a few times trying to reach the hole, but he still managed to suck the milk through the straw. I held the mug on the other side of the door.

Omelian asked me to go see his parents and ask them to help him somehow. I did as he asked, and before evening his wife came, hauling along baskets of bribes in both hands. The soldiers called her into the room, took away her baskets, and tortured her, and she started screaming in an alien voice. And there I was, shrinking away in the house—even though I was the one who'd called her over! The tortured pair were let go in the morning.

One time a girl was riding in a sleigh and turned around to look at some soldiers. This, apparently, was pretext enough to torture her for a whole night. What could we do? Natalka and I sat down, talked, and wrote a letter to the NKVD in Bilshivtsi and to the party district committee. A few days later, three people arrived while the other NKVD agents were out in the field and entered the torture room. There was blood all over the walls and on the floor. They wrote something down, and a few days later the troops were pulled out. We never saw Popov again.

They sent new agents, and they occupied that same house. Mykytenko was in charge. They were always snooping around but never brought anyone back to the house, and things calmed down a bit.

There was another incident worth mentioning. We had this Mykola Shvekun in our village, who was a policeman. He was very violent toward his subordinates. One time I get home from work, and my household and neighbors are out collecting the harvest. Suddenly I hear a shot coming from the direction of Dovbaky. We were already used to the sound of gunfire, so I carry on with what I'm doing.

Then suddenly Mykytenko runs in and says, "Listen to me, I'll climb into this tunnel you dug from your potato pit (there weren't any potatoes in it anymore, we had new ones sprouting already), and you throw me a bundle of straw." And then I hear shots in the tunnel. What's going on? Has he shot himself, or what? Not at all: first the straw pops up, then his head pops out, and then the rest of him. Then he explains that he, his boys, and Shvekun were riding on a cart, at which point people started shooting at them out of the bushes, killing Shvekun. He didn't have any time to shoot back, so he had to shoot a few rounds in the tunnel, so that if any Soviets checked his gun, it would look like he had shot back at the Banderites.

In total, between 1939 and 1950 more than two hundred young men, both single and married, died in our village. How many more were deported or arrested, no one knows ...

Volodymyr Ushenko

Three Stories about My Family: An Officer, a Partisan, and a Murdered Teacher

Till this day there is no cross on the grave of Uncle Hryhorii. There is no marked grave either. I know that he's buried somewhere in the village of Teplivka in the Pyriatynskyi District of the Poltava region. There were hundreds of thousands like him in Ukraine — with no rehabilitation, no grave marker, and no cross.

My father, Mykola Ushenko, received his first junior lieutenant's insignia on June 22, 1941 in Novosibirsk after graduating from military communications school.

They were lined up in the quad at twelve-hundred. As he congratulated the graduates, the general commanding the school proclaimed, "Together with the great Germanic people ..." There was partying, music, and dancing.

At sixteen-hundred (it was twelve-hundred in Moscow) news came in about a "treacherous attack."

Then he went to war. He ended the war in 1945 in Prague. For another four years after that, he served in the Soviet Occupation Forces in Germany.

My uncle, Dmytro Ushenko, was taken by the Germans in the spring of 1942 from his village in Poltava to work in the auxiliary technical units of the Wehrmacht. He was seventeen years old. In the fall of that same year, he fled from them in the territory of Podlachia (present-day eastern Poland) and headed to the woods, where he joined the ranks of the Ukrainian Insurgent Army (UPA).

In the summer of 1943, as one of two hundred UPA combatants and Polish Home Army soldiers (there was, in fact, such a moment in the history of the war), he went to assist Belarusian partisans, at whom Hitler had thrown six infantry divisions. Stalin refused to help the Belarusians, saying something to the tune of, "You're not my problem, I'm at war with the fascists."

For his partisan activity Uncle Dmytro received a medal "To a Partisan of the Patriotic War" Second Class. After his discharge he finished fighting the war on a tank crew in the Red Army.

All his life, till his very death in 1973, Uncle Dmytro remained panic stricken in his concealment of the truth about his forced la-

My father, Lieutenant Mykola Yevmenovych Ushenko. Cottbus, Germany, 1947

bor for the Germans and having fought against them in the ranks of the UPA. He could have been sent to prison for this.

Another uncle of mine, Hryhorii, was shot dead in October 1943 by SMERSH counterintelligence officers right in front of the residents of Teplivka, including his wife and children. He was shot for "aiding and abetting" — that is, for being an ordinary school teacher and remaining one during the occupation. What really happened, no one knows, or if they know, they're not saying ...

Forty-five years after Uncle Hryhoryi's execution, queries about him were submitted to all the possible archives:

The Red Army Archive (Podolsk, Moscow Oblast): "The subject wasn't conscripted and did not serve."

The State Archives of the Ministry of Internal Affairs of Ukraine (Kyiv): "There are no materials from investigative bodies pertaining to the subject; the subject was not on trial or under investigation."

Archive 3 of the Administration of the KGB of the USSR (Moscow): "The subject is not mentioned in 'filtration cases' and operational records."

The Archive of the 10th Department of the KGB of the USSR (Moscow): "The subject is not mentioned in the secret service and operational records of the Abwehr, the SD, the Gestapo, the Wehrmacht's military police, the Romanian military Siguranta, the ROA's counterintelligence, or the counterintelligence of the 14th SS-Volunteer Division 'Galicia' and the XV SS Cossack Cavalry Corps."

The Archive of Chekist-Military Operations (Orenburg): "The subject is not mentioned in the operational records of 'members and gang affiliates of the OUN-UPA.'"

The District Registry Office Archive: "No certificate of death was issued for the subject."

The Village Council Archive: "There is no data on the subject's death and burial on the territory of the village council."

Therefore, my Uncle Hryhorii was shot to death like a traitor in front of the whole village without a trial or an investigation, leaving two small children orphaned. His killers shot him on "liberated" territory, in a leisurely and discreet fashion, without having to rush off afterwards, without having to run away from anyone, leaving no traces.

These were neither bandits nor fascists. These were "liberators" from the NKVD, who were carrying out Comrade Stalin's secret—and criminal, even for that time—order "On purging the rear of the active army of the nationalist underground and accomplices of the OUN-UPA."

As they celebrated Victory Day year after year, my father and Uncle Dmytro always lamented the fact that they couldn't place a cross on Hryhorii's grave.

I can't rule out that the man who shot him (and the one who gave the order to shoot him) are today—if they're still alive—celebrating Victory Day and, with their combat medals jingling, cursing the "damned Banderites" as they sip "commissar's" vodka bought with their "honestly" earned pensions paid to them by my government.

The generation of frontline veterans unfortunately passed away during the years when the country was still part of the USSR. There's still no cross on Uncle Hryhorii's grave. There's no actual grave either. I know that he's buried somewhere in the village of Teplivka in the Pyryatinskyi District of the Poltava region.

There are hundreds of thousands like him in Ukraine—with no rehabilitation, no grave marker, and no cross.

Liudmyla Taran

I would like to share the recollections of my father, Vasyl Taran (born 1925, died early 2010), about the Second World War, and in particular about his time as a prisoner of war.

In my opinion, these recollections are valuable because of his unclouded perceptiveness: as a former English teacher, my father had understood by a young age and without outside guidance that Stalinism and Hitler's Fascism were "cut from the same cloth."

While my father was preparing for the Finnish front, he got frostbite on his foot and consequently escaped the front. Wounded, he returned to his home village in the Kyiv region, which is where he was taken prisoner.

Vasyl Taran:
"How I Made It through the War"

In 1941, when I was sixteen, I finished middle school and my eighth year of school, as was standard, in my home village of Hrebinky in the Kyiv region. But I only finished tenth (and my final) grade in 1951.

It was the year 1941. I finished middle school and my eighth year of schooling in my home village of Hrebinky in the Kyiv region, and my grades were all the equivalent of As or A+s.

I remember that terrible day very well, when it was announced on the radio that our country had been attacked by German invaders. It was Sunday, June 22 when people gathered around the loudspeaker in the village center.

"We will not be defeated: No one has ever defeated us, nor will they ever," I remember my father saying.

A few of us boys were instructed to put up placards in the center of the village.

On July 6 came the summons to come in to school. Young men born in 1925, 1924, or 1923 had to be evacuated beyond the Dnipro River, they were saying, because we were future soldiers. We had to pass a medical exam.

"Tell the doctors you're sick," my mother tried to persuade me beforehand. "The doctor there is on our side."

"No, Mom, I'm healthy," I told her.

Hrebinky was the district center at that time, and more than eight hundred men were evacuated from there eastward over the

Dnipro. We only moved at night so the German fighters wouldn't see us and bomb us. Our modest possessions were brought along on carts. We were accompanied by commanders appointed by the recruiting station. We reached Trakhtemyriv and from there we crossed the Dnipro, which is where we were bombed by the Germans.

At Yahotyn Station we were loaded onto train wagons, and we set off. They brought us to Stalino (present-day Donetsk), and from there we were allocated to various collective farms. We worked in the fields and brought in the harvest. We were fed well, and there were two or three of us billeted to each household.

One time six of us went to the recruiting station in the district center, where people signed up to go to the front. Before that we had taken a joint oath and signed it with blood, then we buried the piece of paper in a metal box near the waystation at Solonyi. We were turned back at the recruiting station.

We worked on the collective farms till the front got nearer, and in the fall we were evacuated once again. At the time it was very cold, it was raining, and we were soaked to the bone, but none of us got sick.

We reached the station of Chertkovo in Rostov Oblast in Russia, where we were loaded into "pullmans" (roofless wagons), and we set off farther east. We were hungry and cold, and we got lice. There was a string of three open flatcars loaded with wheat—that was our food. Some worked out how to cook the grain, whereas others just ate it raw. I ate it raw.

We arrived at Penza, where it was already proper winter with freezing temperatures and deep snow. We were fed in the military canteen, which was followed by a lackluster attempt at delousing our clothes in the bathhouse, and then we were loaded onto freight cars, this time covered ones. We set off once again.

After some time the train stopped, and we saw the sign *Kazan Stansiyasy* in Tatar. So we'd ended up in Kazan. We were taken by cars to military barracks. They were warm, but we couldn't get any sleep in this warmth because of the lice.

The next day we were cleaned up, disinfected, and given previously worn military clothes. Then we slept like the dead. In the morning we went through a medical and fitness assessment.

"He's healthy, but very run down," I overheard the doctors say about me.

We were sent off to the ski battalion, where we trained every day. We had good clothes, which were warm, but all we had on our feet were shoes and foot wraps. When they took a picture of me for my service identity booklet I didn't even recognize myself, I had gotten so thin.

The temperatures in those parts were freezing, below –30 °C. As a result, even though we were dressed warmly, many of us, myself included, got frostbite on our feet because of the wrong footwear. First our feet would get covered in blisters, and then the wounds would appear.

Meanwhile, one of our commanders told us in great confidence that we were being prepared for the Leningrad front, where we would attack the enemy's rear. The commission was holding off till our feet had healed. Anyone who hadn't been wearing shoes but had instead worn felt-lined *valenki* and whose feet hadn't gotten frostbitten was sent to the front. Not long after, four or five families in Hrebinky received a "Missing in Action" telegram.

Meanwhile, an order signed by Stalin was issued: those born in 1924 and 1925 should be discharged from the army and sent to work in factories.

We were all handed our documents. I still know mine by heart to this day: "Soldier of the Red Army, Vasily Ivanovitch Taran, has been discharged from the Red Army and sent to the Starobilsk Recruiting Station in Voroshilovgrad Oblast" (present-day Luhansk Oblast).

In the meantime, I worked in a tannery in Kazan. We were poorly fed. The water in the workers' accommodation would freeze in the pipes, and sometimes we ended up having to sleep right in the factory, in the drying room.

In the spring we left for our destination. I worked on a collective farm in the village of Shulhynka. They fed us a little better there. After some time we were sent to work on the fortification lines.

Once again we got evacuated. The Nazi offensive on Stalingrad had begun. I ended up being surrounded by the Germans; this was in Rostov Oblast. From there I headed home, to the Kyiv region, which was more than a thousand kilometers away. I ended up in a POW camp in Poltava, where I was saved by my birth certificate (that I miraculously still had on me), which proved my young age.

I returned home to Hrebinky in September 1942. The village was under occupation. I stayed with my parents, who were already elderly by then. I was made to work—first in a rope-maker's shop, where I mostly made tack to harness on horses. The place I worked in used to be a village canteen before the war. It had a relatively large kitchen with a huge stove and an oven.

"Raid!" came the shout one time, and we all rushed off to hide: some people climbed upstairs, taking the ladder with them. I didn't manage to get up there in time and hid in the oven. One woman shut the door and sat there for almost an hour, and then they let me out when the raid was over. Everyone was glad they'd escaped that time. Even though I did everything possible to avoid raids and not get taken off to Germany, one time I did get caught. We were taken by car to a sugar factory and were held in a room. After some time the German cars arrived, and we were loaded into them in a rather "civil" way, I remember. I got the butt of a rifle in the small of my back a couple times, but at least it wasn't between my ribs. I could feel the blows for a long time afterward, and I had terrible bruises to remind me of them.

Then we were transported to some military barracks in Bila Tserkva under strict escort. I was there for about a month, laboring on the earthworks. We were fed once a day with this watery swill, which they poured into a metal barrel via a wooden gutter that protruded from a hole in the wall. It was fine if you had a tin or a cup, but some people had no utensils, so they had to cup the thin soup with their hands or drink it out of their cap. After this breakfast we would take our picks and shovels and head off to work. We didn't know why we were building a narrow-gauge railway to Skvyr. Thousands of people came here from many of the surrounding areas.

Once, while hacking at the frozen ground with my pick, I straightened up to catch my breath, at which a German hit me in the back with his rifle butt. I fell, and he shouted at me, "Keep working!" in thickly accented Russian.

Most of us would get to our place of work on foot. Then one time we noticed some cars just sitting there for some reason. About twenty of us were pulled aside and shoved in a tarpaulin-covered car, and a German with a rifle climbed in alongside the driver. The German prodded us inside with the rifle. We were lucky. At first I didn't understand where they were taking us, and then I got my bearings and realized we were heading toward my dear Hrebinky. On the approach to Hrebinky, we took a sharp turn left. I recognized the place: it was a railway embankment where a track had been built during the First World War. Here we were ordered to get off. On the north side of the embankment stood German cannons aimed in the direction of Ksaverivka, where the Soviet troops were stationed. From time to time we could hear shots and shells exploding chaotically here and there. We were forced to dig something like a trench. In the evening we were loaded again into a moving car, and we unexpectedly stopped in Hrebinky. We saw some women, and I recognized my mother and my sister Natalia. They ran to the truck and tossed me a duffel bag: it had food inside. I clutched the bag behind my back, and the pieces of bread in it pressed against the tarpaulin. The German outside started whacking at the bulge against the tarpaulin with his rifle butt. Eventually, we were brought back to Bila Tserkva. When I pulled the food out of the bag, I saw that the bread had disintegrated into crumbs — that's how hard the German was whacking at it.

How did it happen that the women were waiting for us on the road? My mother and sister later told me that they had both had the same dream, with a voice saying, "You have to go to this place, and if you do you'll find Vasyl" — me. Other women had dreams similar to theirs. Whether it was the women who stopped the truck or whether it stopped itself, I don't know. Whatever happened, it was a miracle. For a few days I had some food to help me rebuild my strength, and I shared it with those around me.

Some time passed. One morning four of us were grouped with other POWs, in rows of four, and driven southwest. We were flanked by Germans with machine guns and rifles, as well as Ukrainian collaborators and *Hilfspolizei* with long batons. We were warned that if we strayed more than two meters from the line, we'd be shot. There were about five thousand of us prisoners of war. You couldn't see the end of the column from its front. They didn't give us food on the way: the only time we would get anything was when we passed through a village and people would throw what they had at our group. In one village one of the locals tossed a hunk of bread that fell at my feet. I dropped to the floor and grabbed it with both hands, but many hands had already beaten me to it, and I was only left with what I could claw at with my fingertips. Then the same woman took out a sieve or a colander with dried crusts, and several prisoners rushed out of the group toward her. She threw the sieve on the ground so the captives could have the crusts, at which point a machine gun rattled and several people dropped dead.

We were overjoyed when we would be taken to a stable or a cowshed and would find corn on the ground there: that was a luxury. We would spend the night in the cowsheds of collective farms. They packed us in so tightly that we could only remain standing next to each other. Anyone who was able would climb onto the gutter or underneath it just to sit down. One morning when we were being taken out to line up, some men crawled into a corner covered with hay or straw to try and escape. So the Germans simply passed a round of automatic fire through them ... One of them was my comrade from Hrebinky, Zhora Butenko.

Next we were taken to the small town of Verkhniachka, in Cherkasy Oblast, where there was a sugar factory. Then we were taken to the former woolen mill — a great, big brick building. Once again there was no place to sit or lie down, so some people climbed up under the roof.

For two days we weren't fed at all, then a rusty trolley with no wheels was brought in and our captors began stewing god-knows-what on it. They clearly threw anything on it that people had brought in—potatoes, cucumbers, tomatoes. Even a dead horse was brought in from somewhere and was chucked in as well. We were given this slop once a day without a crumb of bread or any utensils: we would pass around some tins to eat out of. They started recruiting us into the German army, and some agreed, if only to escape this hell. Two people I knew from Hrebinky were lucky enough to escape the army and make it home, but one of them was shot by Soviet troops after not changing out of his German clothes on time.

We spent about ten days in this hell before we were taken to the train station of Popeliukhy, where we were loaded onto freight cars. We were addressed by a German soldier, who said in broken Russian: "You are all going to a place where millions of people like you will be working. Don't think you'll be living on real butter and sausage—but you will get food, and you will work."

They twisted barbed wire around the wagons, and we set off. During the entire journey they fed us by scattering sunflower seeds on us as if we were chickens—and that was it.

We were taken to Przemyśl, our transit station, which had three-story bunks that, like the walls, were covered in scribbles by exiles from Russia, Belarus, and Ukraine. We were kept there for a few days and were "served" mostly by Poles who walked around with whips. They whipped us to work, saying in Polish, "If you sons of bitches don't get in line, you'll get your asses kicked."

Later we were put in a German freight train and were moved on. We arrived in Dresden. We were driven through the city destroyed by American bombers. We passed the Dresden Gallery, which was partially in ruins. Whenever our large group was marched somewhere, Germans would stand along both sides of the road, and it was clear who sympathized with us and who didn't.

We were marched outside the city, where there were already thousands of people like us. There, "buyers" came to the "auction" and bought us in batches, like slaves. Those of us from Hrebinky and neighboring Salyvonky were kept together. We were brought to Kassel, placed in barracks, and the following day taken to a railcar repair works.

For some reason, I was immediately assigned as a student to a German metalworker who worked on an assembly workstation. The German was named Zhora, and he was a good man. He taught me straight off how to make the electrical current cut out so that you could rest a bit while they looked for an electrician to turn on the machine.

I've always been observant by nature, and after being in Germany a little while, I could see that there wasn't much that could set Hitler's Fascism and Stalinism apart. Both had similar party meetings and slogans; the USSR had its Young Pioneers, whereas Germany had its Hitler Youth. They were cut from the same cloth, only the "cut" was a little different: the Germans were National Socialists, whereas the Soviets were more like International Socialists. In German factories the skilled specialists oversaw and were responsible for everything, whereas in the USSR the foreman did. The Nazis wore a small round badge on their jacket lapels, with the words "National Socialist" encircling a swastika. The higher-ranked officers wore brown uniforms with armbands bearing fascist insignia. I now understand that I used this period of captivity as my own sort of "school of life": I gathered the facts and compared the realities of Nazi Germany and the pre-war Soviet Union.

We were fed the same "dish" three times a day: turnip soup, accompanied by two hundred grams of bread made from a wheat-rye mix. We were chronically hungry, which made us steal anything we could exchange for food, often risking our lives for it. I'm still terrified when I remember how I once cut the leather off three chairs in a mail car and gave it to a Czech POW. He then gave me a loaf of bread with caraway seeds, and I can still remember the taste of it now. But had I ever gotten caught while inside that car, I would've been in deep trouble.

There were a lot of units on the large territory of the factory, and they all had to pass a technical inspection, repairs, and so on. Often these carriages were still loaded with something, and during our lunch break we would wander up and down them, sniffing out anything we could live off: a crust of bread, a cigarette butt, or anything else.

German anti-aircraft guns stood near the road back to the barracks, and next to them were two mounds of potatoes covered with earth and straw. My comrade Dmytro Matviienko and I decided to take some of the potatoes. This was a very risky business, since German guards patrolled near the piles—bearing machine guns, of course. There was a blue light there, and the mounds weren't visible from above. We crawled along on our elbows, shoveled as much frozen soil and straw away from the pile as we could, and took some potatoes. If the guards had noticed us, then a second later a round of bullets would have immediately passed through us. But we wanted to eat so badly that we risked our lives without even a second thought.

When we got back to the barrack, one of the *Polizei* noticed us.

"*Halt!*" he shouted in German, then shot at us. We quickly tossed the bag of potatoes under a train wagon, ran in, then lay deadly still in the barracks. Whilst lying there, we took off our outer clothing: the Polizei inspected the barracks but didn't recognize us. That night, even though we knew we might get ambushed, we went back for our concealed potatoes. I remember many other cases like that.

In the spring we went to work on the vegetable patches so that we would get fed: we mostly dug small plots. In general, the ordinary Germans treated us well, sympathizing with us and secretly giving us a little something now and then to bolster our strength.

Once, while I was still on the assembly workstation, the medical station was set up in our workshop, and the medical staff were hanging around. An officer came up to me, and stood and watched as I was on the lathe.

"So, how are things, my Soviet metalworker? How are you being fed and paid?" he asked me in broken Russian.

I thought he must be some agent provocateur, but a second later he said, "*Feiern am*, take a break. Go to wagon number seven."

I asked my colleague who had been working there for a long time for advice, and he told me not to worry: the German just wanted to feed me; the officers had asked him to several times as well. As such, I went to wagon number seven and the officer treated me to ersatz-coffee and a slice of bread with margarine, which I scoffed down in an instant.

"*Noch?*" he asked. "More?"

I nodded.

The officer made another treat, wrapped the piece of bread in paper and gave it to me. I was scared that my goodies would be taken away from me at the security gate, but it was fine. There were more than a few cases like this.

Prisoners from all over Europe worked at the railcar repair works. There were Poles, Czechs, Belgians, Dutchmen, Frenchmen, Ukrainians, Belarusians, Russians, and even some Italians that had been brought there after Mussolini's demise and Italy's subsequent withdrawal from the alliance with Hitler. We called them all "Badoglio," after the Italian *capo* at the time.

Us workers from the Soviet Union and the Italians had it the hardest. The rest had it easier, especially the French — and even the Poles. They treated us "partners in misfortune" well and helped us as much as they could.

Not far from our factory, was our camp, where prisoners from the Soviet Union were kept, and it had a *Natalka von Poltava* sign over the entrance in German, referencing Mykola Lysenko's opera *Natalka Poltavka*. Our camp was surrounded by barbed wire, and we lived quite far away from the factory in the barracks, though these weren't fenced. Between the barracks was a little booth where the Polizei who accompanied us to and from work stayed. The Polizei changed often, and all of them treated us prisoners differently. There were the ones who just shouted at us, and others who beat us without saying anything. We gave each one of them a nickname: "Fox," "Halfwit," and so on.

In the second half of 1944, we were bombed heavily by the Americans. We weren't allowed into proper bomb shelters. One time we were marched into the basement of a four-story warehouse. A bomb flew in and blew up right above the basement. The ceiling fell in and bricks fell in on us, but there were only two exits. We threw the bricks off us and crawled back out onto God's green earth.

There was a bomb shelter on the factory grounds called the "Winkelturm" — a mushroom-shaped concrete structure with a sharp roof and walls one-and-a-half meters thick. We weren't allowed in there. I also remember one time when we were marched onto a wooden deck by a stream that flowed below the factory. A bomb exploded in the distance, and we were scattered like skittles ten or fifteen meters away along the decking. When the factory got bombed, the expensive equipment was evacuated and the Ausländer workers were given different jobs. One crew, which I was in, dug a tunnel into the mountain next door as a sort of bomb shelter; another one was digging a little further on and we were supposed to meet each other. According to the plan, the tunnel was supposed to be U-shaped. Our crew had six Ukrainians, two Italians, one Belgian, and a German — the foreman and specialist.

By 1944 and 1945 the Germans had already realized that Nazism was on the verge of collapse. Some people, especially ordinary people, changed their attitude toward us for the better. "Is it very cold in Siberia?" they would sometimes ask us. Hitler had frightened them by saying that when the Russians arrived, they would be taken off to Siberia.

On the eve of 1945, we experienced very heavy bombing. Many *Auslanders* and *Ostarbeiters* filled the tunnel. We sat there for a long time, as long as there was still enough fresh air. When it became too hard to breathe, we started running out of the tunnel before we suffocated. My head hurt for a few days after that. The Americans also dropped time-lapse bombs that would explode a week later, and they scattered so many leaflets that the Germans gave up on taking them away from us.

Spring came, and we went to the city outskirts to work for some Germans in return for food. We had this *Bauer* friend, and we went to him for extra work in the evenings after work or on Sundays. This German always employed a Polish man, a young Polish woman, and a young Frenchman. This Frenchman stole flour, grain, and, on one occasion, even bacon from his employer—all for us. One time, when we left the Bauer's, two Germans saw us on the city outskirts and called us "*Russische Schweine*"—Russian pigs. We went after them to give them a good hiding, but they scarpered pretty quickly.

A little later in spring 1945, a second front opened, and the Americans and British were on the offensive, so the Germans started evacuating us to the East, accompanied by Polizei. We were scared that we would be taken to the gas chambers, so we agreed among ourselves that if that's where they ended up taking us, we would fight back—that way, at least some of us would remain alive. We were driven about thirty kilometers away, then the Polizei disappeared somewhere, and we were left alone. We began moving east, and the Americans caught up with us—and then we were free.

What a swift change in circumstances! One day we were slaves, and the next we were free—freedom! People who the day before had been prisoners of war and Ostarbeiters were riding around on bicycles and motorcycles, while Americans drove a horse and cart over a Nazi flag. Freedom! We turned back, but we didn't want to walk to Kassel, so we based ourselves in the small town of Gemünden, which had three rivers: the Weser and its tributaries, the Fulda and Vera Rivers. It was a very picturesque place. We were housed in a former camp for German troops. There were representatives of the various peoples of Europe in the camp, but most of them were Ukrainians, Russians, and Belarusians. We were fed more or less decently. The Americans took engines and other military equipment out of a large hangar, and we made a kind of theatre or club out of it. We set up a stage, a tarpaulin curtain, and benches, and every night former POWs from different countries would perform. I think us Ukrainians performed the best: we had wonderful singers and other "*artistes.*"

We were later told that, in Kassel, people were going after anyone who had been persecuting us. There was a female doctor who, whenever a sick Ostarbeiter would come to her, would say, "Go to work. Who else is going to build a great Germany?" She was done away with. They couldn't find Dodoy, the Ossetian cook that would beat prisoners round the head with a ladle; he had run away somewhere.

We stayed in Gemünden for about two months, after which the Americans transported us to the town of Halberstadt and housed us in a former school, the Schiele Lyceum. It wasn't a bad location, being very well equipped with an observatory, two sports gyms, a cinema, beautiful classrooms, a huge lobby, and an assembly hall. According to an agreement they had made, the Soviet forces were to enter the city, and the Americans and the British were supposed to leave—which is what later happened. A few of us men were taken to work at a meat-packing factory. A little later we were drafted into the army, but without uniforms because there was nothing to wear. We were preparing for war against Japan, and we all signed up as volunteer fighters. We stayed in former German barracks, which were well equipped. We were often taken to various cities for unknown reasons. One time we were taken to a former concentration camp where the inmates had been building an underground factory, but we were housed in the place the SS guards used to live. At the end of that summer, in August, we were transported across Poland in Studebakers to the Ukrainian border. We arrived at Volodymyr-Volynskyi, where thousands upon thousands of us were waiting outside the town. Volodymyr-Volynskyi was a rail station. A few days later a freight train arrived, and the next day the train set off with us in it. We made our bunks ourselves by dismantling the abandoned building next to the railway. I don't remember how long our journey was. When we passed through Ustymivka, I saw the chimney of the sugar factory in my hometown of Hrebinky. We were being transported as soldiers in the 25th Workers' Battalion, and we had military commanders with us.

We finally made it to Dniprodzerzhynsk (present-day Kamianske). We were unloaded and taken to the accommodation of the Ordzhonikidze coke plant. The dormitories had been built in the 1930s, like the plant itself, and they were nice-looking buildings. The female dormitories were on the left, the male ones were on the right. The facility had a canteen, a medical center, a night school, and a large lobby. It had a hall with a stage on the first floor, with nice plants all around and a dance floor. We had A major, a battalion commander, and a senior lieutenant were in charge. The major, who looked to be thirty-five or thirty-seven, was a wonderful person who always treated us well, whereas the lieutenant was a hard-nosed drillmaster.

The next day we went to the plant. It turned out to be in ruins. "When will it be rebuilt?" I thought.

It was no matter: we took apart the destroyed one and rebuilt the new one in less than a year, and the plant launched into production. I was put to work as a machinist and tool smith, and I soon made good on their trust. We were paid a wage, like normal workers. We were fed in the canteen, but in the mornings and evenings we had an inspection.

A few days after we were brought to the plant, the major left somewhere and when he came back, he said that the next day thirty men would be granted leave for ten days, not counting the time needed for the journey home.

I didn't make the list. However, a telegram from my mother arrived, saying that she was seriously ill and it had been certified by a doctor. The major preferred it if we approached him about all military procedures. I went to him, and he granted me leave. I took a few freight trains, then walked from Bila Tserkva to Hrebinky (some twenty kilometers) on foot. From the road I walked round the garden, which is where my relatives saw me: my sister Natalia and her husband Andrii ran to meet me, and my mother after them. Agricultural production was low in the post-war years, and we used a ration system. We were malnourished, though we managed to get hold of some food here and there—a kilo of bread, for instance. Then again, all of us were young, and we had fun.

We were transferred to Donbas, to Voroshylovsk (present-day Alchevsk). My friend and I decided to return to Dniprodzerzhynsk. It was winter, with freezing temperatures, and we had a tough time getting there, coupled with getting stopped by the police, but we managed. We were greeted in Dniprodzerzhynsk with open arms, so to speak.

Our battalion had already been disbanded by that time, so we became ordinary workers. Life went on as usual: there was a monetary reform, and the ration system was abolished. I would go to visit my mother several times a year: either after a telegram request or on vacation. I wanted to go home, but to do so I'd have to resign. I went to the factory director to do this several times, but in vain. It was very difficult to resign from work at a factory back then; it was almost impossible. The director even promised me an apartment that I could put my mother into, but he wouldn't let me leave. But in 1949 Soloviov, the foreman of our shop, helped me, for which I am grateful to this day. He was being transferred to another company, and he offered to write me a statement that I was going to go with him.

I took part in everything going on at the factory, I was respected by my colleagues in our shop, I took part in the drama club—but I wanted to go home to my old mother. And so I quit and I finally came home. A few days later I was working in a car repair shop, again as a machinist and tool smith. I went to night school, starting my penultimate grade. In 1951 I finished my final grade. That year I entered the Bila Tserkva Institute of Foreign Languages, graduating in 1955 from Horlivka, to where the institute had been transferred. Immediately upon graduation, I found a job as an English teacher at the high school in Hrebinky, where I worked until my retirement in 1986.

Eduard Zub

The German Attack Wasn't Unexpected: "We All Knew That There Would Be a War. How Did Stalin Not Know?"

Whenever "The Girl Saw the Soldier off to the Front" played on the radio, my grandma's eyes would fill with tears. But she didn't seem to harbor any ill will against the Germans. She said that there were good people among them too, and "had Stalin and Hitler met face to face, there wouldn't have even been a war, but instead they dragged so many people into their mess."

My name is Eduard Ivanovych Zub, and I write a regular historical column for the Kharkiv weekly *Piatnytsia* (Friday). I'm a historian by profession, vocation, and way of life. That's why I understand perfectly well that from the standpoint of source criticism, memoirs are just about the least important type of source.

Nevertheless, when I recall the stories that my grandmothers, God rest their souls, used to tell about the war, Taras Shevchenko's "If old people lie, then so do I" involuntarily comes to mind.

It's possible that my story may include too many pre-war years, but I need to explain how my grandma, Praskoviia Antonivna Zub (née Khrol), born in 1918 in the Kharkiv Governorate, ended up all the way in Halychyna at the start of World War II. "The West," from the point of view of a peasant girl from Slobozhanske since many generations back—that was something!

To be precise, the problems began back in Kharkiv, when my grandfather, Volodymyr Kharytonovych Zub, a teacher at the Ponomarenkivska village grade school, was first recruited onto a mission to "liberate" the Western Ukrainian lands. For a long time after, my grandma would bring up the briefing in the district committee, where they were prepared for their relocation to Halychyna:

"So he asks me, 'Is your child baptized?' I'm sitting there and don't know what to say. I don't want to lie, but I'm also scared to admit that we secretly did baptize the teacher's son [my Uncle Volodymyr, b. 1937]. Then he gives me this look and says, 'Even if he's unbaptized, you tell everyone there that you baptized him. Because the kids there will tease him.'"

The German Attack Wasn't Unexpected 245

Graduation photo, 1934. The only photo of my grandmother and grandfather together. My grandmother is sitting first on the left, and my grandfather is third from the left. He was the teacher, and she was his student. She later became his wife.

They even prescribed the type of clothing the wife of a Soviet teacher was supposed to wear when she traveled! "I'm walking around the village in a big hat. It was the first time I had worn such a thing. Your grandfather forced me to because that's what he had been instructed. I'm walking and crying because everyone's making fun of me—that Pashka's parading around dressed up as God. And Volodka, who's walking behind me, says, 'Get used to it! That's the only way you can walk and be around there.'"

My grandparents left for Halychyna sometime in October or November 1939. They lived in the towns of Yaniv (present-day Ivano-Frankove) and Maheriv. My grandfather, if I'm not mistaken, moved up the ranks to inspector for the district department of public education. "It was a good job," my grandma would jokingly recall. "Whenever he'd go off somewhere, he'd come back with some young chick—sometimes a young hen, other times a duckling."

Teachers were respected there: "As soon as we arrived, we were given an apartment. In the morning I grab an ax to chop firewood, and the landlady runs out, snatches the ax out of my hands, and yells that that sort of thing doesn't befit a teacher's wife."

Regarding the "unexpectedness" of the German attack in 1941, my grandma had her own opinion. She often repeated, "We all knew that there would be war. How did Stalin not know? The German reconnaissance planes were flying wherever and whenever they wanted."

When the bombers started flying past too, my grandfather was recruited into the army, and my grandma and her son were put on a troop train: the families of Soviet workers were being evacuated.

"We passed through Kharkiv and didn't stop. I see that they're taking us to the *katsaps*—the "goats," as we used to call the Russians. Nah, I wasn't going ... I jumped off the moving train somewhere past Kupiansk already and walked back home on foot."

Home was the little village of Khroly next to Kharkiv. She walked a few dozen kilometers with a huge suitcase and a four-year-old child—and already pregnant with my father (born on Christmas of 1942).

Her descriptions of the occupation were a little different from the ones we heard in school. She always exaggerated the "balance" of which side stole more. The Germans took off with however many chickens (I don't remember the exact number anymore), while "our side" confiscated sheep that had them living lavishly during the occupation. In the end it would work out that our side took more. For some time there were Croats stationed in the village: "They didn't speak our language, but we understood them. They were good people. They gave your grandfather a hat and boots for free."

She often described how our *otochentsi*, the soldiers that had been cut off from the Red Army by German encirclements, would knock on the window at night: "Lord! They were hungry, wounded, tattered. Many a time we had to hide them." On one occasion helping them backfired on her: one of the other villagers reported on her activities to the Germans. It's a good thing that her neighbors managed to warn her: "They're heading to your house!"

As Grandma used to describe it, she had had her fill of terror then. The Germans turned the whole house upside down, and then to top it off forgot their machine gun when they left. I'm quoting her verbatim: "When I saw that, I snatched up the machine gun and started chasing them down. I'm shouting, 'Pan, pan!' (Sir, sir!) and thrusting that gun into the air, but they're not hearing a damned thing, they just keep clucking in that language of theirs. When they finally heard me, they took the gun but then wouldn't let me go. They're poking me with that same machine gun: walk in front of us! Well, I think to myself, this is it, Pashka ... When all of a sudden, we reach some corner of the village and they point at a house. That's where the guy that turned you in lives, they said. He ended up moving when our soldiers arrived."

Believe it or not, my grandma knew back in 1939 how the war would end for our family. "Your grandpa and I were walking through what's now Kharkiv's Central Market, and he starts scolding me for something. And a Gypsy woman that was walking by says, 'Don't listen to him. He's not going to live with you either way. And your child will burn up in a fire.' And that's what happened." My grandfather lived out his final years in faraway Western Australia (how he ended up there is a separate and rather dark tale), and the "child" — namely, my Uncle Volodymyr—stepped on a mine and was blown up. He was twelve and was with two other boys from his village when it happened.

My maternal grandmother, Iryna Vasylivna Fartushko (born 1911), was also fond of reminiscing about the past, though more often about collectivization and 1933 than the war.

Grandma Ira with my mother, 1945

Being still in grade school, I was utterly horrified by her stories—and particularly by her traditional "prelude" of, "Listen, grandson, to what they did, those communists, those vermin ..." My mom, upon hearing this type of "education" one time, grew seriously alarmed: "God forbid, he'll let slip some of this in school." I never let anything slip. But I'm starting to now.

About the inviolable fraternity of peoples in the USSR, my grandma described: "The hospital trains were half packed with evacuated Jews. They paid crazy money to the hospital orderlies to get out of there. Then the orderlies would get drunk with that same money and start tossing them out of the moving train."

Here's another ordinary, everyday story: It's the summer of 1941, half of Ukraine is in flames already, and in Kharkiv people are bickering in line for beer. "An orderly gets off our train. He's exhausted, bandaged up himself already, and he is craving that beer badly. He walks up and asks, all civilized, 'Comrades, mind if I jump the line? I'm on duty.' And this one pot-bellied guy says, 'All of us here are on duty!' Oh, he yanked that carbine off his shoulder so fast ... He got his drink alright."

The naturalism of Grandma's stories knew no bounds: "I'm walking with a girlfriend through a field (this was sometime in early 1943, outside Kharkiv). It was right after our Katyusha rocket launchers were brought in and finally made mincemeat out of the Germans; they hadn't been able to drive them out of there for a long time. There are arms and legs lying all round ... And then I see that someone's already been there: the Germans are without clothes. And one of them had been stuck onto a horse, and he froze just like that, naked butt and all. It was very cold. When my girlfriend saw a wedding ring on one of their fingers, she started trying to pull it off, but it wasn't coming off. So she cut off the finger with a knife. 'That's a sin!' I exclaimed, but what did sins matter anymore ..."

My grandmother never told any stories about her husband, my grandfather, Oleksii Oleksandrovych Kolesnyk. I know only that he went missing.

Whenever "The Girl Saw the Soldier off to the Front" played on the radio, my grandma's eyes would fill with tears. But she didn't seem to harbor any ill will against the Germans. She said that there were good people among them too, and "had Stalin and Hitler met face to face, there wouldn't have even been a war, but instead they dragged so many people into their mess."

Unfortunately, no one has yet managed to replay the past.

Vladyslav Faraponov

My Family's War: Their Unheard Memories and Their Heroic Deeds Have Now Been Uncovered.

"You saved scores of lives, but you never bragged about it!" That's what my family could say about a real hero — my great-great-grandfather.

Davyd Moiseievych Brusylovskyi, born in 1890, was an army doctor second rank, a highly-qualified surgeon, and head of medicine at a mobile field hospital. For three weeks between January and February 1942, working eighteen hours a day at the operating table, he provided help to more than one thousand wounded people. With no regard to the passing hours or the fatigue, Comrade Brusylovskyi saved the lives of more than one hundred of his patients.
He has been awarded a state medal for military service.

The strange thing about the above is that for a long time nobody, not even my grandmother (Ryma, Davyd's granddaughter) or my great-grandmother (his daughter, Anna Davydivna), was aware of this distinction. In fact, the only thing they knew was that he had been an army doctor: a surgeon, to be precise. Knowing that your great-great-grandfather saved thousands of lives and allowed many

Davyd Moiseiovych Brusylovskyi

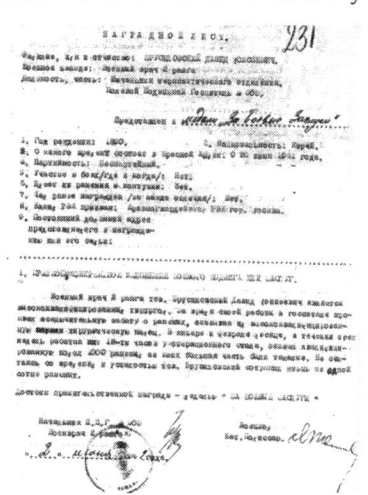

Award letter, June 2, 1942

Photo from the family archive, 1941

generations to exist today is the source of great pride. By Front-line Order No.18, Davyd Moiseievych Brusylovskyi was awarded a medal for military service on August 12, 1942. Unfortunately, our family has never seen this medal, but when they learned about the award, they were proud and glad at the chance to talk about it. After all, it is a central story in our family history and one we will cherish.

It is distressing to realize that your relatives—people you could write a whole book about—will no longer be able to tell you about their own personal history.

It is also interesting to learn that some of your relatives, who became related because of your parents' marriage some thirty years after the war, fought on opposite sides.

For instance, my great-grandmother, Akulyna Vasylivna Pedchenko (later Shyptenko), whom everyone affectionately called Granny Klava, was in the ranks of the Yakov partisan resistance detachment.

Everyone knew this story and it was later corroborated by documentation; the documents underscore the words of Bohdan Stelmakh: "This is the history of our home nation" (from his poem "History"). This is the story of one nation.

My great-grandfather, Ivan Tykhonovych Faraponov, was also awarded medals for fighting in the Red Army, opposite the partisans. He was awarded the Medal "For Courage":

> On the west bank of the river Oder in the Lebus region, working on expanding auxiliary support networks while under enemy fire and enemy bombardment from the air, during February and March 1945 he undertook precise measurements of their lines and accurately calculated their coordinates.

Grandpa Ivan spent the rest of his life working at a village school in Novoshmidtivka in the Novoodeskyi District of Mykolaiv Oblast.

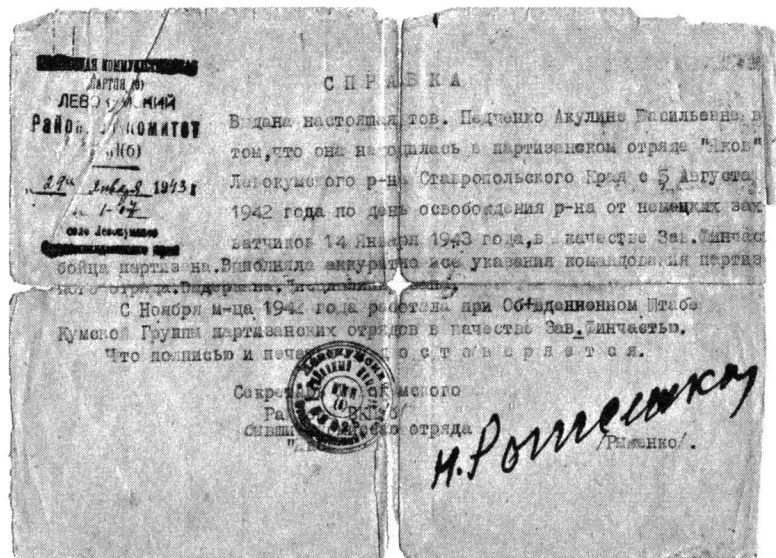

Document certifying that Akulyna Vasylivna Pedchenko spent time with the Yakov partisan detachment. January 29, 1943

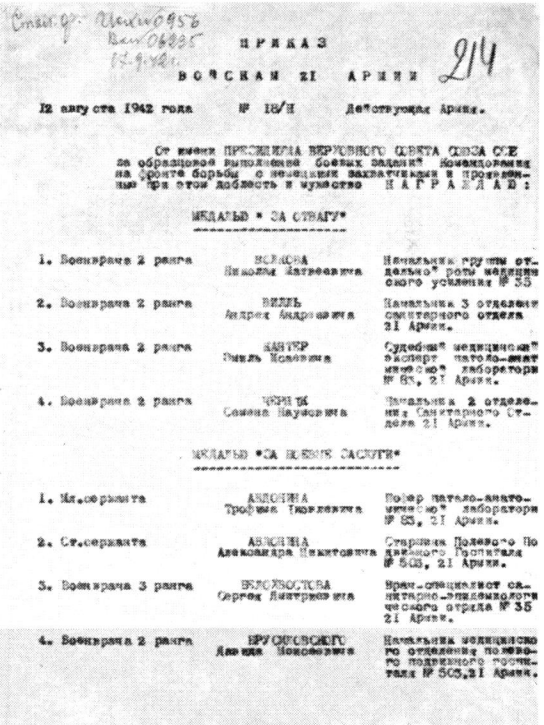

Order No. 18 from August 12, 1942

My great-grandfather Ivan Tykhonovych Faraponov (left), 1985

My grandfather wouldn't be lucky enough to be around today if the wartime story of my great-grandfather, Leonid Semenovych Voloshyn, had been any different. Though this isn't something to hide nowadays, back then Grandpa Leonid tried to conceal his Jewish ethnicity, so after the war he listed it as "Russian." Apart from during the evacuation, we don't know his exact whereabouts between the years of 1939 and 1945. According to some relatives, it's definitely known that he fought with the Banderites after the war and was wounded.

Later I managed to find out that his father and my great-great-grandfather, Semen Hryhorovych Voloshyn, had died in the Battle of Stalingrad in 1943. His son, i.e., Great-Grandfather Leonid, dug his own father's grave in the bitter cold of that winter. He never loved funerals, and it was only on May 9, 2005, the year of his death, that we learned the reason why.

I don't know which of these deeds is more heroic: saving the lives of thousands or saying goodbye like that to one of your own.

For all intents and purposes, all of my relatives, each of whom was affected differently by the war, rarely if ever talked about these events or about what really happened. Some were scared that something would happen to them if they did, whereas others simply could not allow their children to even imagine the kind of grief they had experienced and preferred to forget instead.

The body's wounds have healed, but have the wounds of the heart?

Bohdan Ivchenko

The History of Victory Day in the Soviet Union (1947 – 1965)

Is it true that prior to 1965 the Soviet government didn't celebrate Victory Day to commemorate the surrender of Nazi Germany? The historical facts continue to be confused to the present day, even in publications by historians. This research is based on materials from the Soviet press of the post-war years.

Most ordinary Ukrainian citizens that have no first-hand knowledge of life in the Soviet Union prior to 1965, or that were school-aged children at that time, support the myth spread by the Soviet mass media that Victory Day was only celebrated on a national level in the Soviet Union from 1965 on. Better informed Ukrainians know that for the first two years after the end of the war—that is, until 1947—Victory Day was in fact celebrated, but that this holiday was later terminated by the Soviet government.

The need to write this article arose long ago since historical facts continue to be confused to the present day, even in scholarly circles. For example, in the November 2016 public lecture "St. George's vs The Guards: The Real History of the Victory Ribbon," which was presented as part of the public project Likbez: The Historical Front, Yana Prymachenko, an employee of the History Institute of the National Academy of Sciences, noted that May 9, 1965 was an ordinary day, not a holiday. However, in my opinion, this day wasn't at all an ordinary or simple one prior to 1965, but a day that involved obvious and incontrovertible elements of festivity, which is why in this article I propose to unpack the history of Victory Day celebrations in the Soviet Union prior to 1965.

May 9 was officially approved as the holiday of "Victory Day" in 1945, at which time it became a day off for workers. In accordance with a decree of the Presidium of the Supreme Soviet of the USSR, dated December 23, 1947, Victory Day once again became a working day, but its status as a holiday didn't disappear. For the purposes of an analogy, we can take the Day of Unity of Ukraine, January 22, which in contemporary Ukraine is an official public holiday, yet is a working day.

How exactly was Victory Day celebrated from 1948 to 1964? First, in all of those sixteen years, artillery salutes were performed on May 9 in the Hero Cities[1] and in the capitals of the Soviet republics. It's worth noting that an artillery salute is never performed on an ordinary day — namely, one that is not a holiday. Second, official Victory Day greetings to all those to whom the holiday pertained were published on May 9 on the front pages of both the national and more minor newspapers of the Soviet Union. Had this day not been a holiday, the editors would have had no right to print greetings in their newspapers. Third, every year on May 9, the Minister of Defense issued and officially published a Victory Day order greeting all those involved in the victory over Nazi Germany with the holiday. And fourth, on the pages of those same national newspapers, many articles dedicated to Victory Day were published. It's worth analyzing in greater detail how Victory Day was officially celebrated in those years when the holiday was a day of work.

The year following the cessation of the holiday as a day off for workers, on Victory Day in 1948, thirty-volley artillery salutes were performed in Moscow, in the capitals of the Soviet republics, and in the Hero Cities of Leningrad, Stalingrad, Odesa, and Sevastopol. On this day, by order of the Minister of Defense of the Soviet Union, artillery salutes were also held in Kaliningrad and Lviv, even though these cities were neither capitals of Soviet republics, nor Hero Cities. Why exactly were these cities, from among the Soviet Union's other cities, granted special privileges on Victory Day? We can surmise that a salute was performed in Kaliningrad due to the fact that its capture entailed extremely fierce battles; the participants of these battles were even awarded a separate medal during the time of the Soviet Union. The salute in the city of Lviv possibly may have been due to the fact that Lviv was the governing center of the Carpathian Military District and a sort of capital of Western Ukraine, where anti-Soviet sentiments existed and the Ukrainian Insurgent Army was actively operating at the time, and the celebration of Victory Day was "for show," intended to inculcate local residents with pride in not just the victory over Nazi Germany, but also the victory of Soviet rule in Western Ukraine.

The order of the Minister of Defense of the Soviet Union established Stalin's role as a great military leader and also proclaimed the eternal glory of those who died for the freedom and independence of the Motherland. On that day, the central radio stations of the USSR broadcast a concert commissioned by the Heroes of the Soviet Union, which was followed by a program about the Heroes of the Great Patriotic War and then a concert by the Red Army Song and Dance Ensemble. A second radio program broadcast scenes

---

1   A Soviet honorary title awarded to twelve cities of the Soviet Union for outstanding heroism during World War II.

from a play entitled *The Victors* and a narrative about the storming of the Reichstag. On this day in Kyiv, in addition to the salute, mass festivities took place: Kyiv residents visited an exhibit dedicated to the events of the Great Patriotic War and an exhibit of military equipment seized in battle. In honor of the Victory Day celebrations, various sports competitions were held in many cities.

The following year, in 1949, a Victory Day order of the Minister of Defense of the Soviet Union comparable to that of 1948 was published. On May 9, 1949 on the first national radio channel, poems about Victory Day were read, a musical-literary Hero Cities concert was broadcast, followed by a talk show with Colonel-General Vyacheslav Tsvetayev on "The Great Victory of the Soviet People," after which was broadcast the play *The Final Defense* about the events of final stage of the war against Nazi Germany. Leading up to Victory Day 1949, the film *The Battle of Stalingrad* was shown in Soviet cinemas, which elicited a lively interest from the public. That year, on Victory Day in Moscow, in addition to the artillery salute and traditional evening festivities, numerous sports competitions were held, including for aircraft modelists, motorcyclists, and motorists. A great number of Moscow residents visited the Museum of the Soviet Army that day; the hall with the so-called "Victory Flag," which had been raised above the Reichstag, was of particular attention to the visitors.

In Kyiv the celebration of Victory Day 1949 began on May 8, as it was a Sunday. In Kyiv on that day numerous meetings with war heroes were held, as well as lectures dedicated to Victory Day. A great number of Kyiv residents attended the exhibit "Partisans of Ukraine in the Fight against German Fascist Aggressors." Many others visited the grave of General Vatutin, whose troops liberated Kyiv, as well as the grave of Senior Lieutenant Sholudenko, who was first to enter Kyiv in his tank on November 5, 1943. Numerous sports competitions took place in Kyiv stadiums in honor of Victory Day. On May 9, 1949, despite this being a working day, meetings were held at Kyiv places of employment in honor of the holiday, where employees that had served on the front would speak. The Society for the Dissemination of Political and Scientific Knowledge held lectures at Kyiv factories and plants with rich-sounding titles, such as "J.V. Stalin, the Great Military Leader and Organizer of the Soviet Army's Victories" and "The Generalissimo of the Soviet Union J.V. Stalin's Art of Commanding in the Great Patriotic War." That year in Lviv a socialist competition was launched in the leadup to Victory Day, in which Oleksandr Krutyi, an employee of the Lvivsilmash Factory and a participant in the storming of Berlin, performed remarkably well. From among the other cities and localities of the Soviet Union, of particular note that year were Vinnytsia and Vinnytsia Oblast: a sports parade was held in Vinnytsia on May 9, 1949, in which 25,000 people took part, and similar parades took place throughout Vinnytsia Oblast.

After 1949 the Ministry of Defense of the Soviet Union was divided into two ministries, the Ministry of War and the Ministry of the Navy. As such, two separate Victory Day orders were issued on May 9, 1950, from both the Ministers of War and the Navy, though neither of them differed from the comparable orders of the Minister of Defense of the Soviet Union from preceding years. The Victory Day radio programs were just as saturated with military and patriotic pathos as they had been in previous years. What's interesting is that on May 9, 1950, in addition to the traditional concerts and historical lectures of Victory Day, a radio production based on Oles Honchar's novel *The Flag Bearers* and excerpts from Yuliy Meitus' opera about members of the Young Guard from Krasnodon in the Luhansk region were broadcast.

On May 9, 1951, as in the preceding year, two separate Victory Day orders were published, from the Ministers of War and the Navy. However, whereas from 1948 to 1950 veterans were greeted with their victory over "Fascist Germany," in 1951 the terminology changed somewhat and the Minister of War congratulated veterans for their victory over "German imperialism," while the Minister of the Navy still congratulated veterans for their victory over "Fascist Germany." If we compare the content of the radio programs from May 9, 1951 with those of preceding years, one may notice that the quantity of content dedicated to Victory Day had decreased, but it's worth noting a fact that likely appealed to Ukrainians—that on this day the Ukrainian literary figure Oles Honchar was again recognized with the reading of excerpts of his novel *Golden Prague*. In Kyiv the celebration of Victory Day began as it had the previous year, on May 8.

May 9, 1952 is memorable in that, in contrast to previous years, there wasn't a single radio broadcast dedicated to Victory Day, though the traditional Victory Day artillery salute, lectures, meetings at workplaces and educational institutions, and museum exhibits remained.

The USSR celebrated Victory Day 1953 without its "ingenious military leader" Stalin, who died on March 5 of that year. For the first time in the order issued by the Minister of Defense (in 1952, this position was still called the Minister of War) on May 9, 1953, not a single mention was made of Stalin. An artillery salute was ordered to be performed in Moscow, the capitals of Soviet republics, and the Hero Cities, but Kaliningrad and Lviv were no longer included in the list.

After 1953 Stalin would never again be mentioned in Victory Day orders, and the artillery salutes in Kaliningrad and Lviv would

May 9, 1956. For the first time since 1945, the front pages of *Pravda* showed no headlines about Victory Day.

also be forgotten. The traditional Victory Day lectures and meetings would still be held, just as before. The Minister of Defense's order from May 9, 1954 mentions the role of the USSR's allies in the victory over Nazi Germany for the first time; in the past, Victory Day orders had referred exclusively to the Soviet Union's victory over its enemy. The tradition of holding lectures, meetings, exhibits, and sports competitions for Victory Day still continued.

The first milestone anniversary of the victory, in 1955, was commemorated on a larger scale than the earlier May 9 celebrations. That year the order of the Minister of Defense mentioned the allies of the anti-Hitler coalition and their role in crushing the enemy. On May 8, 1955, on the eve of the holiday, meetings on the anniversary of the victory were held in Moscow, which were attended by the party, state, and military leadership of the Soviet Union. The Presidium sat on the country's main stage during the solemn celebration, against a backdrop of large portraits of Stalin and Lenin, though the Minister's Victory Day order, as in the preceding year, no longer mentioned Stalin. The first to speak at the celebratory meeting was Chairman of the Council of Ministers of the Soviet Union Nikolai Bulganin, who also didn't mention Stalin in his speech, noting only the Communist Party's leading role in the victory over the enemy. The celebration of Victory Day in Kyiv also began on May 8, as May 9 fell on a Monday. A number of sports competitions were held in Ukraine's capital on May 8, 1955 in honor of Victory Day.

Partisan meeting in Moscow on Victory Day, with a speech by ex-commander Sydir Kovpak, 1957.

May 9, 1956 was memorable in that for the first time since 1945, there was no Victory Day greeting printed on the first pages of *Pravda* ("Truth"), the leading newspaper of the Soviet Union. Instead, the initial columns of this newspaper were devoted to a draft of the Law on State Pensions. The traditional Victory Day artillery salute, meetings, and lectures were held, as they had been before, but in 1956 and in subsequent years, only twenty artillery volleys were performed instead of the thirty-volley salute.

The order of the Minister of Defense from May 9, 1956 made mention of the contributions of the anti-Hitler coalition allies in the victory over the enemy, but though the allies were again mentioned in the 1957 order, given the foreign policy situation, the latter order also noted the "aggressive policy of imperialist governments." The traditional Victory Day meetings, lectures, and salutes were held, as they had been in earlier years, but *Pravda* correspondents devoted particular attention to the meeting of former partisans in the square next to the Bolshoi Theater in Moscow, where the celebrated Ukrainian partisan Sydir Kovpak was performing.

On May 9, 1958, as in 1956, Victory Day celebrations were pushed to the background in the news announcements of the Soviet

May 9, 1958. Victory Day is once again pushed to the background behind other news reports in the Soviet press.

press, while a plenum of the Central Committee of the Communist Party of the Soviet Union, which was considering a report by Nikita Khrushchev on accelerating the development of the chemical industry, was highlighted, though Victory Day meetings, lectures, and artillery salutes took place in accordance with tradition. Victory Day 1959 was again celebrated throughout the country, but it wasn't noteworthy in any way in comparison with preceding years.

The Soviet people celebrated the fifteenth anniversary of victory over Germany in 1960. Once again thirty-volley salutes were performed, as opposed to the twenty-volley ones that had occurred from 1956 through 1959. The entirety of the state and party elite of the time gathered in Moscow for a celebratory Victory Day meeting. In Odesa the Monument to the Unknown Sailor was unveiled especially in time for the holiday.

On May 9, 1961 there were again twenty-volley salutes, not ones of thirty volleys, as had been performed on the fifteenth anniversary of Victory Day. This would be the case in years to come. Solemn evening festivities dedicated to Victory Day took place in the monumental Pillar Hall of the House of the Unions in Moscow, that were presided over by the head of the state himself, N.S. Khrushchev. Traditional evening gathers and celebratory meetings with veterans were held in other cities.

The Minister of Defense issued the traditional Victory Day order in 1962, but noted that fascism was witnessing a revival in West Germany. The wonderful threesome of caricaturists known as "the Kukryniksy" published an interesting caricature prior to Victory Day with a message of sorts to the "American aggressors" — that

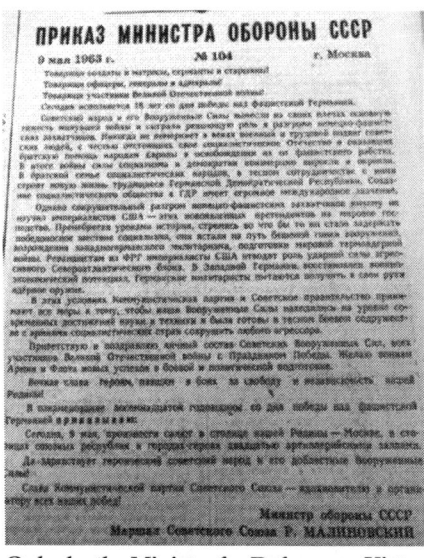

Order by the Minister for Defense on Victory Day, May 9, 1963

they were welcome to repeat Hitler's fate. A solemn evening celebration was held in the Pillar Hall of the House of the Unions dedicated to Victory Day, which was again presided over by Khrushchev. Meanwhile, in other cities festive gatherings and meetings took place on the occasion of the holiday, as they had in the past.

In 1963 the Victory Day order of Minister of Defense Rodion Malinovsky pertained more to the events of the time than to the victory of eighteen years earlier. In his address, the marshal of the Soviet Union focused not on the victory over Nazi Germany but on American imperialists, the revival of militarism in West Germany, and the United States' preparation for nuclear war. The artillery salute in Moscow, the capitals of the union republics, and the Hero Cities consisted of twenty volleys. As always, meetings with veterans, excursions to museums, and the like took place in honor of Victory Day.

The anti-American rhetoric introduced in the preceding years in the Victory Day orders of the Minister of Defense was continued in the order of May 9, 1964, though it wasn't as overt as it had been in 1963. The minister first offered Victory Day congratulations, then noted that the world's "imperialists were trying to thwart the march of communism at all costs." As in previous years, the celebratory salute consisted of twenty artillery volleys.

On May 9, 1965 Victory Day would once more become a day off for workers, as it had been till 1947, and the scale of its celebration would increase significantly, but that is already the subject of a separate study.

Contributing Authors

Taras Antypovych — writer (Poltava — Kyiv)

Boris Artemov — teacher, journalist, writer (Zaporizhia)

Vladyslav Faraponov — student at Kyiv National Economic University (Mykolaiv — Kyiv)

Bohdan Ivchenko — historian, history museum employee (Kharkiv)

Vakhtang Kipiani — journalist, chief editor of the *Istorychna Pravda* ("Historical Truth") website (Tbilisi — Kyiv)

Yevhen Klimakin — journalist (Berdychiv — Warsaw)

Yurii Kolomyiets — poet, member of the New York Group of Poets (Kobeliaky — Chicago)

Danuta Kostura — journalist, civil activist (Vorzel)

Oleh Kotsarev — writer, journalist (Kharkiv — Kyiv)

Eleonora Koval — doctorate, professor of biological sciences (Kyiv)

Dmytro Krapyvenko — journalist, chief editor of the magazine *Ukrainskyi Tyzhden* ("Ukrainian Week"), (Yoleten — Kyiv)

Oles Kulchynskyi — Turkologist, translator (Kremianets — Kyiv)

Anastasia Lebid — political refugee (Matseiv — Vorokhta — Toronto)

Ihor Lubkivskyi — radiophysicist, psychologist (Terebovlia — Ternopil)

Sviatoslav Lypovetskyi — publicist, historian (Ternopil)

Romko Malko — journalist, photo reporter (Ternopil — Kyiv)

Maria Matios — writer, People's Deputy of Ukraine (Roztoky — Kyiv)

Sevhil Musaieva — journalist, chief editor of the *Ukrainska Pravda* ("Ukrainian Truth") website (Dzhuma — Kyiv)

Volodymyr Parkhomenko — local historian (Hlynsk — Kyiv)

Oleh Pokalchuk — military psychologist (Lutsk — Kyiv)

Nataliia Popovych — writer, community leader (Lviv — Toronto)

Stepan Semeniuk (formerly Stepan Dranitskyi) — OUN member, UPA soldier, political prisoner in Soviet and Polish prison camps (Harazdzha — Zielona Góra)

Taras Shamaida — journalist, lawyer, civil activist (Poltava — Kyiv)

Ihor Shchupak — teacher, director of the Jewish Memory and Holocaust in Ukraine Museum (Zaporizhia — Dnipro)

Iryna Slavinska — journalist, writer (Kyiv)

Elina Slobodianiuk — candidate of historical sciences, business and political communications specialist (Vinnytsia — Kyiv)

Pavlo Solodko — journalist, co-founder of the *Istorychna Pravda* website (Kyiv)

Dmytro Stembkovskyi — tour guide (Kyiv)

Valentyn Stetsiuk — retired lieutenant colonel (Kadiivka — Lviv)

Liudmyla Taran — writer (Hrebinky — Kyiv)

Serhii Taran — political scientist (Kyiv)

Volodymyr Ushenko — former KGB officer (Boryspil)

Iryna Yatsyshyn — teacher (Lviv)

Oleksandr Zinchenko — journalist, editor of the *Istorychna Pravda* website (Kharkiv — Kyiv)

Eduard Zub — historian, regional historian (Cherkasy — Kharkiv)

UKRAINIAN VOICES

Collected by Andreas Umland

1   *Mychailo Wynnyckyj*
      Ukraine's Maidan, Russia's War
      A Chronicle and Analysis of the Revolution of Dignity
      With a foreword by Serhii Plokhy
      ISBN 978-3-8382-1327-9

2   *Olexander Hryb*
      Understanding Contemporary Ukrainian and Russian
      Nationalism
      The Post-Soviet Cossack Revival and Ukraine's National Security
      With a foreword by Vitali Vitaliev
      ISBN 978-3-8382-1377-4

3   *Marko Bojcun*
      Towards a Political Economy of Ukraine
      Selected Essays 1990–2015
      With a foreword by John-Paul Himka
      ISBN 978-3-8382-1368-2

4   *Volodymyr Yermolenko (ed.)*
      Ukraine in Histories and Stories
      Essays by Ukrainian Intellectuals
      With a preface by Peter Pomerantsev
      ISBN 978-3-8382-1456-6

5   *Mykola Riabchuk*
      At the Fence of Metternich's Garden
      Essays on Europe, Ukraine, and Europeanization
      ISBN 978-3-8382-1484-9

6   *Marta Dyczok*
      Ukraine Calling
      A Kaleidoscope from Hromadske Radio 2016–2019
      With a foreword by Andriy Kulykov
      ISBN 978-3-8382-1472-6

7   *Olexander Scherba*
     Ukraine vs. Darkness
     Undiplomatic Thoughts
     With a foreword by Adrian Karatnycky
     ISBN 978-3-8382-1501-3

8   *Olesya Yaremchuk*
     Our Others
     Stories of Ukrainian Diversity
     With a foreword by Ostap Slyvynsky
     Translated from the Ukrainian by Zenia Tompkins and Hanna Leliv
     ISBN 978-3-8382-1475-7

9   *Nataliya Gumenyuk*
     Die verlorene Insel
     Geschichten von der besetzten Krim
     Mit einem Vorwort von Alice Bota
     Aus dem Ukrainischen übersetzt von Johann Zajaczkowski
     ISBN 978-3-8382-1499-3

10   *Olena Stiazhkina*
     Zero Point Ukraine
     Four Essays on World War II
     Translated from the Ukrainian by Svitlana Kulinska
     ISBN 978-3-8382-1550-1

11   *Oleksii Sinchenko, Dmytro Stus, Leonid Finberg (compilers)*
     Ukrainian Dissidents
     An Anthology of Texts
     ISBN 978-3-8382-1551-8

12   *John-Paul Himka*
     Ukrainian Nationalists and the Holocaust
     OUN and UPA's Participation in the Destruction of Ukrainian Jewry, 1941–1944
     ISBN 978-3-8382-1548-8

13   *Andrey Demartino*
     False Mirrors
     The Weaponization of Social Media in Russia's Operation to Annex Crimea
     With a foreword by Oleksiy Danilov
     ISBN 978-3-8382-1533-4

14 Svitlana Biedarieva (ed.)
    Contemporary Ukrainian and Baltic Art
    Political and Social Perspectives, 1991–2021
    ISBN 978-3-8382-1526-6

15 Olesya Khromeychuk
    A Loss
    The Story of a Dead Soldier Told by His Sister
    With a foreword by Andrey Kurkov
    ISBN 978-3-8382-1570-9

16 Marieluise Beck (Hg.)
    Ukraine verstehen
    Auf den Spuren von Terror und Gewalt
    Mit einem Vorwort von Dmytro Kuleba
    ISBN 978-3-8382-1653-9

17 Stanislav Aseyev
    Heller Weg
    Geschichte eines Konzentrationslagers im Donbass 2017–2019
    Aus dem Ukrainischen und Russischen übersetzt von
    Martina Steis und Charis Haska
    ISBN 978-3-8382-1620-1

18 Mykola Davydiuk
    Wie funktioniert Putins Propaganda?
    Anmerkungen zum Informationskrieg des Kremls
    Aus dem Ukrainischen übersetzt von Christian Weise
    ISBN 978-3-8382-1628-7

19 Olesya Yaremchuk
    Unsere Anderen
    Geschichten ukrainischer Vielfalt
    Aus dem Ukrainischen übersetzt von Christian Weise
    ISBN 978-3-8382-1635-5

20 Oleksandr Mykhed
    „Dein Blut wird die Kohle tränken!"
    Über die Ostukraine
    Aus dem Ukrainischen übersetzt von Simon Muschick
    und Dario Planert
    ISBN 978-3-8382-1648-5

21 *Vakhtang Kipiani (Hg.)*
    Der Zweite Weltkrieg in der Ukraine
    Geschichte und Lebensgeschichten
    Aus dem Ukrainischen übersetzt von Margarita Grinko
    ISBN 978-3-8382-1622-5

22 *Vakhtang Kipiani (ed.)*
    World War II, Uncontrived and Unredacted
    Testimonies from Ukraine
    Translated from the Ukrainian by Zenia Tompkins and Daisy Gibbons
    ISBN 978-3-8382-1621-8

EAST EUROPEAN STUDIES: JOURNALS AND BOOK SERIES

SOVIET AND POST-SOVIET POLITICS AND SOCIETY

Editor: Andreas Umland

Founded in 2004 and refereed since 2007, SPPS makes available affordable English-, German-, and Russian-language studies on the history of the countries of the former Soviet bloc from the late Tsarist period to today. It publishes between 5 and 20 volumes per year and focuses on issues in transitions to and from democracy such as economic crisis, identity formation, civil society development, and constitutional reform in CEE and the NIS. SPPS also aims to highlight so far understudied themes in East European studies such as right-wing radicalism, religious life, higher education, or human rights protection.

JOURNAL OF SOVIET AND POST-SOVIET POLITICS AND SOCIETY

Editor: Julie Fedor

The Journal of Soviet and Post-Soviet Politics and Society was launched in April 2015 as a bi-annual companion journal to the Soviet and Post-Soviet Politics and Society book series (founded in 2004 and edited by Andreas Umland, Dr. phil., Ph.D.). Like the book series, the journal provides an interdisciplinary forum for original research on the Soviet and post-Soviet world. The journal strives to publish creative, intelligent, and lively writing, which tackles and illuminates significant issues and is capable of engaging wider educated audiences beyond the academy.

ibidem Press

BALKAN POLITICS AND SOCIETY

Editors: Jelena Džankić, Soeren Keil

The book series Balkan Politics and Society (BPS), launched in 2018, focuses on original empirical research on understudied aspects of the multifaceted historical, political, and cultural trajectories of the Balkan region. The series includes:
- Discussions on the political systems of the Balkan states, including single country case studies and comparative research
- Analyses of relevant policy fields
- Studies of the link between contemporary political issues and historical debates
- Historical debates on the Balkan states
- Analyses of the social and economic reality of the region
- Research on the evolution and development of different cultures in the region
- Discussions on the evolution of the various societies in the Balkan

FORUM FÜR OSTEUROPÄISCHE IDEEN- UND ZEITGESCHICHTE

Editors: Leonid Luks, Gunter Dehnert, Alexei Rybakow, Andreas Umland

FORUM is a bi-annual journal featuring interdisciplinary discussions on the history of ideas. It showcases studies by political scientists, philosophers as well as literary, legal, and economic scholars, and books reviews on Central and Eastern European history. The journal offers critical insight into scientific discourses across Eastern Europe to Western readers by translating and publishing articles by Russian, Polish, and Czech researchers.

ibidem Press | Leuschnerstr. 40 | 30457 Hannover | Germany
Phone: +49 (0) 511 2 62 22 00 | Fax: +49 (0) 511 2 62 22 00 | sales@ibidem.eu

LITERATURE AND CULTURE IN CENTRAL AND EASTERN EUROPE

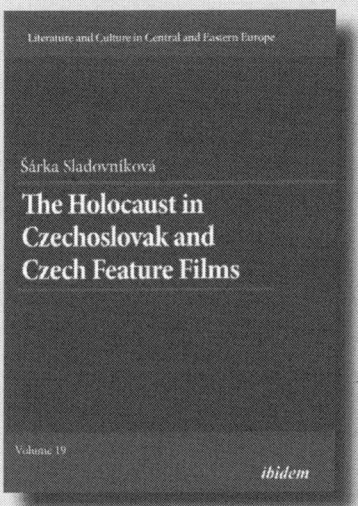

Editor: Reinhard Ibler

The book series Literature and Culture in Middle and Eastern Europe aims to provide a forum for current research on literature and culture in Central and Eastern Europe. It prioritizes a spatial-regional concept over a purely philological one, e.g. Slavic, in order to better reflect the numerous interrelationships that characterize the literature and cultures of Eastern Central, Southeastern and Eastern Europe as well as the German-speaking world. The series aims to uncover these manifold mutual contacts, overlaps, and influences, both individually and as a whole.

JOURNAL OF ROMANIAN STUDIES

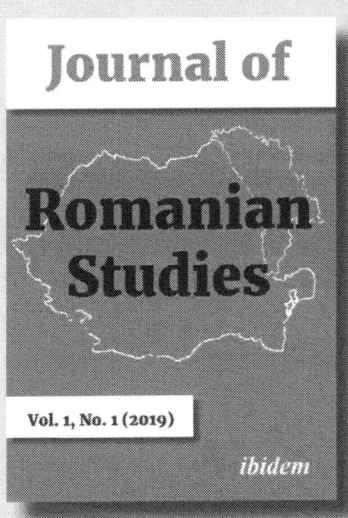

Editors: Peter Gross, Svetlana Suveica and Iuliu Ratiu

The *Journal of Romanian Studies*, jointly developed by The Society for Romanian Studies and ibidem Press, is a biannual, peer-reviewed, and interdisciplinary journal. It examines critical issues in Romanian studies, linking work in that field to wider theoretical debates and issues of current relevance, and serving as a forum for junior and senior scholars. The journal also presents articles that connect Romania and Moldova comparatively with other states and their ethnic majorities and minorities, and with other groups by investigating the challenges of migration and globalization and the impact of the European Union.

ibidem Press

www.ibidem.eu | facebook.com/ibidem.Verlag

ibidem.eu